BISEXUAL SPACES

BISEXUAL SPACES

A Geography
of Sexuality and Gender

Clare Hemmings

ROUTLEDGE
New York and London

Published in 2002 by
Routledge
29 West 35th Street
New York, NY 10001

Published in Great Britain by
Routledge
11 New Fetter Lane
London EC4P 4EE

Routledge is an imprint of Taylor & Francis Group.

Printed on acid-free, 250-year-life paper.
Manufactured in the United States of America.
Design and typography: Jack Donner
10 9 8 7 6 5 4 3 2 1

Library of Congress Cataloging-in-Publication Data

Hemmings, Clare.
    Bisexual Spaces : a geography of sexuality and gender / Clare Hemmings
        p. cm.
    Includes bibliographical references and index.
    ISBN 0-415-93082-0 ISBN 0-415-93083-9 (pbk.)
        1. Bisexuality—Philosophy. I. Title.

HQ74 .H45 20002
306.76'5'01—dc21

                                                                    2001049101

To Ann and John Hemmings,
for your absolute faith

CONTENTS

List of Illustrations   ix

Acknowledgments   xi

Introduction   1

Chapter 1
Bisexual Landscapes   15

Chapter 2
Desire by Any Other Name   53

Chapter 3
Representing the Middle Ground   99

Chapter 4
A Place to Call Home   145

Notes   199

Index   235

LIST OF ILLUSTRATIONS

Fig. 2.1
Author's photograph of Lunaria, lesbian feminist bookstore, 1995   57

Fig. 2.2
Author's photograph of the North Star bar, 1994   59

Fig. 2.3
Flyer for the March against Pornography, April 1989   64

Fig. 2.4
Author's photographs of alternative T-shirts for the 1990 and
1991 Northampton Pride Marches   69

Fig. 2.5
Flyer with theme of 1992 Northampton Pride Marches   70

Fig. 2.6
Flyer with theme of 1993 Northampton Pride Marches   71

Fig. 2.7
Author's photograph of 1994 Northampton Pride March T-shirt   86

Fig. 3.1
Loren Cameron, *Self-Portrait Nude #46A* (2000)   130

Fig. 3.2
The front cover of the 1996 book *Bisexual Horizons*   135

Fig. 3.3
"Bisexuality," *Newsweek* cover July 17, 1995   136

Fig. 3.4
Stephanie Device, *fingerprints* (1997)   140

Fig. 4.1
Author's photographs of the San Francisco Women's Building, on
Eighteenth Street   151

Fig. 4.2
"Are You Ready for a National Bisexual Network?" BBWN flyer
distributed at the 1987 March on Washington for Gay
and Lesbian Rights   163

Fig. 4.3
Advertisement for the 1990 Lesbian and Gay Freedom Day Parade
in San Francisco, from the 1990 National Bisexual Conference
brochure   167

Fig. 4.4
Rachel Kaplan and Keith Hennessy, "'Bi Artists' Manifesto,"
the 1990 National Bisexual Conference brochure   174

Fig. 4.5
Rachel Kaplan and Keith Hennessy, "The Third Path,"
the 1990 National Bisexual Conference brochure   176

Fig. 4.6
Flyer for the Eighth National Bisexual Conference,
Edinburgh, September 7–10, 1990   178

Fig. 4.7
Flyer for the Second International Bisexual Conference, London,
June 23–24, 1992   179

Fig. 4.8
Cover for the Fifth International Bisexual Conference
program, Cambridge, Massachusetts, April 3–5, 1998   180

ACKNOWLEDGMENTS

The research for, writing, and editing of this book has taken place in a number of different institutions, and with a variety of different funding sources. It has also required the love and care of many significant people who have inspired me and critiqued my work, but more importantly have taken time out from their own concerns to engage with me about mine.

Thanks to the British Academy, the Fulbright Commission, the California Institute for Contemporary Arts, and Suntory and Toyota International Centres for Economics and Related Disciplines, for funding, and to York Women's Studies Centre, Utrecht Women's Studies Centre, the Five College Women's Studies Research Center, the University of North London Women's Studies Department, the Sociology Department at Goldsmiths College, and the Gender Institute at London School of Economics for housing me. And to all the colleagues and friends in each context for their support. Special thanks to Hazel, Anne, Ros, and Carl at the Gender Institute for creating a generous and light-hearted working environment, and to Jyl, Arlene, Rosi, and Henry for insisting it be done honestly.

Thank you to all those who went beyond the call of duty to help me identify, create, and analyze sources—Warren Blumenfeld, Lani Ka'ahumanu, Stephanie Berger, Robyn Ochs, Brett Beemyn, Loren Cameron, Stephanie Gill, Jim Frasin, Bet Power and Karen Bellavance-Grace.

A toast to the best readers I have had (I know that now): Jo, Merl, and Ann, who wrote this book with me. And to Karen, Diana, Claire, Jane, and Cath. To David, for writing to me.

INTRODUCTION

This book as a whole offers a critique of dominant formations of gender and sexuality, with bisexuality as the particular way in, and brings to light alternative formations that challenge our current understanding of relationships among sexual and gendered identities, subjects, and communities. My primary aim is to investigate the repeated production of bisexuality within much queer and feminist theory as an abstract and curiously lifeless middle ground. As middle ground, bisexuality is frequently demonized for supporting or even generating fixed oppositional structures of sexuality and gender, and on these grounds is commonly dismissed in both epistemological and ontological terms. Bisexuality is rarely examined as a potentially enlightening analytical tool or starting point for knowledge, nor as a particular subject position that might merit further inquiry by anyone not calling herself bisexual.[1] The absence of discussions of a range of bisexual meanings within contemporary approaches has the effect of consolidating the dominant "bisexual model" of sexuality or gender, while at the same time insisting on its insignificance.

My response to this critical and cultural positioning of bisexuality has three main directions. First, I build on existing theoretical work on bisexual subjectivity that has begun to elaborate a set of epistemologies of the fence rather than the more familiar *closet*. Jo Eadie and Maria Pramaggiore both use this term directly, although I am also thinking of Elizabeth D. Däumer, Amber Ault, Ann Kaloski, Merl Storr, Steven Angelides, and Mariam Fraser as forming an emerging trajectory of theorists concerned with formation of bisexual knowledges both historically and contemporarily.[2] As I delineate in detail in chapter 1, such approaches share my desire to rethink genealogies of sexuality and gender via a central focus on bisexual knowledges, or knowledges *about* bisexuality. Second, and in the process of achieving this first aim, I redraw the map of contemporary feminist and queer studies from this perspective of bisexual knowledge. This process involves identifying bisexual meaning in key feminist and queer texts, thereby creating rather different textual associations than are produced by existing authors and theoretical schools. Instead of grouping together psychoanalytic queer texts, or feminist epistemologists, for example, I account for feminist and queer theorists in terms of which bisexual meanings they reproduce or generate in order that their own texts might function in particular ways. Such an approach allows me to tease out threads of bisexual knowledge where at first glance there might appear to be none. Too often, I want to argue, a particular text is said to ignore bisexuality, when in fact bisexuality is essential to that texts' coherence.

I believe that both of these approaches are important in the development of a critical bisexual theory, but I also want to push my investigation of bisexuality in another direction. The third focus of this book, then, is to consider specific formations of bisexuality in local and national contexts, as a point of marked contrast to the theoretical abstractions that commonly mark its emergence. I am interested in those moments and histories where bisexuality is either not produced as middle ground at all but as a subset of either heterosexuality or homosexuality, for example, or in close association with other subjects or communities. Where bisexuality does emerge as a middle ground, I want to track its appearance between locations other than homosexuality and heterosexuality—between lesbian and gay male spaces, for example.

As is discussed further in chapter 1, I will draw heavily on the epistemologies and methodologies of cultural geography in order to achieve this aim. Thus, this book maps divergent and dissonant bisexual meaning in a range of contemporary sexual and gendered spaces. The three concerns in this book cannot, of course, be addressed separately, and it is precisely through a spatial approach to bisexual meaning that all three directions come together. My emphasis then is not on bisexual spaces per se, but on contemporary sexual and gendered spaces where bisexuality informs the development or specific manifestation of sexual subjectivity, identity, or community, whether or not bisexuality is visible or named as such. I identify the role of bisexuality in fashioning contemporary sexual and gendered spaces, as well as the moments and places at which precise meanings of bisexuality circulate and gain new meaning. To track the emergence or insistence of bisexual knowledges in this way allows for attention to *difference* and *tension* rather than *consolidation* or *transcendence* in bisexual meaning to take center stage.

Bisexual Middle Ground

In the current sexual and gendered imagination, bisexuality is always the middle ground between sexes, genders and sexualities, rather than being a sexuality, or indeed a gender or sex, in itself. Unlike the proverbial no-man's land, however, the bisexual middle ground of contemporary feminist and queer theory is anything but neutral. On the one hand, bisexuality is cast as the pernicious glue maintaining heterosexist gendered, and sexed complementarity. On the other, within much contemporary bisexual theorizing, that same middle ground represents the great "bisexual escape" from rigid sexed, gendered, and sexual oppositions. This latter position seeks to reclaim the bisexual middle ground of contemporary and historical theory, culture and activism, in direct response to the perceived elision of bisexual specificity, but, as I argue below, fails to challenge bisexual abstraction at a fundamental level.

The Great Bisexual Escape

Rather than consolidating sexual and gendered binaries, the middle ground of bisexual writing is imagined as a place from which bisexual subjects can resist and transcend categorization, a space that offers refuge from the perceived tyranny of what has come to be termed "mono-sexuality."[3] In this trajectory, sexual and gendered middle ground has been conceived of in a number of positive ways: as a bridge linking polar and otherwise estranged opposites,[4] as a unique combination of sexual (as well as gendered or raced) differences,[5] or as a space of difference rather than derivation.[6] In the first case, the metaphor of the bridge reproduces the understanding of bisexuality as linking sexual opposites rather than a sexuality in its own right. Inadvertently, conceptualizing bisexuality as a bridge reproduces rather than challenges existing perceptions of bisexuality as either abstract or as a passing phase. Bisexuality becomes real only in heterosexual or homosexual contexts, but has no enduring context of its own: no one stays on a bridge for long. In the second case, bisexual ground is understood as both heterosexuality and homosexuality, as staked out in the overlapping territories where gay and straight cannot be separated. Because it is neither one nor the other it is presumed to transcend both categories, insofar as it is not limited by the boundaries of either. It is not a new territory, then, but a synthesis that is also mapped onto other overlaps—in particular man/woman and black/white. Again, this bisexual ground emerges as oddly abstract, since no attention is paid to the power relations that produce any or all of these categories, and structures of sexuality are too casually mapped onto other binaries as if one opposition were identical to all. It is the final vision of a bisexual middle ground as a site of transformative difference that is the most consistently appealing to bisexual writers. In his article "Blatantly Bisexual: Or, Unthinking Queer Theory," bisexual theorist Michael du Plessis suggests that we might want to conceive of a sexual middle-ground as a "radical . . . site for a new bisexual activism" rather than as the "only place to which bisexuality gets relegated."[7] In this context, bisexual location is conceived of in something like feminist standpoint terms,[8] achieved not through sexual practice or wishful thinking alone, but through political struggle and the transformation of a marginalized perspective. Only in this account does something like a bisexual epistemology begin to take shape, although, as we shall see, this is also not without difficulties of its own.

As an active middle ground, then, bisexuality becomes less a static ground and more a peopled location, less a structural composite and more a conscious fusion. In a contemporary bisexual imaginary, the sexual middle ground is occupied by bisexual subjects who then claim to be able to see "both sides" and articulate themselves accordingly. In chapter 1, I address this understanding of bisexuality as the "critical outside" of sexual and gendered structures, paying particular attention to the lack of reflexivity such a claim necessitates. There are enormous dangers in bisexual subjects' assumptions that they are not constrained by sexual, gendered, and raced oppositions, not least of which is that bisexuals' own exclusions cannot be recognized and thus addressed.[9] Yet despite my criticisms, in developing such a strategic vantage-point bisexuals have been able to refute claims that they do not exist as sexual subjects, or are confused, inauthentic, or damaged versions of other sexual identities, arguing that their location gives a clear perspective of contemporary sexual and gendered terrain. Such assertions have facilitated recognition among bisexuals of themselves as healthy, intact subjects of contemporary political and sexual culture,[10] and advanced the search for a history of bisexual politics and desire despite the consistent refusal of lesbian, gay, or heterosexual subjects to do so. If lesbian, gay, and heterosexual subjects do not recognize bisexual identity, then bisexual subjects will hold up mirrors to affirm each other's reality. In addition, queer theorists' refusal to recognize bisexuality as a valid and enduring sexual identity, and bisexuals themselves as authentic subjects, is redefined by "bisexual advocates" as a deliberate foreclosure of non-oppositional sexuality and held up as evidence of lesbian and gay conservatism and self-interest.

Indeed, the bisexual political move I have described above has been enormously important to me. Writings from the late 1980s and early 1990s were my first introduction to the possibility of articulating a distinct bisexual subjectivity and, more importantly, bisexual desire. The anger at misrecognition expressed in *Bisexual Lives* and *Women and Bisexuality* from Britain,[11] and *Bi Any Other Name* and *Closer to Home* from the United States[12] resonated with my own frustration at the limited terms of a queer debate within which bisexuality could only be represented negatively. More recent anthologies such as *Bisexual Horizons* from Britain and *Bisexual Politics* from the United States have also inspired me in moments,[13] though by the mid-1990s the consistent reinvocation of bisexual marginality in relation to lesbian and gay communities, and the rather glaring lack of critical reflection on the limits of "bisexual transgression" had also begun to raise questions in my mind about the problems with contemporary bisexual tactics for recognition. Similarly, early bisexual theorizing, to which I was and still am a contributor, built rather hastily on this proposition of a privileged bisexual perspective rather than specifying the precise nature of that perspective or the limits of its critical reach. The more epistemologically productive moments of bisexual theorizing of the last decade are frequently undercut by the reinstatement of bisexuality as a marginal identity, itself not needing to be "undone."[14] I have become increasingly concerned that reactive bisexual claims to being more transgressive, perverse, gender bending, or multicultural than other queers not only beg to be excepted, but also force bisexual activists and theorists into a political and theoretical cul-de-sac, the geography of which I sketch more precisely in chapter 1. Bisexuality is thus posited as a consistent and self-evident challenge to lesbian, gay, and straight oppositions, the fluidity and transgressive nature of the former contrasted with the static and conservative nature of the latter.

I experienced this dynamic at the Fifth International Bisexual Conference, which I attended at Harvard University in April 1998. As suggested, bisexuality as transgression was the dominant meaning insisted upon and adhered to. At the opening plenary each mention of the word *bisexual* was greeted with a standing ovation. The emphasis of the keynotes was on the equal exclusions bisexuals face from lesbian/gay and straight communities, and the importance of bisexuality's inherent challenge to a "monosexual" imperative. The presumed ethnic, racial, and cultural diversity of local, national, and international bisexual communities was consistently reemphasized despite, or perhaps because of, the predominantly white and middle-class contingent of the conference. While this may have been experienced as uplifting for many bisexuals present, such repeated rhetorical invocations are in the end rather hollow, lacking as they are in both evidence and specificity. I found myself wondering what ground for action and thought bisexuality would offer if it turned out that bisexuality does not (necessarily) explode or even temporarily expose oppositional categories of sex, gender, sexuality, and race. Would a life of inauthenticity and passing as lesbian, gay, or straight be the only alternative? Is there no other basis on which I might claim my desire to be significant? In a sense, these questions motivated the present project.

Interestingly, the conference body as a whole was not so uniform in its unreserved celebration of bisexual transcendence. A workshop on transsexual/bisexual alliances was critical of such idealization, highlighting the problems this posed for coalition politics around, for example, creating and accessing HIV/AIDS resources within the local (Boston) community. Merl Storr and I presented papers focusing on the problematic and ahistorical collapse of structures of race, gender, and sexuality within bisexual organizing and theorizing, and were pleased at the enthusiastic response both presentations received. The development of such critical spaces within the conference as a whole was greeted positively, despite the returning and rereturning to an untheorized bisexual promise at each plenary. It is my belief that bisexual theorizing urgently needs to engage with the complexity and sophistication of the experiences of many bisexuals, whose multiple locations cannot be so simply understood as transgressive of, or even self-evidently different, from, the locations of other sexual subjects.

Although much of this book is highly critical of contemporary bisexual politics and theory, my interest in this book is not in displacing bisexual theorizing to date, but in building on its insights and political motivation. I want to critically interrogate the emergence of contemporary political bisexuality in the United States and Britain, as well as those queer and feminist approaches that seek to reduce bisexual meaning to its dominant Western formation. At this point in time, I am as unhappy with the pervasive bisexual strategy of resignifying the sexual middle ground to create an alternative bisexual location as I am with strategies that seeks to reduce bisexuality to its most conservative meaning. In the first place, I am not convinced that bisexual subjectivity bears no relationship to sexologically and psychoanalytically rendered bisexuality, nor that one need take this position in order to assert the validity of bisexual inquiry. It is entirely myopic to imagine that bisexuality has no role in the maintenance of dominant structures of sexuality. There is, as Jonathan Dollimore has remarked, a tendency toward "wish fulfillment" among bisexual theorists,[15] a desire to distance ourselves entirely from the power-imbued oppositions we are accused of maintaining.[16] I want to argue in line with Merl Storr that it is important to examine "not just [bisexuality's] potential for opening up new ways of understanding gender and sexuality, but also its potential for obscuring or even foreclosing new understandings."[17] Thus, in this book I insist that presumptions of de facto bisexual transgression have as foreclosing an effect on the range of bisexual knowledges and ontological possibilities as do presumptions of de facto bisexual consolidation, and I examine the concrete problems such assumptions have raised in particular contexts.

Bisexual Consolidation

As suggested above, the misguided search for a great bisexual escape must be placed within the context of its dismissal within queer elaborations of sexual and gendered knowledge. I want to return here to the contemporary insistence within sexuality and gender studies that bisexuality can only consolidate hierarchical and polarized sexual and gendered divisions. I remain suspicious of the determination on the part of contemporary theorists of sexuality and gender to see but one kind of bisexual meaning without imagining alternatives. I want here to examine this writing off—or writing *out*—of bisexuality in two queer trajectories. First, I discuss the location of bisexuality within queer epistemology, which advocates genealogical and historiographic methods in the researching of queer subjects. Second, I examine the positioning of bisexuality within work on queer performativity which seeks to adapt a psychoanalytic perspective for poststructuralist understandings of the sexual and gendered subject. These themes recur throughout the book, and so what I aim to do here is introduce my concerns through a brief exploration of bisexual meaning for the theorists most commonly associated with these two approaches: Eve Kosofsky Sedgwick and Judith Butler, respectively.

In queer epistemological terms, bisexuality as middle ground enables and consolidates a heterosexual/homosexual dyad, and is thus directly implicated in dominant historical and contemporary "epistemologies of the closet."[18] For Sedgwick, it is precisely bisexuality's location as bridge or predisposition that maintains sexuality as an effect of gender difference—a link she most emphatically, and I believe rightly, wishes to undo[19]—and that provides sufficient justification for foreclosing further consideration of bisexuality's parameters.[20] In line with Sedgwick, I do not dispute the long histories of sexology and psychoanalysis that rely on bisexual predisposition in order to imagine and insist on the differentiation between various sexed, gendered, and sexual manifestations and behaviors, with a view to fixing the array of difference into the decidely familiar categorizations of man/woman, masculine/feminine, and heterosexual/homosexual. Further, I am indeed convinced of the link that Merl Storr insists on between this form of bisexual meaning and the creation of imperialist racialized topographies, where undifferentiated bisexuality remains the state of members of primitive societies, while the prevalence of monosexuality becomes the marker of civilized cultures.[21] Yet in keeping with, rather than contrary to, queer epistemology, such acknowledgments seem to me to mark just the beginning of necessary inquiry into bisexuality. To my mind, it is precisely the discursive dominance of bisexuality as the naturalized middle ground from which adult sexuality (and indeed Western civilization) proceeds that makes the task of tracing its contemporary emergence and history so urgent.

To approach this issue from another angle, if participation in and reproduction of dominant norms is sufficient grounds for refusal to consider a particular location within sexual hierarchy further, one might be forgiven for wondering why such a stringent test is not equally applied to homosexuality. To extend Sedgwick's logic, homosexuality's structural opposition to and maintenance thereby of heterosexual dominance should preclude further consideration of homosexuality. Yet lesbian, gay, and queer deconstruction of identity categories has resulted in a veritable explosion of published work and archival collections documenting innumerable strategies, commitments, and practices of subjects of same-sex desire historically and in the present that cannot simply be reduced to their location in opposition to heterosexuality. In fact, the desire to find same-sex, or differently gendered, knowledge or expression in a variety of cultural and historical milieux—despite homosexuality's implication in dominant structures—could be said to define the contemporary queer historiographic project. And as a result we now benefit, not only from a plethora of gay and lesbian, but also fag, effeminate, molly, femme, and butch knowledges, to name just a few.

In this vein, I want to argue that it is not enough to trace the history of same- and opposite-sex desire simply in terms of its perceived effects—oppositional heterosexuality and homosexuality, masculinity and femininity, hierarchized racial topographies. To do so at once obscures and reproduces the naturalized understanding of bisexuality as predisposition, and thus heterosexual/ homosexual oppositions as natural and inevitable. Oddly then, existing queer approaches that dismiss bisexuality assume a direct relationship and continuity between meanings in the present and those in the past, reducing bisexual present and past to a single dominant meaning in the process. The approach I take in this book follows Sedgwick's suggestion that theorists need "[r]epeatedly to ask how certain categorizations work, what enactments they are performing and what relations they are creating, rather than what they essentially mean."[22] Here it is not only effects of bisexuality as middle ground but also the conditions that enable bisexuality's repeated reproduction in the same and different forms that require our attention. Judith Halberstam interprets Sedgwick's genealogical approach, or "perverse presentism,"[23] by advocating a method of analysis through which we interrogate "in the first what we think we already know, and then . . . move back toward the question of what we think we have found when we alight on historical records of so called lesbian desire."[24] Likewise, a queer bisexual genealogy must identify discontinuities or absences of meaning in the present, in order that different bisexual meanings and their effects might be traced. Thus, again rewriting Sedgwick, a bisexual genealogy denaturalizes the present "to render less destructively presumable '[bisexuality] as we know it today'."[25]

Despite her own, and indeed Halberstam's, reservations about bisexuality, I have found Sedgwick's queer epistemology and historiography enormously helpful in the development of my own project. It is Sedgwick who urges us not to privilege dominant sexual configurations, nor to assume that "homo-, hetero-, [or] bisexual" people experience "gender meanings and gender differentials" in the same way, or as significant at all.[26] This distinction between dominant structures and the subject of those locations (and others) is important. Sedgwick herself, in other words, proposes a means of thinking about a bisexual subject who sits at odds with dominant meanings of bisexuality as pseudo-hermaphraditic gender merging. Indeed, she cautions against the epistemic violence that is both a cause and effect of imposed meaning from outside marginal experience, particularly where that directly contradicts the articulation of experience from a subordinate location. She writes, "to alienate conclusively, *definitionally*, from anyone on any theoretical ground the authority to describe and name their own sexual desire is a terribly consequential seizure."[27] Unless the "anyone" invoked here is always already a lesbian or gay subject—a gesture that would foreclose rather than open up questions of knowledge, ontology, and power that Sedgwick proposes so provocatively—I can only presume this could also apply to bisexual subjects. In terms of her own argument, here, Sedgwick's insistence on bisexual normativity in the face of consistent bisexual refusal of that singularity can only work if one assumes in advance, and without question, that lesbian and gay subjects unfailingly produce "less normative and therefore riskier, costlier self-reports"[28] on the conditions and possibilities of their existence in the world than do bisexuals. Such an insistence would be directly at odds with Sedgwick's larger epistemological project.

I want to turn now to the arena of queer performativity, examining its own particular relationship to and production of bisexual meaning. As many readers are no doubt aware, performativity is a queer methodology used to expose heteropatriarchal normativity as a pernicious fiction. While queer epistemologists usually do acknowledge bisexuality as significant within dominant structures, even if they do not consider any form of bisexual resistance, performativity approaches fail to engage with bisexuality in any substantive way, either not mentioning it at all or referring to it obliquely and often with hostility.[29] Yet these same approaches commonly utilize a repudiative model of the formation of gendered and sexual subjectivity that relies on a prior acceptance of human bisexual predisposition as the ground for sexual development. I have come to understand the implicit assumption of bisexual collusion in or reproduction of binary opposites as an alibi facilitating queer theorists' continued use of bisexual predisposition as the unacknowledged ground for their own theoretical inquiry.

In *Gender Trouble*, for example, Judith Butler discusses the ways in which the butch/femme pairing exposes rather than replicates the constructed nature of the heterosexual matrix through parody. She writes, "The replication of heterosexual constructs in non-heterosexual frames brings into relief the utterly constructed status of the so-called heterosexual original. Thus, gay is to straight not as copy is to original, but, rather, as copy is to copy."[30] Despite the fact that bisexual subjects might well be considered to make even closer copies of this fictional "heterosexual original," Butler restricts her imagination of that parody to lesbian or gay frames. In Butler's and other queer theorists' schemas,[31] specific gender performances are enabled by the repudiation of heterosexual or homosexual object choice,[32] and embodied as loss in a homophobic social order. The fact that a bisexual subject consciously makes both object choices must therefore either be ignored or taken to indicate a failed or flawed engendering. Bisexuality is thus problematic on two counts: Butler requires bisexuality as psychoanalytic ground to facilitate her own model of gender performativity,[33] and cannot acknowledge a gendered bisexual subject as a possibility. The latter does not simply provide an alternative to the former meaning; in this context it challenges the assumption that this must be how engendering works.

The queer accusation that bisexuality "reinscribes [oppositional] categories,"[34] then, can be read as a displacement of queer theory's own investment in bisexual meaning remaining singular, dominant, and, most importantly, unacknowledged. The notion of gender performativity and hence queer transgression requires this. Amber Ault rightly notes that "Butler rescues lesbianism from Julia Kristeva's 'prediscursive, psychotic,' apolitical abyss but leaves bisexuality mired there."[35] To put this rather more forcefully (though less eloquently), I would argue that "real" (i.e. lesbian and gay) queer subjects occupy the parodic high ground of contemporary sexual culture and theory both at the expense of bisexual difference and through the reinscription of bisexuality as the undisputed middle ground of heteronormativity. Without this displacement, the queer performative subject cannot remain lesbian or gay.

Queer consolidation of bisexual meaning occurs on two levels. The first, as I have delineated, is structural. Historiographically, bisexual meaning remains assumed, so that a heterosexual/homosexual dyad can be said to regulate sexual knowledge. Performatively, queer theory's framing of a transgressively gendered subject relies on bisexuality as structural middle ground to underpin both object choice and repudiation. Inevitably enough, there are echoes of this dynamic on an interpersonal level, too; for what is the extraordinarily common reiteration of the stereotype of a bisexual woman—that she will always leave her lesbian lover for a man—but the discursive manifestation of an a priori assumption that the bisexual woman has already made that object choice without repudiating it? For psychoanalytically informed queer theory, opposite-sex object choice is made and repudiated (lesbian and gay subjectivity), or it is made through same-sex repudiation (heterosexual subjectivity). Since the bisexual does not repudiate opposite-sex object choice, she must therefore *be* heterosexual. There is no question here that one might choose to make a same-sex object choice, without having "first" made and repudiated the all-important opposite-sex object choice; or indeed, that one might make an opposite-sex object choice without having "first" irretrievably lost the primal, and socially precluded, same-sex object. The conclusion reached in the rhetorical invocation of habitual bisexual behavior above seems to be that without repudiation, there is apparently no reason a bisexual would not or could not settle (back) into heterosexuality.[36] Ault identifies a similar discourse in the way her lesbian interviewees talk about bisexuality, concluding, "What is at stake is not so much whether a woman will leave her woman lover for a man as whether the dissemination and institutionalization of a bisexual identity category during the present period constitutes a hegemonic move that could incorporate lesbians into dominant cultural systems."[37] In effect, bisexuals become the theoretical and cultural carriers of heterosexist hegemony within lesbian and gay, or queer, community—the cultural embodiment, or perhaps better, *hologram*—of a psychic model of sexual subjectivity that privileges opposite-sex object choice as impossible to refuse without repudiation and desire as mirrored by a concomittant loss.

Any reader who is the subject of her own particular bisexual positioning will no doubt be familiar with how this displacement plays out in practice. As Sedgwick points out so astutely and movingly, marginal subjects learn to negotiate difference through the development of complex "nonce taxonom[ies] for mapping out the possibilities, dangers, and stimulations of their human social landscape."[38] Sharing information about how to negotiate queer space is a commonplace of bisexual-bisexual interaction (at least in the U.K. and U.S. circles of which I am a part), because the price of getting it wrong is direct and intimate. Bisexual nonce taxonomies include an unreliable sixth sense about when one should broach the subject of one's bisexuality, and how this differs depending whether the person in question is a friend, a colleague, or, critically, a hoped-for lover. In addition, bisexuals need to learn how to read such lesbian and gay statements as "My last lover was bisexual," since it is often difficult to tell if the speaker is particularly hostile toward or open to engagement with bisexuals. Bisexuals know, because we need to know, that nothing stops the progression of a flirtation, political bond, or camaraderie quite like the "realization" of bisexuality, which in that moment is coextensive with the "realization" of betrayal, founded on a "realization" of the inevitability of the heterosexual return. Yet to withhold that critical information may simply be to delay the same process and have it revisited on one's head twofold at a later date. Bisexuals know, because they cannot help but know, that at some point there will be a need to "confess," and that that confession risks interpolating them as subjects that they will not recognize themselves to be.[39] In both structural and interpersonal contexts, queer theory's reliance on bisexuality as heteronormative underscores its determination that despite the rejection of identity, the opposition to heterosexual normativity should remain the privilege of a distinctly gendered lesbian or gay male subject. Anxieties about any lingering sexual and gendered oppositions that could compromise queer transgression can thus be displaced onto a hypothetical and abstracted bisexuality without contours or history rather than engaged with directly. It is my hope that one effect of this work will be to make queer theorists think (at least) twice about what they think they already know about bisexuality.

An Outline of the Chapters

As indicated at the beginning of this introduction, the rest of this book is concerned with bisexual meaning in sexual and gendered spaces. To narrow down the scope of this project, I examine the emergence of this "bisexual territory" in the contemporary United States in the late 1980s and early 1990s. In both published work and activism at this time bisexuality becomes a dense site through which concerns around sexuality and gender are debated. My chosen time frame provides a useful starting point for a contemporary history of contested bisexual meaning. The late 1980s and early 1990s saw a dramatic increase in both published work on bisexuality and in campaigns for local and national bisexual political visibility,[40] and discussion of bisexuality in local and national lesbian and gay publications was also more frequent and direct than it had previously been. I also focus on contemporary urban or theoretical spaces because the existing queer and feminist material I revisit in this book usually analyzes a subject occupying urban settings, and/or engages a subject positioned in a largely theoretical or conceptual terrain. Four main chapters of this book follow.

In chapter 1, *Bisexual Landscapes*, I provide a detailed history of contemporary bisexual theorizing in the United States and Britain, focusing on the emergent themes that typify this body of work, some of which I have already signaled. I pay particular attention to the development of bisexuality as middle ground, and to sets of tensions within bisexual theorizing currently. I identify these tensions as especially dense in consideration of bisexual elision or presence, epistemological and identity approaches, and the location of bisexuality within or beyond existing identities and communities. In addition, I introduce the reader to key ontological assumptions that a "bisexual intervention" urges us to reconsider: linearity and identity formation, visibility politics, and questions of the authentic sexual subject. Following this exploratory mapping of bisexual theory, I lay out my theoretical, epistemological, and methodological framework for the rest of the book, focusing on how what I term *bisexual partiality* and *bisexual presence* suggest a potent fusion of poststructuralist and spatial approaches to the study of sexual culture. Following recent work within sexual geography, I make the case for considering bisexuality as it exists within, and in part structures, spaces where it is not always named. I suggest that in response to differences that coexist in particular sites the subject is formed through a series of cultural (as opposed to unconscious) repudiations. Such an approach enables a consideration of bisexual subjectivity as something other than the embodiment of psychic merging. Chapter 1, together with this introduction, forms the theoretical backdrop to my forays into the formation of bisexual space in subsequent chapters.

Chapter 2, *Desire by any Other Name*, takes up the concerns already raised vis à vis the production of contemporary bisexual meaning, in relation to lesbian space in Northampton, Massachusetts. I trace the history of lesbian space in this area from the mid-1960s, with a particular focus on the role bisexuality (in both its abstracted and concrete forms) has played in its formation. The main body of this chapter analyses the Northampton Pride March debates, which took place between 1989 and 1993 and concern the issue of named bisexual inclusion in what was formerly the annual Northampton Lesbian and Gay Pride March and Committee. The furious battles over community, visibility, and identity in the local and national press change the nature of lesbian space in Northampton, and bring a range of bisexual meanings out into the open. First, I chart the positioning of bisexuality as middle ground in the construction of lesbian space, with a particular emphasis on the systematic depoliticization of bisexuality in order to establish the limits of "lesbian territory." More specifically I am interested in the ways that bisexual women are located between lesbian and heterosexual male territory, and thus come to signify a masculine threat to lesbian safety. Secondly, I trace a slightly different trajectory that locates bisexual space as emerging initially from within lesbian space, becoming its opposite only through these Pride March debates. Finally, I look to the conceptualization of bisexuality as transgressive middle ground within a developing queer community in Northampton.

In chapter 3, *Representing the Middle Ground*, I chart the location of bisexuality through its association with transsexuality within contemporary U.S. and U.K. queer and feminist, political and theoretical approaches. How are bisexuality and transsexuality placed and to what (or whose) ends? What effects does the association of bisexuality with transsexuality have on emergent bisexual and transsexual subjectivities? This approach deliberately foregrounds the fact that cultural space is not necessarily geographically locatable, and that contemporary theories of sexuality and gender constitute a distinct space of differences within which bisexual subjectivity takes shape.[41] I begin by charting in more depth the history of bisexuality as middle ground in sexological theory, sociobiology and Freudian psychoanalysis, and link these perspectives to the production of bisexuality as middle ground in contemporary lesbian feminist and queer political theories. In the process, I examine bisexuality's production as heteronormative middle ground as precisely that which links it, historically and contemporarily, with transsexuality. This chapter thus marks a return to the examination of the effects of dominant bisexual meaning. I am particularly interested in tracing the similarities and differences in the ways that both bisexuality and transsexuality are understood as exhibiting reductive gender traits via their association with heterosexual femininity, or as subverting raced oppositions as well as gendered and sexual divides. The final section of this chapter focuses on the limits and possibilities of transsexual and bisexual photographic representation, which offer an exemplary site through which to examine the materialization of these different productions of transsexual and bisexual meaning.

Chapter 4, *A Place to Call Home*, takes up the issue of a concrete bisexual ground for community and identity in relation to the creation of bisexual space in San Francisco. Instead of focusing on the role of bisexuality in the creation and maintenance of "other" spaces, here I consider the steps taken to establish a specifically bisexual territory that can be differentiated from lesbian, gay, or straight spaces. In a similar vein to that taken in chapter 2, I trace the history of an emergent bisexual community in San Francisco from the early 1970s onward, looking at its relationship to the sexual freedom and feminist movements, and charting its transitions in light of the HIV/AIDS epidemic. The primary focus for this chapter is the First National Bisexual Conference in 1990, which I analyze in terms of organization and execution, and in terms of its role in the creation of a national U.S. bisexual network (BiNet). As with previous chapters, I approach this material in terms of bisexual abstractions and concrete bisexual spaces. My interest here is first, to trace the location of bisexual space in San Francisco in relation to lesbian and gay spaces and second, to interrogate the influence of contemporary understandings of bisexuality as transgressing opposites of sex, gender, sexuality, and race in the formation of the 1990 National Bisexual Conference space. What difficulties does such abstraction present when dealing with material differences that cannot simply be transcended?

Tracing concrete bisexual manifestations in all of the above chapters provides both a critique of what we think we already know about bisexuality and a fresh challenge to the presumption that heterosexuality and homosexuality, masculinity and femininity, male and female reside in clear opposition to one another. If bisexuality can be located "elsewhere," what uncharted heterosexual and lesbian or gay knowledges might also emerge?

CHAPTER 1

Bisexual Landscapes

I have spent almost ten years thinking about the relationships among feminist theory, queer theory, and bisexuality, inspired initially by what I perceived to be an absence of literature engaging substantively with the subject. To a certain extent this remains true today: consideration of bisexuality has not generated anything like the volume of work on feminist, or lesbian and gay, subjects, despite the boom in the publishing industry of titles addressing gender and sexuality in various ways. This chapter is an attempt to come to grips with what it is that makes bisexuality, as an object as well as subject of inquiry, so difficult to address in empirical, theoretical, representational, and political terms, despite the fact that in our everyday lives bisexual behavior is anything but a rarity.

Part 1 of this chapter, "Bisexual Histories," provides an analytical history of thinking about bisexuality, focusing on writing in the United States and Britain. In the first instance, I provide a critical and political background for readers not familiar with bisexual thought, and a critical summary of these approaches for readers who are.[1] Particular attention is paid in this section to the emergence of contradictory bisexual meanings suggested in the introduction. I then discuss bisexual writing thematically, tracing a shift from bisexual theorizing that adopts an identity-based approach to one that emphasizes bisexuality's challenge to existing structures of sexuality and gender. This split (between epistemology and identity) remains unresolved, and reflects bisexuality's structural position as middle ground within contemporary thought. Part 2 of this chapter, "Bisexual Epistemologies," sets out my framework for theorizing bisexuality in the rest of the book, mapping the various disciplinary and methodological influences I have drawn on. I discuss the relationships among, in particular, poststructuralist feminist epistemology (historiography and genealogy), sexual geography, and the reflexive traditions within feminist and lesbian inquiry, and their application to my own work. This second part of the chapter situates my own work firmly within feminist epistemological, and methodological tradition, and insists on the importance—indeed, *necessity*—of conducting empirical and archival work from a poststructuralist perspective.

Part 1: Bisexual Histories

There has been very little bisexual theory to date that is not based in psychology, empirical sociology, or sexual-identity politics. When three influential works on bisexuality were published between 1975 and 1978—Margaret Mead's "Bisexuality: What's It All About?" Charlotte Wolff's *Bisexuality: A Study*, and Fritz Klein's *The Bisexual Option*[2]—a virtual silence about bisexuality was broken.[3] This silence, or more properly, lack of work directly on bisexuality, had stretched since Alfred Kinsey and Wardell Pomeroy's findings in the late 1940s and early 1950s that "only 50 per cent of the population is exclusively heterosexual throughout its adult life, and . . . only 4 per cent of the population is exclusively homosexual throughout its life."[4] As a result of this research, Kinsey and Pomeroy developed what became known as the "Kinsey Scale,"[5] which numbers 0 to 6, 0 being exclusively heterosexual, 6 being exclusively homosexual. The true bisexual is understood to be a "Kinsey 3," equally attracted to men and to women.[6] While Kinsey's findings shocked America in the late 1940s and early 1950s, the implications of a bisexual continuum did not take root in the public imagination, such that twenty seven years later Mead must remind her readers that "[t]he time has come . . . when we must recognize bisexuality as a normal form of human behavior."[7]

Prior to Kinsey, bisexuality was predominantly represented and produced in early-twentieth-century sexological or psychoanalytic texts, or in fictional works from the same era.[8] Thus, in the medico-psychoanalytic literature, bisexuality has been read as physical or psychical hermaphroditism, [9] as psychical androgyny,[10] or as the ground from which heterosexual or homosexual adult sexual orientation evolves.[11] The only early sexological work to address itself directly to bisexuality was Wilhelm Stekel's *Bisexual Love*, which also posited bisexuality as a sexed and gendered mélange.[12] Unsurprisingly, fictional works from the same period, most notably Virginia Woolf's *Orlando: A*

Biography and Radclyffe Hall's *The Well of Loneliness*, both written in 1928, confirmed this medical view of bisexuality as a transhistorical blending of male and female, masculine and feminine traits in a single body.[13] The understanding of bisexual predisposition that plays itself out in both texts is what allows Orlando to move from one sex and gender to another while remaining quintessentially Orlando, and Stephen Gordon to understand herself as gender inverted. Only Mary Llewellyn, Stephen Gordon's feminine lover, represents the emergent meaning of bisexuality as a combination of heterosexual and homosexual desire.

After the late 1970s, bisexuality seems to disappear once again as a public subject of discussion. There is virtually no writing in English on bisexuality as a viable personal and political concern or choice until the late 1980s. In the last decade, however, there has been an explosion of popular bisexual writing in the United States and Britain, begun by the Off Pink Collective's *Bisexual Lives* in Britain, and Thomas Geller's *Bisexuality: a Reader and Sourcebook* in the United States.[14] The creation of a new body of work on bisexuality has been particularly notable in the United States, and at the beginning primarily took the form of edited anthologies of personal histories or political perspectives.[15] In Britain, Sue George's *Women and Bisexuality* was the first book by a single author to be published on women's bisexuality for almost fifteen years, and the Off Pink Collective published a companion volume to *Bisexual Lives* in 1996.[16]

There is a predominance within popular publishing of bisexual work that engages the relationship between feminism and bisexuality, or that focuses on the historical and first-person experiences of bisexual women. Work in this vein tends to argue that bisexuality is an ideal subject of feminism, insofar as it foregrounds women's independence from men and challenges the assumed relationship between gender and sexuality.[17] Elizabeth Reba Weise's perspective is typical, she writes,

> Those of us who consider ourselves feminist are excited about the possibilities of a bisexuality informed by the understanding that sex and gender are classifications by which women are oppressed and restricted. We see bisexuality calling into question many of the fundamental assumptions of our culture: the duality of gender; the necessity of bipolar relationships [. . . and] the demand for either/or sexualities.[18]

In line with this conviction, women-only bisexual groups count for a large part of U.S. and U.K. bisexual support networks and political movements.[19] This work has not been matched by a corresponding focus on bisexual men qua bisexual men: male bisexuality has tended to be addressed in mixed-sex volumes, through psychological or sociological structural vectors,[20] or in relation to HIV and AIDS, for obvious reasons.[21] Notable exceptions to this rule include the work of David

Lourea, who before his death always insisted on discussing the personal and interpersonal implications of bisexuality, and HIV and AIDS, in public and in private,[22] and the special edition of the recently launched *Journal of Bisexuality*, "Bisexuality in the Lives of Men."[23] Since the mid-1990s, popular writing by bisexuals has begun to move away from personal narrative stories and toward identifying the importance of bisexuality in other spheres of life, though this is by no means a seamless transition, as the above special edition suggests. In particular, the connections between bisexuality and the sex-work industry and sexual libertarianism have been given a good deal of attention, as have explorations of the link between bisexuality and spirituality, and the political alliance of bisexual and transgendered people.[24]

In line with this increase in published work, local, national and international bisexual activism also increased dramatically from the late 1980s on in both Britain and the United States. In March 2001, Britain's national bisexual newsletter advertised sixteen bisexual support groups nationwide, a national bisexual phone line, a nationwide umbrella organization (the British Bisexual Federation), Bisexual Sexual Health Action, and the Bi Parents Network.[25] The U.K. national bisexual magazine, *Bifrost*, folded in 1995, but was replaced by the newsletter *Bi Community News*, which published its forty-eighth issue at the end of March 2001.[26] The U.K. National Bisexual Conference (BiCon) is held every year, usually attracting between two hundred and four hundred people.[27] In the United States there are local bisexual groups in almost every large city, a national bisexual network (BiNet), and a national magazine, *Anything That Moves*.[28] The first National Bisexual Conference in the United States was held in San Francisco in July 1990, the fifth National Bisexual Conference in Boston in April 1998,[29] and the first North American Conference on Bisexuality, Gender and Sexual Diversity in Vancouver in August 2001.[30] Bisexual space has also been created on the Internet, with user lists, websites and chat rooms proliferating.[31] In addition, in both U.S. and U.K. national contexts, bisexual activism has resulted in an increasing acceptance of bisexuality as a valid sexual identity within existing umbrella organizations. Thus Outright Scotland, the democratic lesbian, gay, bisexual, and transgender rights organization, now explicitly includes bisexual and transgendered people, and advertises in *Bi Community News*. And in 1999 the Gay and Lesbian Historical Society of Northern California (a local and national queer archive), changed its name to the Gay, Lesbian, Bisexual, Transgender (GLBT) Historical Society after a number of years of resolutely refusing to do so.[32]

Likewise, bisexual theorizing has begun to make its mark within academia, despite Merl Storr's correct assertion that bisexual theory still needs to pay more attention to the problematics of bisexuality rather than continuing to reassert its validity as a subject or object of study.[33]

In 1992 Elizabeth Däumer published her article "Queer Ethics; or, The Challenge of Bisexuality to Lesbian Ethics,"[34] in which she situates both her writing and bisexuality as part of a queer narrative existing in tension with lesbian/feminism. This was the first U.S. or U.K. publication to theorize bisexuality in relation to queer and feminist theory, and it swiftly became one of the most influential articles for the development of British bisexual theory. Several British bisexual writers, researchers, and academics (myself included) met at the eleventh National Bisexual conference in Nottingham in 1993, and formed the U.K. national network for research on bisexuality, Bi-Academic Intervention. Bi-Academic Intervention's purpose was to create a space for the development of bisexual theory, as well as to "intervene" bisexually in academic discussion of sexuality. The group held a series of small one-day conferences and distributed a newsletter, providing a valuable space for bisexual theorists to develop and share their ideas. Bi-Academic Intervention disbanded all but nominally in 1995, in part because none of its founder members remained convinced of the need to continue theorizing bisexuality as a separate arena of inquiry (from, say, feminist, queer, or film studies).[35] The editorial collective Bi Academic Intervention was formed from within this group, however, publishing the first U.K. volume of bisexual theory and a special issue on bisexuality of the U.S.-based *Journal of Gay, Lesbian, and Bisexual Identity* in 1997.[36] British authors have extended bisexual theory by providing histories and overviews of its frameworks, and engagements with and critiques of their usefulness,[37] as well as a wide range of articles in journals and anthologies (see below). What characterizes the British contribution to bisexual theorizing is an interdisciplinary approach drawing more heavily on critical and cultural theory than on empirical sociological approaches.

In the United States, two edited volumes of bisexual theory have been published—Donald E. Hall and Maria Pramaggiore's *Representing Bisexualities* in 1996, and Paula C. Rodríguez Rust's *Bisexuality in the United States* in 2000.[38] The former was the first anthology of bisexual theory to draw on contemporary poststructuralist, and in particular, queer epistemologies and methodologies to examine bisexuality and its representation in literature, film, and cultural milieux. The latter brings together some of the key U.S. social science writings on bisexuality, with social science being understood almost entirely empirically. Indeed, the majority of bisexual research in the U.S. remains faithful to the concerns of structural sociology and psychology, rather than to an interrogation of bisexual meaning per se.[39] It is no coincidence, then, that the U.S. work that does take a critical stance, interrogating bisexual knowledge from a variety of angles, is not included in Rust's "comprehensive" anthology, even where, as in the case of Amber Ault's work, the author is clearly located within the empirical social sciences.[40] Rust's reader, then, oddly recircumscribes rather than opening up both disciplinary inquiry and bisexual identity. In too much U.S. bisexual research, I would contend, it is assumed that we all know what bisexuality is, and that this self-evident bisexuality needs to be spoken and written about in order for (bi)sexual liberation to occur. A case in point is the *Journal of Bisexuality*, recently founded by the father of bisexual psychology, Fritz Klein. The first issue emphasizes the significance of bisexual activism in recent history for the current sexual landscape of San Francisco, provides a critical view of bisexual representation in the media, and examines the experience of being bisexual in sex therapy.[41] What is markedly absent is any critical account of the terms through which bisexuality is being reproduced, or any suggestion that bisexuality might not always be a fundamentally wonderful thing. Even the articles that at first glance promise a slightly more critical perspective never move beyond the assertion that what we really need are *more* meanings, *more* presence, *more* bisexuality.[42] Chicago University Press has recently published Steven Angelides's work on the historical conditions of emergence of bisexual meaning, though the author himself lives and works in an Australian context.[43]

This increase in bisexual theoretical production is not confined to either single-author books or anthologies that focus directly on bisexuality. Throughout the 1990s, bisexual theorists have been asked to contribute articles to lesbian and gay anthologies, typically, but also to anthologies and journals concerned with sexual space,[44] sexology,[45] and feminist theory and politics,[46] to give just three examples. For the most part, such contributions are understood as wholly additive, with the bulk of queer material and the general framework remaining unchanged and unchallenged by the single bisexual, or transgendered, contribution. As a result, bisexual writing can often be found nestled among pieces that otherwise refuse bisexual existence, or rely on its disavowal, creating an interesting, though probably not enormously productive, tension within the text itself.[47] A number of editors go a step further to include work on bisexuality as central to a particular anthology or journal's vision,[48] although this is most often the case only where the editors themselves identify as bisexual.[49] In their own work too, lesbian and gay writers have begun to refer to bisexuality, although their engagement usually remains restricted to the gloss "lesbian, gay, and bisexual."[50] Indeed most queer writers continue to code and recode "queer" as exclusively lesbian and gay (and sometimes transgendered where this overlaps with lesbian and gay subjectivity) in their work. Bisexual theorists know well that to raise the question of bisexuality in public queer academice space is to risk blank stares, dismissal, or, remarkably frequently, to be accused of "being difficult" or "aggressive" (harkening to the bisexuality of children or criminals?). It is rare indeed for lesbian and gay writers to theorize bisexuality other than to illustrate a related point, or as a rhetorical gesture that highlights the instability of identity categories generally, and lesbian or gay identity categories in particular. For example, in *Getting Specific: Postmodern Lesbian Politics,* lesbian theorist Shane Phelan makes the quite remarkable statement that for the lesbian community to understand its own history it will need to acknowledge "'bisexuality,' the inevitable supplement of sexual categorizing, at the *center* of lesbian experience."[51] Yet Phelan goes no further in exploring her own thesis— that bisexuality is both inevitable supplement and unacknowledged center—mentioning bisexuality only twice in her book, the second time to stress rhetorically, once again, that bisexuals "introduce another other, not at the margin but at the heart of lesbian theory."[52] Two important exceptions to this invoking of the supplemental but critical bisexual are Pat Califia's "Gay Men, Lesbians, and Sex: Doing It Together," and Julia Creet's "Anxieties of Identity: Coming Out and Coming Undone."[53] Both writers interrogate the founding of lesbian desire and identity on bisexual repression, and Creet in particular advocates the acknowledgment of bisexuality as an important part of the process of creating a conscious, non-Freudian lesbian sexuality.[54]

A central development within bisexuality theorizing of the last decade that I would like to develop now is the increased interest in bisexuality as not only, or not even, a sexual identity, but as an ontological or epistemological location from which to critically survey the current field of queer and feminist studies. This push has been precipitated in part by Marjorie Garber and Jonathan Dollimore's work on bisexuality.[55] Garber's epic, *Vice Versa: Bisexuality and the Eroticism of Everyday Life,* may seem an unlikely choice of advocate for a critical bisexual epistemology, since she finds bisexuality quite literally everywhere. Garber discusses bisexuality's role within sexology, psychoanalysis, and psychology, its function in relation to literature, art and culture, and the furthest reaches of its possible meanings, asking her readers to contemplate, for example, whether desire for a grapefruit might constitute bisexual attraction. Given that Garber's bisexuality emerges as a trope for discussing any form of sexual deviation from fixed gender of object choice, in any time and place, one of the effects of *Vice Versa*'s sheer scope is to distance bisexuality from a specific link with identity per se. This is where Garber's theoretical contribution begins and ends, however, and her work is unlikely to change many queer scholars' minds about the importance of bisexual theory to sexuality studies. *Vice Versa* is extremely well researched, engaging in tone, and pleasurable to read, but aims to be theoretically grand without the sustained argument needed to support such metanarrative leanings. Garber uses a number of different bisexual meanings interchangeably, and presents bisexuality as the way to resolve restrictive notions of sexuality and society generally, without providing any examples of how such a resolution would work in theory or in practice. As Storr asserts, "Garber's major theoretical claims ... are not set out rigorously or at sufficient length, and tend to be reiterated rather than elaborated."[56]

Jonathan Dollimore engages the question of bisexuality and identity from quite a different angle, examining the limitations and constraints that structure bisexual identity, in direct contrast to more celebratory work by bisexual authors. In "Bisexuality, Heterosexuality, and Wishful Theory," Dollimore documents the defensive position bisexual theorists have been forced into, and relentlessly critiques the tendency of some bisexual theorists (myself included) to be "more postmodern than thou" in the attempt to bring bisexuality some queer recognition. Instead, Dollimore suggests that we follow Garber in confronting "the challenges and difficulties of the actual desiring encounter with difference, as distinct from the comfortable theoretical invocation of it."[57] Dollimore thus alters the questions bisexual theory asks, from the closed inquiry—how might the parameters of bisexual identity best be asserted or inscribed to benefit bisexuals?—to the rather more open—what does a bisexual know (or not know) in practice? Despite my disagreement with Dollimore over Garber's achievements in *Vice Versa*, Dollimore's critique can now be seen as a turning point for bisexual theorizing. As I delineate later in this chapter, the disagreements between identity and epistemology approaches to theorizing bisexuality are partly what structure "bisexual studies." But before discussing these trajectories in more depth, I want to backtrack slightly to address some of the problems of bisexual signification that have contributed to the lack of development of bisexual theorizing, and their significance for sexual subjectivity more generally.

Bisexual Meanings

The relative lack of contemporary bisexual theorizing can be partially attributed to the range of seemingly contradictory meanings that the term *bisexual* carries. So many definitions of bisexuality proliferate in twentieth-century U.K. and U.S. culture that merely disentangling one meaning from another is problematic. Malcolm Bowie provides the three most common definitions of bisexuality:

> *bisexuality* This term has at least three current meanings, and these can easily produce confusion. As used by Darwin and his contemporaries it presented an exclusively biological notion, synonymous with hermaphroditism, and referred to the presence within an organism of male and female characteristics. This meaning persists. Secondly, bisexuality denotes the co-presence in the human individual of "feminine" and "masculine" psychological characteristics. Thirdly, and most commonly, it is used of the propensity of certain individuals to be sexually attracted to both men and women.[58]

As I suggested at the beginning of this chapter, *Orlando* and *The Well of Loneliness* represented and reproduced these three meanings of bisexuality in 1928. Kinsey recognizes these meanings but disputes the association of bisexuality with intersexuality, hermaphroditism, or androgyny, preferring to think of heterosexual, bisexual, and homosexual as adjectives qualifying sexual behavior rather than as predisposition.[59] Kinsey's warnings have not been heeded, however, and these three meanings retain their dominance today. Providing an interesting precedent for Sedgwick's "axioms,"[60] Kinsey remarks that the term *bisexual* "should, however, be used with the understanding that it is patterned on the words heterosexual and homosexual and, like them, refers to the sex of the partner, and proves nothing about the constitution of the person who is labelled bisexual."[61]

The three meanings of bisexuality that Bowie identifies combine in particular ways to make conceiving of an adult bisexual identity—a possible fourth and more contemporary meaning—difficult. In fact, and as I suggested in the introduction, meanings of bisexuality as the middle ground for gendered and sexed merging, or sexual predisposition, can work in opposition to a clear conception of bisexuality ontology. For example, in a recent seminar I taught on bisexuality, a number of students validated their perception that "we're all bisexual, really" by reference to the increased acceptance of androgyny in night-clubs, which meant that the gender of the person they desired was not always clear. None of these students acted contrary to their perceived sexual identity, however. Their "latent bisexuality" allowed heterosexual or homosexual desire for either sex to surface; they could appreciate the "other side" of themselves. A bisexual potential functions here as inclusive of heterosexual and homosexual desires, and draws on the other meanings of bisexuality as physical or psychic hermaphroditism. Yet the invocation of bisexual potential acts counter to consideration of an adult bisexual identity. The wrong object choice, here, would simply be a "mistake," understandable because of a general human bisexuality, rather than one of a range of bisexual object choices. Similarly, the use of the term *AC/DC* to describe bisexuals retains ambivalence around bisexual meaning. The term clearly denotes a "dual current" in the bisexual herself, though whether this is sexed or gendered remains undecided. Unlike hermaphroditic representation, however, a "dual current" indicates most favorably a vacillation (first one gender, then the other), or most demonizing a lack of stability, inconsistency, or unpredictability. Yet *AC/DC* also carries that other meaning of "dual attraction," which suggests less about the bisexual subject themselves, and more about their changing object choice: the person who is *AC/DC* "swings both ways." The term itself, then, carries all three (and to some extent four) dominant meanings of bisexuality, together with a range of concomitant cultural connotations encompassing untrustworthiness and potential disloyalty, as well as the "good-time gal" situated historically at some point during the "swinging sixties."

Lack of consideration of bisexual identity is not only a question of displacement or substitution of one meaning for another, however. There are additional reasons why bisexuality is rarely conceived of as an adult sexuality. First, the sex or gender of object choice cannot signify bisexuality, where for heterosexuals, gay men, and lesbians it can, in representational and structural terms at least. Although we know that factors other than the gender of object choice influence sexual identity, it is rare for these to be seen as the defining factor of sexual identity. Historically and contemporarily one is heterosexual, lesbian, gay, or indeed bisexual, because of who one has sex with. Non-gender-specific sexual behavior is rationalized within psychoanalysis as a secondary "deviation" of the sexual aim. Thus, Sigmund Freud states that some degree of fetishism is "habitually present in normal love," and that such a deviation becomes pathological only "when the longing for the fetish passes beyond the point of being merely a necessary condition attached to the sexual object and actually takes the place of the normal aim."[62] Within this dominant framework, people whose sexualities are formed primarily through fetishism or sadomasochism, or intergenerational or interracial dynamics, to suggest just a few possibilities, are difficult to account for. Their desires are often figured as perversion, or marginalized as additional desires within a primary heterosexual or homosexual frame.

In Britain, since legal attacks beginning in 1990, most famously in the Spanner trials in which gay men were prosecuted for consensual acts of sexual "violence," sadomasochists have come increasingly to see parti-cular practices as germane rather than peripheral to identity.[63] Such moves help to expose the fallacy that the sexual self is formed through sex and gender alone, although it is still rare for SM or other "deviations" from the primary sexual aim to displace prior identification on the basis of preferred gender of object choice. I want to speculate that in the case of active bisexuality, in these Freudian terms, opposite-sex and same-sex object choice must both be "deviations," since they cannot both be the "normal aim." The danger of bisexuality to this normative sexual paradigm is that what is considered the normal sexual aim, opposite-sex object choice, may itself be a secondary deviation in many cases. Thus, the foreclosure of bisexuality as active sexual behavior is a profoundly protectionist move. Only if bisexuality remains structural predisposition, or sexed-gendered merging, can the "normal aim" be preserved from becoming the fetish.

Second, in an inversion schema where masculinity and femininity must remain sexual complements irrespective of heterosexual or homosexual object choice, bisexuals' inconsistent gender of object choice presents further structural difficulties. Lesbian or gay male sexuality can be heterosexualized through such terms as "mannish woman" and "effemi-nate man," and by association with their correlate "opposite-gendered," if not opposite-sexed, object choices. Butch or femme desire clearly does not always conform to this pattern: femmes desire femmes, butches desire butches, and so forth. But this is not my point; I am talking in terms of the available models of heterosexual sexual and gendered development within which homosexuality signifies, rather than the cultural or social forms that desire may create as its own. If one's gendered subject position determines and is determined by a consistent, opposite-gendered (whether same or opposite-sexed) object choice, a bisexual's structural lack of finite object choice throws her own gendered position, as well as that of her partner(s), into question. If this is true in relation to presumptions of gendered complementarity, it is also true in relation to the individual process of becoming gendered. To understand gendered object choice as precisely that, *choice,* is to challenge the presumption of sexual development, both in terms of sexual aim and objects, and also in terms of process—that is, the repression and melancholic incorporation of the lost object on which gender identity is supposedly founded and maintained.[64] To return to a point I made in the introduction, failure to repudiate one or other gendered object is thus constituted as a failure of identity, and transformed into variations on other identities (failed homosexuality or heterosexuality), or a temporary state in the process of proper identity formation (becoming homosexual or heterosexual). To underline my argument here: Without a normal aim (both sexed and gendered), and without due process of repudiation in the formation of a gendered and sexual self, bisexuals fail to become proper *sexual* and proper *gendered* subjects.

The difficulties do not end here. Even if one can imagine the formation of a bisexual sexual and gendered subject in relation to the above schema—as exception, say, or as vacillation, where the subject has mastered both heterosexual and homosexual forms of desire and identification as similar to two separate languages[65]—bisexual temporality still poses difficulties. One of the conditions for sexual subjectivity is that its aim be consistent over time. Third, then, the formation of sexual identity requires not only that one make a particular gendered and sexed object choice but that one *continues* to make that choice. The present can only be validated by the anticipated future, which can only be validated by a past that is retrospectively given meaning according to the present. One rewrites the past, or at least selects from the past aspects of identity that are consistent with one's present location, to create a sense of continuity between experiences in the past and in the present, a past self recognizable to the present self. Thus, a future that resembles the present is assured through narrative continuity secured in a past that reflects the present. It is less a question of what one actually did in the past, but how those actions or experiences felt. So, for example, a lesbian who comes out in her fortieth year can maintain that she has always been a lesbian, as long as a past containing opposite-sex object choice may be resignified as undesired, unquestioned, or strategic. And a heterosexual woman may understand her brief early affair with her best girlfriend as a case of mistaken identity (desire for friendship), or experimentation in preparation for the real thing, without compromising her own, or other people's, understanding of her as heterosexual. One is allowed mistakes as long as they are seen *as mistakes,* as mere interruption to the narrative of one's true sexual identity. The crucial factor here is that the moments (or years) one disowns from the past must be differentiated from those one claims: the latter are authentic, the former inauthentic, where truth is intimately related to experience. Interestingly, and as Mariam Fraser suggests, the confession of that truth (in this case the mistakes one has regretted making as a way of marking those one wants to claim as authentic) is constitutive of sexual subjectivity, not the site of its undoing.[66] Contemporary lesbian and gay coming out narratives commonly follow this chronology, of course, constituting in many ways the exemplary template of sexual subject formation, and indeed modern subject formation more generally.[67]

In the traditional lesbian coming-out narrative, affairs with bisexual women in the past form one of a range of passable mistakes that guarantee one's status as a bona fide lesbian in the present. As Ann Kaloski indicates, the bisexual woman's "place in the collective lesbian history is only symbolic: she is retained as past 'mistake,' but not as 'real person.'"[68] A lesbian's own inauthentic past experiences are projected onto the bisexual woman, who herself becomes the subject of inauthenticity. As well as carrying lesbian subjects' disavowed inauthenticity, bisexual subjects cannot display the requisite consistency of object choice, to become recognizable sexual subjects in their own right. For bisexuals, the different sexual object choices they have made are precisely what allow them to occupy bisexual subject positions, and to imagine themselves continuing to do so. It is a present with only one lover of one sex, not a past, that poses the most problems for a bisexual identity. What if this is the last person I desire? How can my future bisexuality be assured?

In response to these problems of temporality, bisexuals have striven to create a "before" and "after" that lends validity to their present self-perception. In a narrative typical of this, one woman notes, "For the first time I felt like a whole person. . . . My sexuality has caused me problems because it was too broad to be acceptable to me, as I was trying to force it into narrow definitions—first heterosexual, and second, lesbian.'"[69] This example follows much the same redemptive line as lesbian and gay narratives since it claims an innate but repressed bisexual self and/or a moment of bisexual revelation, together with a previously inauthentic mistaken identity. The problem of the "monosexual" present is often resolved through nonmonogamy: lasting attractions to people of both sexes figure prominently in bisexual self-narratives. Thus, one of the contributors to *Bisexual Lives* insists on the authenticity of her bisexuality through an ingenious mingling of the past and the present:

"Amanda (for two and a half years), Paul (for four and a half years)," and the list continues.[70] Here is a real bisexual, dedicated to multiple object choices of both sexes, steadfast in her endlessly mutable bisexual desire. The present is no longer a slightly embarrassing interruption, but a heroic demonstration of bisexual dedication. There are clearly a number of problems with this bisexual heroism. First, it is but a short step from here to the stereotype of the bisexual as necessarily non-monogamous and only representable in threes (or more). Many bisexuals are monogamous or even celibate (intentionally or otherwise). Second, imagining for a moment that this stereotype were not politically problematic, it would nevertheless be hard to live up to such an ideal, even if the flesh were willing. Third, even supposing that all bisexual desire could be expressed through the simultaneous, unbroken desire for both sexes, the gender complementarity necessary for bisexual desire to be heterosexualized would still be missing, resulting in a lack of narrative closure.[71]

Our "bisexual subject," then, cannot be structurally produced or endorsed through gender of sexual object choice, gendered subject position or chronology of sexual identity, and hence cannot be understood as an adult sexual identity under these terms. In terms of sexual citizenship, too, the inability of bisexuals to argue that they were "born that way" without risking being relocated in the middle ground of predisposition and hence not identity, makes rights claims within the public sphere especially problematic. This is true not just in the face of virulent societal homophobia, but also in relation to lesbian and gay desire for assimilation. The problem is compounded by the fact that theorists of sexual citizenship for the most part also presume that the sexual subjects that one is seeking public recognition for are unequivocally lesbian and gay. Momin Rahman, for example, discusses the impact of queer theory on claims for sexual citizenship in terms of difference, not sameness, but still assumes that it is lesbian and gay subjects, in all their difference, who will take up their citizenship rights.[72] Yet the inclusion of bisexual perspectives in theories of sexual citizenship would complement approaches that highlight the dangers of naturalizing claims for recognition and anticipate dominant strategies of incorporation.[73]

Theorizing Bisexuality

As discussed above, in response to structural and cultural exclusion most bisexual writers argue that bisexuality is a valid sexual identity in its own right, with its own internal consistency, its own coming out narratives (discussed above) and its own unique (and often separate) culture. Mead asserted in 1975 that "there is not, and it seems unlikely that there will be, a bisexual liberation movement. For the truth is, bisexual men and women do not form a distinct group, since in fact we do not really recognize bisexuality as a form of behavior, normal or abnormal, in our society...."[74] Yet despite this assertion, bisexual theorists frequently adopt identity and visibility tropes to advance notions of a discrete bisexual identity and community. In this section, I outline some of the discursive tactics employed by bisexual theorists to produce a viable bisexual subject and highlight the difficulties that these tactics present.

In the first instance, bisexual activists and researchers have begun to use the concept of *monosexuality* to distinguish between bisexuals (who desire more than one sex) and *monosexuals* (who do not). The term *monosexuality* is defined in a number of key ways in order to situate bisexuality as both different from and preferable to it. Wilhelm Stekel's declaration in 1934, "'*There is only bisexuality.... There are no monosexual persons!*'" clearly suggests a mutually exclusive opposition between the two terms,[75] yet importantly does not consider monosexuals to be real or genuine. For Stekel the term *monosexual* is intended to denote surface sexual behavior, under which lies bisexuality, the real sexual ground of the individual: there are no monosexuals. Contemporary bisexual writers have taken the term rather more literally. Thus, in the glossary of *Bi Any Other Name*, *monosexual* is defined as "a term used for both heterosexuals and homosexuals—i.e., all people who love only one gender and take for granted the sexual dichotomy set up by the patriarchy. Bisexuality calls this system of categories and divisions into question."[76] Here monosexuals are both real, rather than really bisexual, and, unlike bisexuals, politically duped into believing in a two sex, two-gender system. In Loraine Hutchins and Lani Ka'ahumanu's definition bisexuals escape patriarchal conditioning, challenging the "categories and definitions" that are the by-products of social misogyny. This redefinition of monosexuality positions bisexuals as occupying the transcendent, politically progressive, yet strangely neutral middle ground of sexed, gendered, and sexual culture.

The strategic importance of the term monosexuality for the development of bisexual community is that it allows for the creation of a sense of common bisexual ground: As Liz A. Highleyman notes, "It may be ... appropriate to regard those for whom sex/gender is a deciding factor in selecting or ruling out partners (homosexuals and heterosexuals, sometimes collectively referred to as monosexuals) as more similar to each other than either is to those bisexuals for whom sex/gender is of little or no importance or relevance in their relationship choices."[77] Not only are bisexuals linked by their difference from monosexuals, we are also uniquely oppressed by *monosexism*—"the belief that people can and should be attracted to only one sex/gender and that there is something wrong with those who cannot or will not choose."[78] A rather cynical reading of Mead and Highleyman together suggests that bisexuals need their behavior to be pathologized in order to secure a group identity from which to assert the normality of bisexuality.

I am only too well aware of the difficulties that bisexuals face in asserting our desires as legitimate, and more importantly, can see that a denial of those desires can have dangerous consequences. The assumption that one is lesbian, gay, or straight can be damaging or even fatal when that translates into lack of adequate HIV/AIDS prevention material aimed at people who have sex with men and women, for example.[79] It is also indeed the case that bisexuals face stigma from both queer and straight communities, although I would want to insist that that stigma is not the same in both contexts. I am deeply concerned by the discursive and political effects that the creation of the monosexual/ bisexual binary has, and believe that arguments for the specificity of bisexual desires need to take a less defensive and potentially divisive form. To term all non-bisexuals *monosexuals* erases the differences between lesbians/gay men and heterosexuals, equating the power dynamics that exist between bisexuals and lesbians/gay men with those between homosexuals and heterosexuals. Such a gesture refuses to acknowledge the social hierarchies of sex, gender, and sexuality that have historically influenced, and continue to influence, subject and community formation. In terms of gender relations alone, establishing bisexuality as the oppressed half of the monosexism binary erases the differences between a lesbian feminist position and a heterosexual male position in relation to structures of power.[80] In a bid to claim minority status, the fact that lesbians and gay men do not have the same definitional, social or economic power as heterosexuals is conveniently ignored. Additionally, the very real cultural, political, and semantic violence bisexuals face from heterosexual and queer communities becomes undifferentiated, and therefore impossible to pinpoint and tackle, as do a variety of bisexual privileges. As Amber Ault saliently remarks, "to universalize the dynamics of oppression, and to present each social site as a fractal image of the larger binary system" is, in effect, "to read from the dominant position."[81] As one might expect, the (bisexual) likelihood of occupying a position of privilege is enhanced not reduced in the moment of assertion of (bisexual) escape from "the social structures and ideologies that govern both gender formation, and sexual-orientation formation."[82]

The second technique through which bisexuality is posited as a credible identity and movement is in its description as *more* authentic than lesbian, gay, or straight sexualities. Thus, bisexuals have been erased from history, wrongly represented, and politically decried, not because bisexuality is rare, but because it is everywhere repressed. Sue George's argument in the first chapter of *Women and Bisexuality*, that bisexuality is historically and contemporarily "excluded and absent" is typical, as is Amanda Udis-Kessler's assertion that negative stereotypes of bisexuality need to be replaced with more positive and therefore truer depictions of bisexuality realities.[83] Marjorie Garber extends these approaches to their logical conclusion in *Vice Versa*, insisting that sexuality and bisexuality are, in fact, synonymous, and, further, that "[b]isexuality is that upon the repression of which society depends for its laws, codes, boundaries, social organization—everything that defines 'civilization' as we know it."[84]

If bisexuality has been erased, then the task for bisexual writers is unambivalent: to rectify the historical record by unearthing historical figures that have hitherto been ignored, or repositioning figures previously imagined to be lesbian, gay, or heterosexual as more correctly bisexual. The history of sexuality is thus rewritten through a process of bisexual reclamation and naming that is itself a rewriting of the lesbian and gay liberation maxim "We Are Everywhere!"[85] Sappho, Oscar Wilde, and Virginia Woolf can be reclaimed as bisexual because of their relationships with more than one biological sex. In fact, anyone whose desires have not been wholly restricted to single-sex object choices throughout their lifetime might well be included in this bisexual history making. To take Oscar Wilde as an example, both Fritz Klein and Garber highlight Wilde's relationships with women as well as men, Klein in 1978 and Garber in 1995. Klein is unequivocal about his view of Wilde as bisexual,[86] while Garber is aware enough of the theoretical problems of historical revisionism from a contemporary standpoint to qualify her documentation of Wilde. She writes "Since Wilde's genius lay in inventing himself as an apostle of perversity, of transgression as such, to "reclaim" him as bisexual instead of gay would be merely to repeat the gesture of fragmentation and compartmentalization, the gesture of essentializing, that is contrary to his own practice and thought."[87] Yet Garber's argument in *Vice Versa* as a whole is that any desire or behavior that is not exclusively focused on one sex or gender is bisexual, and since she does not adequately or consistently distinguish between behavior and identity in her book, Wilde finally emerges, according to her own approach, as unquestionably bisexual. In response to this drive to create an overarching history of bisexuality, peopled with bona fide bisexuals, the editors of *The Bisexual Imaginary* write in contrast that the contemporary task should not be to relinquish negative stereotypes and replace them with more truthful—that is, more positive—representations, but to conduct analyses of "the ways in which [bisexual] meanings accrue; and [to ask] what strategies can be used to effect a more useful or enabling range of meanings."[88] In this light, the editors suggest it might be more helpful to argue that, however he self-identified in his lifetime, Wilde is now "important in the constitution of a bisexual imaginary *and* a gay imaginary."[89]

To critique the "lost bisexuals" discourse further, such approaches are also in danger of reproducing the worst excesses and exclusions that attend an emphasis on identity. At this point in time, a political and theoretical trajectory that posits a discrete bisexual subject is already thoroughly known, its final destination contained within its own terms. Its limits are marked, policed, and then undone in ways that are not just exclusionary (we will presumably need to ask who decides which figures count as bisexual and which do not), but also, frankly, banal. It feels as though we have been rehearsing these circular debates for decades. In methodological terms, too, even if one could "go back" and find consciously or unconsciously elided bisexuals, with all the problems of retrospective historical process implied, and then simply add them to the contemporary picture, a new set of problems emerges. Such an additive, inclusive politics and theory is linked to a larger politics of cultural redress, which even in terms of its own logic creates a never-ending necessity for identifying the next excluded other to be incorporated. Currently we know that in a sexual/gender political theory register, transsexuals and intersexuals are claiming a similar authentic subjectivity that deserves its own particular cultural, political, and legal recognition,[90] but we would be naïve to imagine that inclusion could ever be complete. Not only does that adding of new identities maintain the structure of inclusion/exclusion, itself productive of minoritization, but such a vision is ultimately distopian, since its vision can never be accomplished. This search for the intact, transhistorical bisexual subject, while seemingly confrontational, engages the production of bisexual meaning at a surface level only. It is as if the perceived historical and cultural elision were simply an error to be corrected, a deliberate (but presumably forgivable) absenting—in short, a failure of historical and cultural memory, rectifiable by "remembering" bisexuality and setting the historical record straight. As I will argue later in this chapter, I remain unconvinced as much by the presumption of bisexual elision in the first place as by the proposed means to amend it.

The third way that some bisexual writers have advanced bisexuality as distinct from other sexualities is by shifting from a focus on bisexual identity to one of bisexual epistemology. The question is therefore less who bisexuals are and where they might be located, but rather how bisexuality generates or is given meaning in particular contexts. This epistemological focus tends to ask how a bisexual perspective may be useful as part of a deconstructive project concerned with highlighting the limits of critical discourses of sexuality and gender. I identify three primary forms that a bisexual epistemological approach takes, although individual writers may not be restricted to only one form. The first locates bisexuality as outside conventional categories of sexuality and gender; the second locates it as critically inside those same categories; and the third focuses on the importance of bisexuality in the discursive formation of "other" identities.

The first approach seeks less to explain or define bisexuality than to locate it on the critical edge of, in particular, feminist, lesbian and gay, or queer discourse and politics, as a tool uniquely suited to highlighting the structural problems within sexual identity. Thus, Elizabeth Däumer proposes that "we assume bisexuality, not as an identity that integrates heterosexual and homosexual orientations, but as an epistemological as well as ethical vantage point from which we can examine and deconstruct the bipolar framework of gender and sexuality in which, as feminists and lesbian feminists, we are still too deeply rooted, both because of and despite our struggle against homophobia and sexism."[91] Mirroring Däumer's arguments, I wrote in 1993 about a late twentieth-century feminist "bisexual body" that I envisioned as "a signifier of the possible reconfiguration of the relationships between sexes, genders and sexualities."[92] I articulate this bisexual (woman's) body as a "double-agent" within heterosexual and lesbian communities and present bisexuality as transferring knowledge rather than being produced by the intersection of knowledge and power. Similarly, Maria Pramaggiore draws on the work of Eve Kosofsky Sedgwick to envision bisexual theory as an *epistemology of the fence* that "open[s] up spaces through which to view, through which to pass, and through which to encounter and enact fluid desires."[93] For Pramaggiore, "fence-sitting" provides the bisexual with a unique vantage point allowing her "to reframe regimes and regions of desire by deframing and/or reframing in porous, nonexclusive ways."[94] Such abstract metaphorizations of bisexuality have been critical necessities in the move to theorize bisexuality not simply as an elided identity requiring redress, but as a location from which theory and politics are produced. In addition, the move toward a bisexual perspective as conscious and deconstructive, rather than preconscious or given, is one I welcome. Yet in the above accounts the value of a bisexual perspective continues to reside in its detachment from less complex, less fluid approaches, usually identified as lesbian and gay, or heterosexual. The aim is still to delineate the unique, separate insights bisexuality itself has to offer us rather than critically evaluating bisexual emergence. As with Garber's surface insistence on the problems with claiming Oscar Wilde for a bisexual history, the bisexual theorists above know better than to claim unique identity status for bisexuals, and thus tend to force the difference between perspective and identity in ways that ring rather hollow. The abstraction is a clue in a sense, as is the passive construction of Pramaggiore's *encountering* and *enacting* of desires (rather than directly desiring), a technique presumably designed not to overdetermine the identity of the subject possessing or utilizing this bisexual perspective. There are two possible results borne of this technique. It is either successful, and a bisexual perspective becomes disembodied and two-dimensional (a proposition, not an experience), or it is unsuccessful, and the reader, without signposts to the contrary, simply reconstructs the most plausible relationship between perspective and subject—that is, that they are the same: a bisexual perspective is held by a bisexual subject. Despite the desire to uncouple bisexuality and identity, then, conceptualizing bisexuality as a *critical outside* repositions bisexuals as occupying a transcendent or neutral middle ground, implicitly if not explicitly suggesting that they are not "imbricated in the homo/hetero binarism that structures the rest of society,"[95] that they are more fluid and visionary than other sexual subjects.

This problem of bisexual epistemology reproducing the terms that it seeks to critique is the starting point of the second set of approaches, which endeavors to position bisexuality, its subjects, practices and histories, as *fully imbricated* in the sexual and gendered binaries under consideration. Theorists in this vein argue that the very ability to think about bisexuality as a critical outside is facilitated by existing structures of sexual identity that, as I have argued throughout this book so far, facilitated through bisexuality's abstract positioning as "otherworldy" middle ground. Thus, for Merl Storr, bisexual predisposition in nineteenth-century sexology is precisely that which facilitates racial as well as gendered hierarchies,[96] and for Mariam Fraser, bisexual coming-out narratives continue to mark sexual confessions as necessary rights of passage within the discursive production of the (sexual) self in the 1990s.[97] Both authors view bisexual meaning as generated within rather than outside of sexual norms, and as implicated in both the foundation and perpetuation of those norms.

What it means for interpersonal relationships to consider bisexuality as a critical inside is explored in two very different genres by Jonathan Dollimore and Janice Williamson. As I outlined earlier in this chapter, Dollimore's article rejects bisexual "wishful theory" in favor of an interrogation of "the challenges and difficulties of the actual desiring encounter with difference, as distinct from the comfortable theoretical invocation of it."[98] Dollimore thus advocates bisexual theoretical attention be given to the "mass of tangled desires and identifications" that he believes constitute bisexual practice, and that the bisexual abstractions he critiques disavow.[99] While never moving much beyond stern fatherly advice to bisexual researchers, Dollimore does briefly illustrate his position by imagining for us a bisexual scenario in which "a bisexual male partakes of a threesome in which he watches a man fucking with a woman."[100] For Dollimore, this scene is not one of transcendent celebration, but of difficult, psychically determined, contradictory identifications—the bisexual man wants to be both the man and the woman; he also wants to *have* both the man and the woman. This instability is precisely what makes the bisexual voyeur's position worthy of our attention, in Dollimore's eyes; analysis of this instability is often foreclosed by bisexual theorists' insistence that bisexuals are not confused or undecided, but beyond the constraints of identification and desire.[101]

Janice Williamson's "autobifictograph," "Strained Mixed Fruit," could

be read as a fictional refusal of the bisexual resolution Dollimore de-
plores.[102] As with Dollimore's "bisexual man," resolution within
Williamson's bisexual narrative is always deferred, and never completely
satisfying. Bisexual narrative is never experienced as separate from other
discourses, is cross cut, undermined even, by other narratives, or
understood as fantasy or frustration. So, just at the moment when the
protagonist is about to come out as bisexual, her mother beats her to it
by telling her about having sex with her own best friend once. Not only
is coming out as an independent rite of passage denied the heroine, her
mother supplements her confession by insisting that the experience was
not an enjoyable one. As her "bisexual daughter . . . chokes on [her]
lettuce,"[103] the mother continues, "'She was drunk you know. Reminded
me of your / Father—DRUNK.'"[104] Desperately trying to circumvent her
mother's erasure of difference between unwanted opposite-sex rites and
same-sex experience, the bisexual daughter suggests, "Perhaps if you tried
it again, you might like it."[105] But her mother remains unconvinced:
"No." she says, "I won't."[106] When our heroine finally does come out,
her mother reiterates a recognizable homophobic response, in telling her
she will have "an unhappy life."[107] The difference is that this warning
could as easily be read here as a reflection of the mother's story of sexual
misery that she has already mentioned—a sharing of common experience
rather than a denial of the same familiar cliché. The mother interrupts
the flow of her daughter's story once more by mentioning her own
mother, whom she says she thought was a lesbian: "When she made my
clothes, she stood me on a chair to fit them to me. / Then she stuck pins
in me. Touched my nipples. Made me cry."[108] Is the protagonist's
grandmother an incestuous SM lesbian? Is her mother in turn coming out
as an incest survivor? Or is the grandmother a fabrication of the mother's
homophobic mind? The reader cannot be sure how to interpret events
that would ordinarily point to a straightforward single meaning. In
narrative terms, the mother's interruption again prefigures our heroine's
second coming out, this time as an incest survivor: "[a]s I begin to work
on child sexual abuse narratives and my own suspected incest experiences,
I feel some pressure to renounce my sexual past."[109] More ambivalence—
this time, the narrator suspects rather than is certain about incest in her
past, and is under pressure rather than willing to renounce that past. In
both sexual narratives, which we are surely not intended to think of as
discrete, the daughter's confessions are tempered by her mother's more
dramatic declarations and unequivocal memories, which punctuate and
frustrate the former's uncertainty.

Like Dollimore, Williamson offers us no celebratory bisexual closure;
hers is a multilayered text riddled with anxiety, false starts, and interruptions. Where Williamson differs from Dollimore, however, is in her
concern with a bisexual desire that is psychically complex, but also
historically and socially located. While I concur with Dollimore's petition

for bisexual theory to pay direct attention to the difficulties of bisexual desire, I am less convinced by his belief that this complexity might best be read in the psychoanalytic processes of both wanting and wanting to be. Williamson's bisexual woman's experiences are explicitly historicized through the 1970s and 1980s, and are set against a backdrop of AIDS, racism, and police violence in Canada, while Dollimore gives us no indication of time or place to guide our reading of his bisexual man's experiences. What is valuable about the deconstruction of bisexual identity in the critical inside approaches to bisexual epistemology is the challenge to the notion that bisexuality is always and everywhere the same, or can be known as a static, boundaried identity. The attention to both the constraints upon and the differing forms of bisexuality is indeed welcome.

The third set of epistemological inquiries shares this desire to complicate bisexual meaning and context, and in addition focuses on separating the theorization of bisexuality from bisexual identity. The central premise in such a line of thinking is that bisexuality has discursive impact both with and without the presence of bisexual subjects. Bisexuality is thus worthy of investigation not because bisexual realities have been misrepresented or elided, but because narratives of bisexuality constitute an affective discourse in their own right, one that shapes meaning as well as becoming shaped. Following Sedgwick, Stacey Young succinctly makes the case for this manner of bisexual theorizing; she suggest that we ask a different set of questions: "[W]hat other functions does bisexuality perform in discourses on sexuality? When does it get invoked, and how? When and why does it disappear, and with what effects? What other issues seem to attach to it, what questions does it perennially raise? What complications that appear when we theorize bisexuality actually exist for, but are obscured in theories about, lesbianism, male homosexuality, and male and female hetero-sexuality?"[110] Jo Eadie makes a similar point when he argues that instead of attempting to place bisexuality outside its stereotyped representation, it would be more fruitful to examine that "set of hegemonic conceptions of what bisexuality means which structure for all of us the perception of bisexuality."[111] Both Young and Eadie explore contexts of contemporary theoretical and cultural representation in which bisexuality is a trope for "something else"—typically confusion, madness, or greed. Its metaphorical presence or invocation is thus frequently a way in which anxieties at the heart of other identities may be played out.

The foregrounding of bisexuality as discursively key in the development of other identities has primarily been examined in the context of lesbian identities and communities. This must in part be attributable to the number of bisexual women writers who previously identified as lesbian, and the sustained engagement with feminism, and particularly lesbian feminism, in bisexual theory. Such a move within bisexual theory can also be read as a fleshing out of Shane Phelan's undeveloped comment that bisexuality resides "at the *center* of lesbian experience."[112] Thus, Ann Kaloski highlights the central role that bisexuality plays in lesbian coming-out fiction: bisexuals are that which must be transcended or rejected in order for a lesbian to become herself.[113] Stacey Young, Paula Rust, and Amber Ault are also concerned with the bisexual-lesbian relationship, but more particularly with the variety of techniques that lesbians employ to continue to differentiate themselves from bisexuals, and particularly bisexual women.[114] Young emphasizes the role bisexual exclusion plays in drawing clear boundaries around lesbian community,[115] while Rust uses lesbian talk about bisexual women as a means to understanding "the political and cultural ideology of lesbianism and the structure of the lesbian movement."[116] Ault identifies a range of ways that lesbians position bisexuality, homing in on its discursive function as a means of perpetuating lesbians' own self-hatred, which she locates in lesbian insistence that bisexual women will unfailingly leave a lesbian lover for a man.[117] These are just a few examples of how thinking about bisexuality epistemologically, rather than in identity terms, might help theorists of sexuality and gender to explore the discursive construction of identity and community more fully. These approaches point to ways in which a gendered, sexual subjectivity cannot be said to be formed through psychic mechanisms of repudiation alone, but through a series of repeated *cultural repudiations* that secure identity in recognizable, and often heteronormative, ways.

One of the difficulties with the above approaches is that bisexuality continues to be metaphorized. It is for this reason that I do not only wish to consider bisexuality as it appears in the development of more recognizable sexual subjects and communities, important though this task clearly is. As I outlined in the introduction, I am equally as concerned in this book to identify places where or moments at which bisexual differences might be traced. In certain respects, then, I aim to do in this book what Williamson does in her anti-narrative: I aim to provide a history of bisexual experience without sacrificing the complex and conflicting ways in which that desire is experienced by the individual or group. Like Garber, I want to focus on the bisexual knowledges produced in the margins of dominant discourse, but I also want to connect those to one another through something other than an assumed bisexual universal. I do not want to find bisexuality everywhere in the same form, but look at its contradictory manifestations in a number of parallel arenas, including where it is not named. Part 2 of this chapter develops the epistemologies and methodologies that I have found useful in this endeavor, locating my work firmly within the gender and queer studies traditions of interdisciplinarity and mixed methods.

Part 2: Bisexual Epistemologies

The process of conducting the research for this book has raised questions central to ongoing debates within feminist and queer epistemology and methodology, and in particular the question of "experience" for both the researcher and researched. In this section, I make the case for the importance of poststructuralist feminist and/or queer epistemologies in providing a framework to make sense of the everyday, situated experiences of bisexual subjects. By way of introduction, I focus on two conceptual splits within this field that make bisexuality difficult to theorize. These are, first, a theory/politics divide within feminism, and its correlate within the academy, a theory/empiricism divide; and second, a queer/feminist epistemological division, where gender is assumed to "belong" to feminism, and sexuality to queer studies.

In the first case, my intervention reflects my frustration and dissatisfaction with feminist debate where it proceeds as if poststructuralist methodologies are in necessary opposition to the materialist feminist desire to highlight the lived experiences of women. An endlessly reproduced "split" between theory and politics within feminism, where these terms are sloppily mapped onto poststructuralist theoretical approaches on the one hand, and empirical research on women's lives on the other, results in an impasse foreclosing consideration of the complexities of subject formation and maintenance in the social world. Has anyone been to a feminist conference in the last decade where a theory/practice tension has not been reproduced as *the* structuring tension within feminism, and further, where this imaginary split—none the less powerful for this—has *not* been cited as a key reason for the lack of a current feminist political movement? Interestingly, the insistence on poststructuralist feminist work (rarely referenced) as unable to attend to the "lives of ordinary women" is matched only by the equally unreferenced and glib gesture toward what has become known as "1970s feminism" within poststructuralist work. This imaginary divide is a discursive mechanism alarmingly effective in its capacity to disarm feminist power to explicate the lived social conditions marked by gender, sexuality, race, and class. In other words, it is the repeated invocation of a feminist theory/practice divide, rather than its truth, that could be said to constitute feminist political impotence.

Not only do I believe, with Elspeth Probyn, that gendered and sexual experience needs to be more fully theorized,[118] I also contend that the failure to develop models of experience as partial, fragmented, and contradictory limits our ability to make sense of and thus transform gendered social reality. A feminist epistemology that maintains *a priori* assumptions about what constitutes gendered or sexual experience, and thus subjective location, is necessarily attuned only to dominant gendered and sexual subject formations, and is ill-equipped to produce ethical research on subjects whose knowledges are produced from a variety of different social locations. I will argue that without feminist post-structuralist perspectives, it is not possible to make sense of the peculiarities of bisexual social and political existence, since there are no finite sexual or social practices that adhere to or inhere in a bisexual identity. The nature of bisexual social existence is always partial, most often experienced within communities that do not recognize bisexuality as discrete or viable, and filtered through competing discourses of identity. Thus, when Claudia Card states that bisexuality is "a good *example* of inauthenticity in a lesbian,"[119] or Elisabeth Wilson expresses confusion as to what kind of "effective political identity" bisexuality might be,[120] both writers presume that identity and politics author each other in transparent ways. These perspectives mark the limits of lesbian feminist accounts of experience as much as they express a myopic view of contemporary social and political landscapes. As a transitive subjectivity bisexuality will always be theorized as "something else" at the same time as lesbian, gay, or straight subjectivity becomes over-burdened with "lived realities" that do not resonate with their specific sexed, gendered and sexual experiences.

With reference to the queer/feminist split I mentioned earlier, any reader well versed in contemporary feminist and queer epistemological discussions cannot fail to notice that I mix and match references to sexual and gendered epistemologies here. Queer epistemologists have, of course, made a series of convincing arguments for analyzing gender and sexuality separately. Heavily influenced by Gayle Rubin's "Thinking Sex," queer theorists have pointed to the ways in which feminists frequently subsume "the sexual" under "gender" as an area of concern on the basis that oppressive sexual relations are the effect of oppressive gender relations. As a result, epistemologies of sexuality are relegated to the realm of "special interest." In response, queer theorists have provided genealogies of the effects of a primary, Western homosexual/heterosexual dyad that cannot be reduced to gender binaries, insisting that the concerns of feminist and queer theorists are not always the same, or even mutually supportive.[121]

While I concur with the queer project of foregrounding the central role of sexual discourse in the formation of contemporary subjectivity, one of the unfortunate side effects of such a separation can be concomitantly to reduce feminist inquiry to the pursuit of gendered meaning only. Thus, Eve Kosofsky Sedgwick notes that feminist inquiry is "gender-centered" while antihomophobic inquiry is "sexuality-centered,"[122] and Henry Abelove, Michèle Barale, and David Halperin contend that "[l]esbian/gay studies does for sex and sexuality approximately what women's studies does for gender."[123] What is interesting to me in these statements is not whether each inquiry prioritizes one or the other object, but the fact that this separation becomes resonant at a time when to speak of "gender" as the privileged object of feminist inquiry is rendered unacceptably exclusionary within feminism itself. As Judith Butler points out, such a distinction between the "proper objects" of feminist and queer inquiry can only have a circular effect, epistemologically ensuring that feminism "remain" heterosexist (or indeed racist or classist) in its concern for gender equality above all else.[124] One effect of this gender/sexuality separation is to position queer feminist theorists as queer rather than feminist, thereby positioning their critiques as coming from outside rather than within feminism. This is certainly true of Butler's work, which is commonly institutionally taught as highlighting the inadequacies of feminism, rather than as part of a feminist critical trajectory.[125]

My reasons for resisting the common divisions between feminist and queer objects are twofold. First, I seek to remain faithful to Rosi Braidotti's insistence that postmodern feminist epistemologists need to pay (visionary) attention to the contradictions played out in transitions between sites rather than situating themselves exclusively within a single domain.[126] And in fact, many of the writers I have found most useful in developing a framework for bisexual feminist epistemology—Donna Haraway, Elspeth Probyn, and Rosi Braidotti, as well as Judith Butler— are themselves queer feminist scholars who are unwilling to overinvest in a single subject of inquiry. Each of these theorists is concerned to articulate an understanding of the subject in process (for example the cyborg or nomad[127]) who is formed "through experience,"[128] and not prior to it: whether sexuality, gender, or neither emerges as a key object or effect cannot be assumed in advance. Second, since the subject and object of my own inquiry in this book is bisexuality, I feel I could not prioritize sexuality over gender, or vice versa, even if I so desired. Bisexual meaning, as I have suggested through this book so far, is generated precisely through the slippage among sexed bodies, genders, and sexualities, both historically and in the present: its role in facilitating, maintaining or challenging heterosexist oppositions is as much a question of gender as it is of sexuality.

Bisexual Experience

Before moving on to look in more depth at the intersection of bisexual and poststructuralist feminist and queer epistemologies, I want briefly to give an indication of the parameters of the approaches I am concerned with. I do not wish to retrace already well-trodden paths within approaches to feminist epistemology here.[129] Thus, I will not be rehearsing debates about feminist standpoint and the challenges to "experience" as the authentic ground of feminist intervention,[130] preferring to indicate what I consider to be the most productive points of engagement between feminist poststructuralist theories and my own research.

One of the myths surrounding feminist poststructuralist perspectives is that experience is no longer considered a valuable category of analysis, being replaced by attention to a free-floating "gender performance" not grounded in the female body. In fact, though, the category of experience is anything but abandoned by feminist poststructuralist epistemologists, who pay careful attention to the different ways in which experience might be theorized, and its importance for feminist subjectivity. Probyn, for example, urges feminists to subject "experience" to particularly rigorous analysis, not in order to displace its central role in feminist thinking, but so that it can remain a productive site of engagement.[131] She begins this project by proposing that we make an analytical distinction between ontological and epistemological experiences of "being sexed," where "at an ontological level, the concept of experience posits a separate realm of existence—it testifies to the gendered, sexual and racial facticity of being in the social. . . . [and at] an epistemological level, the self is revealed in its conditions of possibility; here experience is recognized as more obviously discursive and can be used overtly to politicize the ontological."[132] The productive self, for Probyn, emerges as an effect of the tension between these levels,[133] a reflexive subject cognizant of the differences that constitute herself. Similarly, for Braidotti, what marks a postmodern conception of the subject is its formation through recognition and experience of difference rather than sameness.[134] Our subjectivities are not static grounds of certain knowledge but the endlessly renewed and renewable result of connections with other people, places, and expressions. Bradotti figures this contemporary feminist subject as a "nomad" whose transitions are not the site of her undoing, but are "precisely the reason why she can make connections at all. Nomadic politic is a matter of bonding, of coalitions, of interconnections."[135]

Despite the enormous differences of approach within poststructuralist feminist accounts of the relationship between experience and subjectivity, what they have in common is their emphasis on the partiality and transitory nature of experience that cannot be known in advance,[136] but is rather an effect of power relations. As for earlier standpoint theorists, knowledge derives from experience, but the argument is for "politics and epistemologies of location, positioning, and situating, where partiality and not universality is the condition of being heard to make rational knowledge claims."[137] The feminist theorists I am engaging with here are particularly careful to stress that partiality, difference, and transition are distinct from sloppy relativism, allowing for accountability in the present rather than an assumption of predetermined hierarchical difference. It is the situating of these knowledges, the tracking of nomadic trails, and the politicizing of differences within experience that allow us to see how the self is engendered, and what the effects of this engendering are.[138] One effect of such an approach is that one cannot assume in advance which subjects and knowledges will have foreclosing, and which transformative, effects. If this loss of the *a priori* subject seems disquieting, Doreen Massey, for one, has little sympathy, writing, "Those who today worry about a sense of disorientation and a loss of control must once have felt they knew exactly where they were, and that they *had* control."[139]

Of course, such epistemological perspectives have enormous impact on the questions that guide our research on sexual and gendered subjectivities. The questions we ask must necessarily be other than "What is the woman's or lesbian's experience in this context?" or even "What is the feminist or queer reading of this context?" Such questions assume that there is a single experience or single reading that will be identifiable and knowable. Instead, the task is to examine the knowledges that emerge from interactions among and between sexual and gendered subjects, and to assess the political and ethical value of such knowledges. As Sedgwick suggests, the task of queer epistemology must be "[r]epeatedly to ask how certain categorizations work, what enactments they are performing and what relations they are creating, rather than what they essentially *mean*."[140] As I discussed in the introduction, this process is one of queer feminist genealogy, a way of tracing sexual and gendered knowledges at variance with dominant discourses, rather than knowledges we recognize at first glance. Inevitably this will often involve tracing lack of knowledge, or taking the assumed knowledge of the critic as object rather than as identifiable "other." These poststructuralist feminist and queer epistemologies are not in conflict with feminism; nor are they "antifeminist." They should be seen as a part of the time-honored feminist tradition of challenging established "truths" about gender and sexuality. Their aim is to identify the barriers to a politically engaged queer feminist subjectivity and create myriad languages through which progressive female subjectivity can be conceived.

In light of the above, what could easily become the primary question when thinking about bisexuality—"What is bisexual experience?"—is necessarily displaced as impossible to answer, indeed duplicitous with dominant narratives of identity and desire, and a different set of questions is asked, in line with the theorists I have been discussing. Following Haraway, I ask, "Where is bisexuality positioned in the contemporary sexual/gendered field, and how does it position other knowledges?" Following Probyn, I ask "Between what differences is a bisexual self formed and reproduced, and how might we make ethical evaluations concerning this self?" Following Braidotti, I ask, "From which terrains are bisexual subjects expelled and into which welcomed? Which terrains do bisexual subjects traverse or keep conceptually distinct?" And finally, following Sedgwick, I ask, "What different bisexual knowledges circulate currently, and what do they allow and disallow? Which subjugated knowledges can we trace in order for a bisexual genealogy to have resonance in the present?"

In light of these research questions, I want to return to my earlier assertion that without poststucturalist approaches to gendered and sexual knowledge bisexuality is difficult to theorize as anything other than a failed lesbian, gay, or heterosexual subject. I make this argument not just because I want to examine bisexual meaning without relying on the presence of bisexual subjects to validate that inquiry, but also because of the particular form of contemporary ignorance of what constitutes bisexuality. Against both the queer refusal to see bisexuality as anything but a projection of its own anxieties, and the correlate bisexual insistence on a reclaimable, positive, linear bisexual history, I want to emphasize the *consistent partiality* of bisexual experience, and its *consistent presence* in the formation of "other" sexual and gendered subjectivities.

As I have already indicated, the partiality of bisexual subjectivity is commonly construed as evidence of its inauthenticity. Bisexuality is thus understood as unfinished—either as a pre-oedipal potential that will allow for, or become, same or opposite sex object choice, or as a contemporary vacillation that will always change and cannot remain static (a bisexual will always leave you, it is just a question of when). The temptation on the part of bisexual theorists to insist that bisexual subjectivity can be traced as distinctly and authentically bisexual is understandable, but, as I have maintained, unnecessarily reactive. The accusation of inauthenticity must in part derive from an acknowledgment that bisexual subjectivity is historically and culturally formed almost exclusively in lesbian, gay, or straight spaces. The minimal bisexual spaces that do exist—such as bisexual conference spaces and support groups—are recent, often temporary, and do not always feed into a larger bisexual community. Very often, bisexual subjects come to think of themselves as such in spaces that do not recognize them in name. One could think of this lack of recognition as the sign par excellence of a juvenile community, which will, in time, develop and begin to make its presence more clearly and visibly felt. I have already discussed the theoretical and political problems that I have with such a position. But one could also argue that this partiality is in fact a condition of bisexual subjectivity both historically and contemporarily, a sign of its transitivity and continually reformation.

Clearly it is not only bisexual subjectivity that is partial; all subjectivity is formed and reformed in different spaces, has a history of different sexual and nonsexual interactions that make up the particularities of location. But a focus on the specifics of bisexual partiality is useful because bisexual subjectivity is formed *through* its partiality rather than that partiality being the site of its undoing. Precisely because of bisexuality's production as "inauthentic," and due to the lack of separate bisexual spaces, passing as lesbian, gay or straight (whether intentionally or not) is inevitably a formative part of what it means to become bisexual. Epistemologically, the insistent partiality of bisexuality makes visible the process by which we all become sexual and gendered subjects. For example, a bisexual woman in a relationship with a man embodies two central tenets of contemporary subjectivity. First, she provides empirical verification of Sedgwick's reminder that gender of object choice does not wholly determine subjectivity.[141] Second, she dramatizes the temporal nature of all gendered and sexual subjectivity; in order for her bisexuality to make sense to herself, she must give her subjectivity a *conscious history of transition*. Without making this history of transition and difference from herself conscious she would be indistinguishable to herself from a heterosexual woman. To become a bisexual subject, then, partiality and transition (and therefore translation of one culture into another) must be placed at the center of subjective meaning. My insistence on partiality and consciousness of transition as formative of a bisexual self may seem rather too close to home, given the accusations of disloyalty and untrustworthiness that bisexuals commonly encounter. This is, in effect, why I find poststructuralist approaches that eschew authenticity without rejecting political accountability helpful. It is certainly the case that, like Donna Haraway's "illegitimate offspring," the postmodern cyborg,[142] a bisexual subject's allegiances cannot always be anticipated. Rather than seeing this in a negative light I would argue that a contemporary bisexual (rather than cyborg) myth could also be refigured, not as betrayal, but "about transgressed boundaries, potent fusions and dangerous possibilities which progressive people might explore as one part of needed political work."[143] It is precisely a bisexual subject's close resemblance to "other" sexual and gendered subjects that make these "potent fusions" possible.

My concern with partiality in the formation of bisexual subjectivity has also lead me to reject the assertion that bisexual history has been ignored, or knowledge of bisexual subjects repressed. My research suggests that bisexuals are in fact everywhere a *consistent presence* in sexual and gendered culture, not necessarily in a body blazoned with bisexual banners and flanked by lovers of both sexes, but within the cultural and political spaces that take other identities' names. In addition, the boundaries for feminist or queer community are frequently marked by the consideration of bisexual inclusion—whether the result of that consideration is an opening up or reconsolidation of identity and community boundaries—and the specificities of lesbian and gay identity ensured by comparison with real or imagined bisexual subjects. Thus, the question of bisexual subjectivity emerges as a fundamental concern of contemporary feminist, lesbian and gay, and queer politics, culture, and theory. To insist on a discrete and traceable bisexual identity is to miss the social and political conditions that determine its current emergence, as well as the complexities of interaction and community that mark bisexual subjectivity in those moments where it does emerge as distinct. Instead, and in line with epistemological inquiries discussed earlier in this chapter, I investigate the particular conjunctions of differences that give rise to contemporary bisexual meaning whether or not a bisexual subject is a result of those differences.

Bisexual Cartographies

> Do bisexual epistemologies go further than trendiness, charting the politics of sexualities in Western culture, redistricting and redistributing desire, and creating new cartographies for our cultural erotics?
>
> —Maria Pramaggiore, "BI-ntroduction I: Epistemology of the Fence"

My assertions of bisexual partiality and presence inevitably have a direct effect on my research methodology. Following Probyn and Braidotti once more, it is my belief that the nuances of bisexual experience can best be glimpsed through a spatial, or cartographic, approach that prioritizes juxtaposition over displacement, genealogy over linear history, difference over sameness, transition over permanence or indeed systematic, progressive agendas. Cultural geography is regulated by a postmodern shift from analyzing social and cultural life through a focus on time—grand narratives, linear history and so forth—to centering on "the logic of spatial organisation"[144]—temporary connections, local sites, and the like. Thus, Fredric Jameson argues that "our daily life, our psychic experience, our cultural languages, are today dominated by categories of space rather than categories of time, as in the preceding period of high modernism."[145] For Dick Hebdige as for many other spatial theorists, space is of course not neutral, but a site of competing power relations requiring analysis. Thus, he posits, "Spatial relations are seen to be no less complex and contradictory than historical processes, and space itself is refigured as inhabited and heterogeneous, as a moving cluster of points of intersection for manifold axes of power which can't be reduced to a unified plane or organised into a single narrative."[146] Indeed, it is precisely the insistent difference of and within "space" that has ensured its appeal both as subject and object of poststructuralist research. Spatial theory is appealing to me in part because it draws together my engagement with feminist and queer epistemologies, theories of the subject, and community formation. In this regard, Nancy Duncan suggests that the close relationship between feminist epistemology and cartography can be explained through feminists and geographers' mutual concern with location and situation in the formation of gendered, sexual, raced, or displaced subjects.[147] Cultural geography could be seen as offering spatial methodology as a way to enhance or complement feminist and queer epistemologies, in its detailed attention to discourse and difference in local, national, or international contexts. Feminist geographers have thus paid specific attention to the relationship between a gendered subject and her multiple environments, the spaces she traverses, and the conflicts between spaces and the subject evolving through its presence within those spaces.[148] In a sense, then, spatial geography offers an appealing alternative to psychoanalytic models of the subject, without disregarding the dissonance between the subject and the social spaces she occupies, as many constructionist accounts of the subject are wont to do. Indeed, it is often in the pages of cultural geography journals, such as *Gender, Place and Culture*,[149] *Professional Geographer*,[150] or *Area*,[151] that the most interesting and sustained attempts to apply poststructuralist feminist or queer understandings to material contexts occurs.

The overlap between sexuality studies and spatial theory has also proven extremely productive. Michel Foucault is perhaps most strongly associated with early moves within sexuality studies toward a consideration of social space rather than linear time. In "Of Other Spaces,"[152] Foucault writes on methods for "interpret[ing] human geographies as texts and contexts,"[153] and discusses the interplay between geographic and historical imaginations: "The present epoch will perhaps be above all the epoch of space," he writes. "We are in the epoch of simultaneity: we are in the epoch of juxtaposition, the epoch of the near and far, of the side-by-side, of the dispersed. We are at a moment, I believe, when our experience of the world is less that of a long life developing through time than that of a network that connects points and intersects with its own skein."[154] Foucault's earlier work on genealogy began this move from time to space in its challenge to conventional historical narrative.[155] His later work on spaces provides a further critique of linearity, combining his genealogical commitment to subjugated knowledges with a desire to excavate both the past and the future through their placement in the present—a genealogy of the present. It is this link between space and genealogy that I have found particularly useful in my own work, since it allows for a connection between and among spaces while resisting unitary, or universal, meaning. More recent work on sexuality and space that emerges from this tradition assumes not that "sexuality acts itself out in space," but that "the question of space [is] already inscribed in the question of sexuality,"[156] since sexuality is enacted in relationship to others, regulates public/private boundaries, and gains meaning in relation to community. In other words, sexuality (as well as gender) is particularly amenable to a spatial approach.

Queer scholars of sexuality and space have used sexual cartography as a way of exploring the importance of sexual identity for social and spatial actors, without necessarily seeing identity, sexuality, and community as fused. In this vein, Foucault's understanding of "heterotopia" is particularly pertinent to the study of lesbian, gay, queer, or feminist understandings of sexual spaces.[157] A heterotopia is a site of "mixed, joint experience,"[158] acting as a mirror for the self, a real and imaginary space at once. Heterotopias are linked, but not reducible to, normative spaces. Queer spaces—such as the imaginative gay space of a post-Stonewall America, or the general notion of shared queer culture, as well as bars, clubs, and support groups—are understood as spaces of both identity and survival, as spaces that allow queer identity to flourish in the relative safety of other queers. Thus, as Gordon Brent Ingram, Anne-Marie Bouthillette, and Yolanda Retter posit, "Queer space enables people with marginalized (homo)sexualities and identities to survive and to gradually expand their influence and opportunities to live fully."[159] The theorization of queer space has also allowed for material consideration of many of queer theory's most compelling arguments, and for a convincing consideration of the overlaps among the sexual, gendered, and raced spatial realities that we each inhabit.[160] Sedgwick's and Butler's insistence that we challenge the centrality of simple identity in the lives of sexual beings is in turn translated into the following questions: How do sexual, gendered and raced subjects "take up space"? What is the relationship between dominant and subcultural locations? How are queer subjects produced in both discursive and actual spaces? What imaginative as well as actual geographical spaces do the disenfranchised create and occupy? Thus, the delineation of queer cultural, social and theoretical spaces has allowed for a theoretical and material focus on difference and everyday realities rather than identity and ideal behaviors, without sacrificing attention to diverse and intersecting inequalities and power relations.[161] And in keeping with their postmodern roots, sexual cartographers have been as concerned with how specific sites generate forms of resistance as with the site-specific production of constraint.

As I have suggested, queer and feminist cartographic approaches to the subject and community seem ideally suited to my own avenues of inquiry. Thinking spatially opens up the possibilities of exploring further my concerns with bisexual difference, the generation of bisexual meaning rather than identity per se, and bisexual involvement in lesbian and gay communities. Yet bisexual and spatial theorizing do not always sit comfortably with one another, and in many ways the overlaps raise more questions than they solve. There are no explicitly bisexual spaces in the same way as there are lesbian and gay spaces. As I delineated at the beginning of this chapter, bisexual support groups and conference and resource spaces have developed in the last ten years or so, but public, social bisexual spaces, named and recognized as such, do not exist. As a result, bisexual self-identification is not directly related to an external bisexual "home" in the same way as lesbian and gay self-identification often is, or at least can be, particularly in urban areas. While this lack of bisexual home may open up opportunities for challenging the exclusivity of presumed lesbian and gay enclaves, bisexuality can still be difficult to pin-point. Given that my desire in this book is to trace specificities of bisexual difference in contemporary culture and theory, finding bisexuality "every-where and nowhere" could be counterproductive, and could reconfigure bisexuality simply as a carrier of difference for lesbians and gay men. In this respect, too, bisexual difference disappears, since a range of subject locations and practices, transsexuality or child love, for example, serve this function within lesbian and gay spaces as well. In addition, to refer back to my discussion of multiple and often conflicting bisexual meanings earlier in this chapter, where one locates bisexuality is also apt to rein-force one or other dominant bisexual meaning, even while challenging "other" identity-space configurations. For example, it would be possible to argue all of the following depending on which bisexual meaning one was prioritizing at a given juncture:

1. Both gay and straight spaces are also bisexual spaces.
2. Neither gay nor straight spaces are bisexual spaces.
3. Bisexuals are on the margins of both gay and straight space.
4. Bisexuality is at the center of gay and straight space.
5. Bisexuality marks the boundary between gay and straight spaces.
6. Bisexuals move between gay and straight spaces.
7. Bisexuals breach gay and straight spaces.
8. Bisexual space encircles gay and straight spaces.

Small wonder, then, that Marjorie Garber finds bisexuality, in some form, to be present almost everywhere. The key issue for me here is that each starting point, or conclusion, provides a different reading—not just of bisexuality, but of sexual and gendered space as a whole—and that these readings are political readings.

Analysis of a small drawing by Joan Nestle graphically displays some of the problems bisexuality presents when reading sexual space. Nestle's drawing appears in *Queers in Space* and is an illustration of the gay and lesbian beach she used to frequent at Riis Park, New York, in the late 1950s and early 1960s. Nestle describes how the safety of this space of lesbian and gay desire was always restricted and demarcated by hetero-sexual onlookers, from the wall behind the beach, from the straight part of the beach, and by police patrols.[162] In Nestle's drawing (and in the sexual imagination more generally) gay and straight spaces are separated by a thin line on the beach, and a double line to denote the wall. Where is bisexual space, either actually or imaginatively, and what difference does it make where one locates it? Is bisexual space in the thin line in the sand, occupied by people who are not sure where their allegiances lie? Are bisexuals the voyeurs behind the wall getting a good look before going home to their opposite-sex spouse? Is bisexuality rife but undisclosed within either the gay or the straight territories Nestle demarcates? Or is it a common, acknowledged set of practices that causes no problems for either camp? Is it inside Nestle's changing rooms, on the softball fields, inside the police vans? Is bisexual space entirely absent, or is it perhaps all-inclusive, allowing gay and straight to coexist, albeit in tension, and marked by the four straight lines forming the boundary to the map itself? Each location denotes and reproduces particular bisexual meaning: bisexuality as potential preceding sexual identity, as bridge or middle ground, as closeted or pornographic, as an integral aspect of queer culture.

These are abstract questions if one thinks of these spaces as merely geographical. But Nestle's lines are intended imaginatively, rather than as a representation of actual boundaries. The gay and lesbian spaces Nestle sketches are not concrete or absolute. The lines separating straight from gay can be transgressed or ignored, and clearly not only in terms of bisexuality. The gay beach is there under sufferance, as the presence of the police vans and the onlookers indicate. As Nestle states, "[W]e were always watched."[163] Neither is this gay space permanent. Nestle renewed her annual summer pilgrimage "sometimes as early as May but surely by June."[164] In the winter months the bars of the city became, once again, the only gay space. The imaginative extent of the gay beach at Riis Park is brought to the fore in an incident described by Nestle. She writes, "Only once do I remember the potential power of our people becoming a visible thing, like a mighty arm threatening revenge if respect was not paid. A young man was brought ashore by the exhausted lifeguards and his lover fell to his knees, keening for his loss. A terrible quiet fell on our beach, and like the moon drawing the tides, we formed an ever-growing circle around the lovers, opening a path only wide enough for the police carrying the stretcher, our silence threatening our anger if this grief was not respected. . . . The freaks had turned into a people to whom respect must be paid."[165] Determination that the man's grief will be respected transforms the gay space of the beach, unifying its members and solidifying such that transgression of that space (through mockery) would be courting violence. While gay space here transgresses its boundaries, the imaginative geography carved by loss and the threat of violence divides the beach starkly. In such a context the fact that it matters enormously where bisexuals are located, or locate themselves cannot be ignored. They question "Which side are you on?" could not be more urgent. But equally importantly, that side cannot be decided in the abstract on the basis of preceding knowledge about bisexuality, or where one believes bisexuality should be located. And neither is bisexual location dependent on whether a particular man has an opposite-sex spouse at home or a particular woman is planning to leave her lesbian lover for a man later that day, or indeed if lesbian and gay culture is the only home either has ever known.

The unity of movement in Nestle's narrative is formed through immediate cultural connectivity. Identification with the adaptive community in this instance occurs not along pre-discursive gendered lines, but through knowing where one belongs. If the loss and threat are meaningful, then participation in the circle around the lovers will be a learned instinct.

In my reading of Nestle's cartography, I am reminded why it is that spatial theorizing is so appropriate as a means of pursuing my goals in this book. Nestle's moving account of the meaning of cultural space raises a series of issues that I am in interested in addressing. First, the problem of bisexual location is implicitly posed by the organization of gay/straight spaces in Nestle's drawing. Second, heterogeneity of sexual spaces is implied by the fact that bisexuals are likely be located *somewhere* on the map. Third, and most important, it becomes critical to think about sexual location in specific and not abstract terms, since so much is at stake in any consideration of sexual space. The significance of place and space, and particularly of "home," is not geographically defined or predetermined, but resonant with meaning and emotion. This seems to me to be a productive way of thinking about the consequences of what bisexuality means, and for whom, without universalizing those meanings.

In subsequent chapters, then, I will employ a spatial approach in a dual manner. As outlined in my introduction, each chapter can be seen as a discrete cartography within which I locate the production and significance of bisexual meaning for the space as a whole. In addition, I highlight the challenges that specifying bisexual location poses to its continued reproduction in dominant terms as middle ground between sexed, gendered and sexual polarities, building a bisexual genealogy through the analysis of each space.

The research required to map this bisexual difference reflects my concern with both partiality and space. Wanting to find bisexual meaning in spaces where it is not necessarily named has raised a set of interesting research problems in its own right. Archives are commonly organized according to recognizable identity or community categories, both for ease, and, in the case of the queer archives I consulted, to facilitate investigation of usually hidden histories. In both cases the process of cataloging tends to reproduce contemporary categories and understandings of sexual and gendered subjectivities. Of the primary archive collections I consulted, two were collections put together by bisexual individuals or collectives—the David Lourea Archives held at the San Francisco Public Library,[166] and the holdings at the Boston Bisexual Center. The other two were lesbian and gay or sexual minorities collections, where the location of "bisexual materials" was ambivalent or in transition. At the time of conducting the majority of my research what is now The Gay, Lesbian, Bisexual, Transgender (GLBT) Historical Society in San Francisco was then the Lesbian and Gay Historical Society of Northern California (LGHSNC).[167] The board of the LGHSNC had vigorously resisted several attempts to alter its remit to include other sexual or gendered minorities, and this was reflected in the archive cataloging (*lesbian + x, gay + y,* or chronological under specific events). In terms of research, what this means is that both bisexual identity and bisexual meaning could be, and indeed are, located anywhere, once the joys of a handful of dusty old newsletters from the San Francisco Bisexual Center (in the David Lourea Archives) had been exhausted. In contrast, the Sexual Minorities Archives in Northampton, Massachusetts changed its name from the New Alexandria Lesbian Library in 1992 better to reflect the content of the archive and its users, and at the time of conducting my research was in the process of trying to re-classify its holdings accordingly—instead of "lesbians and health," for example, the classification now read "health and sexual identity." The problems of conducting research in bisexual archives were conversely reflective of the desire to rewrite sexual history with bisexuals at its center. Too little bisexuality on the one hand, too much on the other—in neither context is bisexual *meaning,* as opposed to *identity,* foregrounded.

A focus on partiality has meant I have had to look farther afield in terms of tracing the trajectories that make up a contemporary bisexual subject in progress. The materials I consulted in each context include newspaper articles, photographs, interview transcripts, political flyers, letters, accounts of personal experience, audiotaped workshops, audiovisual materials, fiction, feminist and queer theory, newsletters, and a host of other archive material from a number of different geographical locations. The eclectic, piecemeal nature of the body of my research is true to the conditions of bisexual partiality and constitutes a necessary "cultural theft." My genealogy of bisexuality is, in effect, a process of scavenging from "other" locations, to flesh out a bisexual subject whose presence in those locations has been difficult to trace from a more conventional historical perspective.

Given my own location as a self-professed bisexual subject, and my passionate engagement in feminist research, it would be disingenuous not to consider what my involvement in this research means. Thus far, I have been concerned with the bisexual epistemology and methodology, paying little attention of the role of researcher in articulating the bisexual experiences I am interested in. The end of this chapter considers how to theorize my own impact on the bisexual research I have engaged in, and more particularly the impact bisexual research has had on my own bisexual subjectivity. How do I pay attention to the shifting locations I variously occupy through the sexual and gendered landscapes I inhabit, and the bisexual knowledges that emerge from the resonance of differences and similarities between field and researcher?

To a large extent, my focus on the particular sexual spaces outlined above is a reflection of my own interests and investments. The spaces I choose to explore are familiar ones I have traversed or immersed myself in. I am not a dispassionate flâneur. I provide one particular link between the three spaces I delineate in the rest of this book. I am one of these spaces' "own skein[s],"[168] since I have lived in both Northampton and San Francisco, and have been a part of bisexual and transgendered communities in the United States and Britain. My own sense of self as bisexual has been negotiated primarily in relation to these lesbian, gay, queer, and transgendered social and political spaces, and the spaces I have chosen to focus on in this book reflect those experiences. As Colomina argues, "Space is, after all, a form of representation,"[169] and I trace these spaces not only in an attempt to locate bisexuality, but also as a representation of my own location. The lack of consideration of heterosexual spaces could be understood in that light, but also as a reflection of the relative lack of spatial theorizing of heterosexuality to draw on.[170] The relationship between researcher and researched is an ongoing one, too. Historian Dell Upton writes evocatively of this process that "an individual's perception of a landscape changes with the experience of moving through it."[171] In a similar vein, Probyn suggests evocatively that her own desire is shaped both by being a lesbian and by desiring lesbians.[172] My own movement through the landscapes I delineate has been, as you will see, anything but a neutral passage. My thinking about bisexuality, and indeed my sense of bisexual self, has changed due to my travels in and through these particular sexual and gendered landscapes.

Given that I am committed to understanding bisexual experience as formed in the interfaces among different sexual, gendered, and raced locations, and that my own location is clearly formative, I cannot ignore the fact that the tracking of my own location is one of the findings of my research. The place of the personal voice, either of the research subject or the researcher, is anything but self-evident, to be slightly painfully confessed at the outset of the account of research, never to be returned to again. But in line with the poststructuralist queer feminist theorists I discussed earlier on, rather than abandoning experience as a useful intervention or ground for analysis, I have tried to explore the interfaces among different locations throughout this book. In each chapter I ask how different bisexual locations, including my own, inflect one another or produce one another, and to what effect. What does bisexual experience mean in relation to lesbian, gay, feminist, queer, and transgender experience? Thus reflexivity, for me, is less about *demonstrating* one's position than it is about being open to the ways in which collision, collusion, and conflict with one's research bodies shape one's own position and give it meaning. In this I am, of course, influenced by Adrienne Rich's "Notes Toward a Politics of Location."[173] Rich argues seductively that one should begin "not with a continent or a country or a house, but with the geography closest in—the body," [174] while issuing the warning that one's own feelings "are not *the* center of feminism."[175] Rich's desire to locate herself in her writing, a desire I share, inflects my genealogy of bisexual spaces with a feminist ethics, a feminist politics of location. It is my hope that my attention to my own position of engagement throughout this book will prevent a tourist-like separation between researcher and researched in uncharted territory,[176] and may indeed provide fresh perspective on places I thought I already knew.

Chapter 2

Desire by Any Other Name

I begin this work on bisexual cartography by exploring the overlap and differences between women's bisexuality and lesbianism in Northampton, Massachusetts. Since the late 1960s, Northampton, and the surrounding areas of Amherst, South Hadley, and the valley hill towns—together known as the "Happy Valley," from the Connecticut River Valley—have been home to a thriving lesbian community. Northampton came to the eyes of the U.S. public in a feature article "Strange Town Where Men Aren't Wanted" of the *National Enquirer* in April 1992.[1] The sensationalist article dubbed Northampton "Lesbianville, U.S.A.," and gave the exaggerated impression that a third of Northampton's population is lesbian. More conservative estimates are that between one tenth and one fifth of the population is lesbian or gay (whether these statistics include bisexuals is never stated).[2] Whatever the actual figure, Northampton holds a prominent place in the lesbian imaginary, serving as a focal point for notions of lesbian identity, community, and possibility within the United States and beyond, much as San Francisco does for gay men.[3] As Michael Lowenthal notes, "Northampton is something of a lesbian Mecca, to which all dykes must make at least one pilgrimage during their lives,"[4] and an article in the *Los Angeles Times* suggests "common wisdom holds [that] 'All lesbians pass through here at least once.' "[5] A bisexual women's community has never established itself in Northampton, however, though there are numerous bisexual women living there and the attempt has been made to forge such a community on a number of occasions.

In this chapter I focus on events and writings between 1989 and 1995, during which time a series of heated debates took place concerning the named inclusion of bisexuals in the annual Gay and Lesbian Pride March. My emphasis is less on the perceived success or failure of this endeavor than on the extent to which it is marked by its particular lesbian context. The ripples of disruption caused by these debates spread throughout lesbian communities in the United States, and had implications for both lesbian and bisexual identity and community more generally. In the context of this project as a whole, a consideration of bisexual and lesbian space in Northampton provides a rare opportunity for analyzing the attempt to carve out bisexual space within a lesbian community. This is one of the first times that bisexuality has been discussed at length within the contemporary U.S. lesbian and gay community, and the Pride March debates create the first space for overt discussion about bisexuality in Northampton's contemporary lesbian history. Stacey Young remarks that "the controversy over the Northampton Pride March brought us [bisexuals] a long way. The thoughtful and sustained public discussion of bisexuality and the role of bisexuals in queer communities/movements was unprecedented, coming as it did before the publication of any of the bisexual anthologies."[6] I want to argue alongside Young that a "close look at the Northampton controversy and *Gay Community News*'s (*GCN*) coverage reveals a good deal about some of the different ways that identity and community are conceptualized within lesbian and gay politics."[7]

Although the debates I attend to in this chapter surround the *Lesbian and Gay* Pride March, the discussions almost exclusively concern the relationship between lesbians and bisexual women, and the lesbian and bisexual communities. Both bisexual men and women took part in the debates, but gay male opinion is curiously absent, although several gay men resigned from the 1990 Lesbian and Gay Pride March Committee following its decision to exclude bisexuals.[8] My analysis focuses explicitly on the relationship between bisexual women and lesbians as outlined in and created through these debates.

Part 1 of this chapter, "Personal and Political Locations," provides a cultural and historical background to the debates that I analyze in more detail in the rest of the chapter. First, I interweave the narrative of three decades of lesbian community and culture with my own experience of living in Northampton and begin to trace a history of bisexual women's identity and community there. Second, I outline the history of debates about bisexual inclusion and exclusion in the Northampton Lesbian and Gay Pride March and Committee, and the ensuing debates in the national and local press. In particular, I pay attention to the ways in which lesbian identity, community and space are secured through the discursive positioning of bisexual women as sexual rather than political, and as embodying heterosexual privilege rather than subcultural knowledge. In part 2, "Divided Loyalties," I examine the differing uses that bisexual women and lesbians make of visibility discourses to consolidate and contest Northampton's sexual territory, asking whether "inclusion" is necessarily the outcome affording most opportunity for the development of bisexual meaning. I end this chapter by reflecting on the lesbian and bisexual experiences expressed through three different narratives, in which the presumed relationship among desire, identity, and community is problematized. As a whole, this chapter continues to challenge the abstract positioning of bisexuality as middle ground between oppositional terrains, insisting on bisexual subjects' significance for and participation within lesbian community, and the importance of analyzing local as well as dominant knowledge formations. I also continue to stress the value of utilizing a model of cultural rather than object-choice repudiations in the formation of sexual identity and community, for lesbians as for bisexual women.

The texts that I work with in this chapter are drawn from the Northampton Collection, located at the Northampton Sexual Minorities Archives (NSMA) in Massachusetts. The NSMA is a grassroots resource, run by curator Bet Power from his home by the river on the outskirts of Northampton. The archive has an interesting history. It began life as the New Alexandria Library for Lesbian Women in 1974, its title later shortened to the New Alexandria Lesbian Library [NALL], and became the Sexual Minorities Archives in 1992, coinciding with Power's own transition from butch lesbian to transgendered man.[9] The Northampton Collection is a rich, ongoing, local collection of personal papers, cassettes, slides, and newspaper clippings, documenting lesbian, gay, bisexual, and transgendered events, political discussions, celebrations, and personal relationships in the Northampton area from 1968 to the present. It is made up of general files in date order (from 1968 to the present), files on particular individuals and groups, and material on particular issues (e.g. several files concerning sadomasochism). In part 1 I make use primarily of the general files and special collections; in part 2 I focus on the local and national newspaper and magazine debates (1990–1991) that emerged from and partly comprise the Pride March controversy. As well as using the Northampton Collection I follow comparable debates in a number of lesbian and feminist journals, in particular *Sojourner* and *Lesbian Connection*, to highlight the fact that the issues I am identifying in this local context are also relevant in national and international contexts. In addition, I consulted materials at the Stonewall Center,[10] and the files on Northampton housed at Northampton's queer bookstore, Pride and Joy. My personal experience of being a bisexual woman in a predominantly lesbian town has also influenced the writing of this chapter.

Part 1: Personal and Political Locations

Lesbian/Bisexual Territory

Northampton's contemporary lesbian community began in the early 1970s, with the establishment of women's and lesbian feminist cooperatives. Many lesbian feminists studied at the women's colleges—Smith (in Northampton) and Mount Holyoke (in South Hadley)—and stayed on after graduation. This is still common today. In the 1980s the lesbian influence on Northampton became more firmly incorporated into the town, mainly through the establishment of local lesbian entrepreneurship and cultural events. Lesbian-owned businesses—bookshops, craft shops, lingerie shops, restaurants and bars—proliferated. As a result, other businesses began to target the burgeoning lesbian market, offering "dyke discounts" and dyke-friendly ambience.[11] Lesbianism is big business in Northampton. Before and during the 1995 Lesbian Festival in Northampton—which had been an annual event run by WOW Productions, a lesbian-run entertainment promotion company—many of the town's storefronts sported bright pink festival posters and flyers, saying "Welcome to Northampton's Lesbian Festival." Being lesbian friendly is an advantage, not a hindrance, to small businesses struggling to thrive here. Culturally, the town offers lesbian music, dances, films (at the local arts cinemas), theater, readings, and academic papers—and this is set within a more general liberal, arts-positive milieu.

A walk through the streets of Northampton gives a fuller impression of the town.[12] Northampton is certainly no metropolis: it maintains its small-town feel. As a friend from San Francisco notes, "It feels a bit like they're going to take the set down at the end of the day." Walking up Main Street from Market Street, under the bridge with lesbian graffiti (two entwined women's symbols) emblazoned in red,[13] you pass Praktically Worn, a secondhand clothes store, two well-known town dykes behind the counter, the piercing service advertised in the window (Navels and Nipples—Reduced). Continuing up Main Street, a left onto Pleasant Street brings you to the Pleasant Street Theater arts cinema, which shows independent, foreign, and queer movies. A couple of blocks down Pleasant Street is Sylvester's, a rather up-scale breakfast diner, where groups go every Sunday a.m. en masse, the sidewalk bursting with queers nursing their hazelnut-vanilla coffees and reading the *New York Times*. A short walk farther down Pleasant brings you to the mostly gay male SM store Primitive Leather.

Just around the corner on Pearl Street is the Pearl Street nightclub, which hosts a lesbian and gay night every Thursday. Back up to the main intersection and out onto King Street is Lunaria, Northampton's (lesbian) feminist bookstore, which housed the "Lesbians for Lesbians" group influential in the debates about the inclusion of bisexuals in the Pride March (Fig 2.1). A sign over the lesbian fiction section asks men not to browse. Lunaria has long been a site of controversy within the lesbian community, insisting on a no pornography or SM materials policy. Popular urban myth has it that in 1989 two lesbians went into Lunaria and began to enact a public SM scene. This act of provocation resulted in the *Calendar*, the local lesbian listings newsletter, refusing to advertise Shelix (Northampton's woman-to-woman SM group) in its pages.[14]

Coffee shops predominate on Main Street, ranging from the rather exclusive café, Curtis and Swartz,[15] for the more chic lesbian couple, to the Haymarket café, which offers a slightly younger and trendier experience. On the right off Main Street is Center Street, home to Northampton's own lesbian lingerie store, Gazebo, offering the 10 percent dyke discount. Just down the road from Gazebo is the Iron Horse, a predominantly straight bar and performance venue where lesbian, gay, and queer acts from all over the country also come to play, despite its small size.[16] Further up on the left off Main Street, on Crafts Avenue, is Pride and Joy, the town's only specifically queer (mixed) bookstore. Pride and Joy also stocks videos, sex toys, magazines, badges, T-shirts, and cards,[17] and serves as a community base for information.

Continuing up Main Street toward the imposing edifices of Smith College at the top of the hill, you pass the Unitarian Church. The church steps provide the unlikely site for a daily congregation of young butches,

Fig. 2.1. Author's photograph of Lunaria, lesbian feminist bookstore, in 1995.

decked out in their casual yet precise teaming of white T-shirts and low-slung 501 blue jeans, drinking coffee and projecting their group gaze outward, as much to mark out their own territory as to cruise. Past the church on the left is the old stone building of the Academy of Music, now an alternative theater, film, and performance venue.[18] Walking past Smith College on your right, up to West Street, you can see the North Star ahead of you (fig. 2.2). The North Star bar and dance club is Northampton's lesbian bar, owned and run by and for lesbians and gay men for almost ten years.[19] My favorite time to go to the North Star is 5 P.M., arriving straight from Smith's Neilson Library. At that time of the day, the sweat of the previous night still hangs in the air. Sitting at the bar with a friend, joining the few other regulars in the place, camaraderie develops as we nurse our "Buds" and watch reruns of 1950s sitcoms playing on the TV behind the bar. From beginning to end of my walk to the Green Street Café, an upscale restaurant run by two gay men which prides itself on serving "only the best" French cuisine has only taken me fifteen minutes. As the waiter shows me to my friend's "usual table" in the window and I consider the menu, two women walk by the window hand in hand. This is such a common sight that I barely even register the moment; it is only now, in writing, that I remember.

The picture I am painting here is one of a vibrant, well-serviced lesbian community, with the emphasis most definitely on *serviced*. It can be extremely difficult for new women in town to meet other women, precisely because most lesbian spaces are so commerce-oriented, and require company for you to feel part of the community.[20] For lesbians and bisexual women, sitting in a coffee shop surrounded by lesbians, is, perhaps, only a joyful community experience if you are with someone; it is not necessarily the best environment in which to meet new people. Specific lesbian events in Northampton tend to be organized around a theme. The *Calendar* lists endless potlucks and group therapy meetings, but few political or purely social events. In this respect the very public nature of Northampton's lesbian community can make coming out a very isolating experience. Perhaps this is where the nostalgia I experience when writing about the North Star's lingering sweat comes from. I think that what I liked about five P.M. at the North Star was the residue of a subcultural queer experience that is otherwise lacking in Northampton generally. There are few treacherous heterosexual urban territories to negotiate, queer haven all the sweeter for its distinctness. The brash commercialism of Northampton's lesbian community—although selling rainbow earrings and aromatherapy rather than computers or fast food—can be linked to, say, the bright lights of Grand Opening (Boston's women's sex store), where what was hidden and marginal is made visible and central. Yet for those not wanting another cappuccino, or a dyke shopping or filmgoing experience, there are paradoxically few other public expressions of same-sex desire. For people whose desires cannot be separated from the contexts in which they have more traditionally found expression, these Northampton's consumer opportunities can be about as exciting as a cold shower.

The *CNN* and *20/20* television coverage of Northampton presented the town as entirely homophobia free, and interviewed only prosperous professional women. Yet, Northampton is not the totally safe lesbian haven that the tabloids, and my own narrative above, would have you believe. The sensationalism of Northhampton's status as "Lesbianville" can cause problems in itself. One woman talked openly of her experiences at the hands of the National Enquirer journalists. She was photographed under false pretenses and had no idea that the picture of her with her lover was going to be nationally reproduced in the tabloid.[21] The town-wide ban on smoking in public places serving food, effective since summer 1994, has also had the unanticipated effect of forcing hetero-sexual male smokers onto the streets, thus increasing the levels of homophobic harassment lesbian and bisexual women receive. A lesbian friend of mine talks of how she began to find walking past Bart's and Coffee Connection (two coffee shops on Main Street) intimidating, because of the comments and harassment she endured from the men

Fig. 2.2. Author's photograph of the North Star bar in 1994.

sitting outside smoking. She notes that walking by used to be her femme opportunity to catch a butch's eye, but that this has been ruined now that the smoking ban has taken effect. In Northampton, lesbian moral, physical, and mental health also provides a major source of lesbian income. In every issue of the *Calendar* there are well over forty advertisements for lesbian health practitioners and counselors. Nevertheless, the economic and consumer base of Northampton's community remains precarious. As should be clear from my tour of Northampton, lesbian and gay businesses often follow a pattern of opening, closing, and reopening; lesbian arts and media tend to share a similar fate. The 1995 Lesbian Festival was the last one in Northampton: WOW Productions took a financial loss at the festival from which it never recovered. So far, no other organizations have been set up to take over the responsibility for putting together the festival, which was one of only two annual women's festivals in the United States (the Michigan Womyn's Music Festival being the other). More recently, the lesbian newsletter, the *Amazonian*, established in May 2000, folded less than a year later in April 2001.[22] While there is always a client base for lesbian venues or alternative health practices, there is not a regular enough cash flow to secure the long-term health of social, cultural, and political ventures. Much of the reason for this is lesbian poverty. In her discussion of the 20/20 reporting, Liz Galst emphasizes that the prime-time TV show failed to mention that in 1994 Northampton's unemployment rate reached an all-time high, at 7.5 percent. Neither did the program represent the large number of "professional lesbians" delivering pizza or working in coffee shops in order to afford to live in the Happy Valley.[23] Valle Dwight suggests that "Northampton's national reputation as an accepting environment for gays and lesbians has . . . meant an increase in visitors," resulting in the local Lesbian and Gay Business Guild "working with other groups to bring tourists to the area year-round, especially in the traditionally slow winter months."[24] It is the lesbian tourist trade that sustains Lesbianville's alternative economy, not, in fact, the lesbian 10 to 20 percent of Northampton's more permanent population.

Northampton is also no idyll immune from incidents of homophobic violence. A 1977 article in *Lesbian Connection* on Northampton's lesbian community—"Analysis of a Lesbian Community—Part One"— discusses the creation of an "attack and defense patrol" in August 1975.[25] The patrol was established in response to several weeks of harassment, "culminating in an attack by several men with a shovel and a machete, at a neighborhood bar where lesbians hung out."[26] In late 1982 and early 1983, the New Alexandria Lesbian Library, Womonfyre Books, and individual lesbians prominent in Northampton's lesbian community became the targets of homophobic harassment in the form of death threats left on answering machines and in letters.[27] A videotape made by Heramedia on violence against lesbians includes a section on the

1982–1983 violence in Northampton. Violence against lesbians is explained in the videotape as the result of men's feelings of exclusion: "lesbian by definition excludes men and this is seen as a threat to male prerogative and masculinity."[28] Community organizing and the resulting pressure on Northampton's mayor and police force in early 1983 resulted in the arrest and conviction of the perpetrator of the death threats in October of the same year. Robert Kremensky was convicted of violating the rights of lesbians, and was given a one-year jail sentence. This was the first such sentence under the state civil rights law for a violation of a person's civil rights. That year's Pride March—"Come Out For Justice: Come Out For Good"—was entirely comprised of speakers talking about violence: Bet Power on the homophobic violence against NALL; Gwen Rogers on behalf of All People's Congress; and the People's Anti-War Mobilization, on the link between violence against lesbians and violence against other communities.[29] In March 1993, "a 21-year-old Northampton woman [was] punched in the face ... by a man who made obscene references about her being a lesbian" outside the Pearl Street nightclub.[30] Once again, the perpetrator was prosecuted under a civil rights violation with bodily injury and battery, and, once again, the lesbian community immediately rallied around the victim, holding a candle-light vigil at the scene of the crime.[31] Clearly Northampton lesbians do face homophobic violence. The difference between Northampton and many other towns, however, is the extent to which the community as a whole responds to such incidents. Pat Califia makes a similar point about queer areas in San Francisco "being simultaneously under attack and yet often well-defended."[32]

The failure of the Domestic Partnership Ordinance to pass the town referendum in November 1995 also indicates that homophobia can be mobilized when right-wing factions feel that the town's lesbians and gay men have stepped over the imaginary line separating cultural and political autonomy. As the report in Britain's *The Guardian* suggested the day before, "a dream of sorts" was on trial: "By Wednesday morning, [lesbians] will know if their safe haven is still safe."[33] The failure of the ordinance by only 87 votes—4,770 to 4,683—was particularly shocking since the ordinance itself would not have guaranteed health insurance benefits for partners, but merely allowed same-sex couples to gain a certificate attesting to the nature of their relationship. Responses to the defeat of the ordinance varied from "This is a city of great hope and spirit," to "I'm surrounded by people who don't support me at best and at worst hate me."[34]

"Analysis of a Lesbian Community—Part Two" also mentions some of the internal tensions of a lesbian community that aspires toward unity but necessarily includes people with different politics, experiences and needs, particularly those of class and ethnicity.[35] The importance of discussion, respect, and inclusion, particularly with regards to race and ethnicity, is highlighted in this early article. While Northampton itself is a white middle-class area, there are established communities of Puerto Ricans and Latinos in the areas surrounding Northampton, and in particular in Florence Heights. But little attempt has been made to examine the reasons why there are very few people from those communities who consider themselves to be a part of the Northampton area's lesbian community. There is a strong Jewish lesbian cultural and political as well as religious presence in Northampton, which makes the situation rather more complicated than a simple black/white split,[36] but in the present day Northampton's lesbian community remains over-whelmingly white and middle class.[37] In an interview about the wave of homophobic violence in Northampton in 1982–83, Kiriyo Spooner and Bet Power mention racist attacks perpetrated against the Hispanic community at around the same time.[38] When asked why links between the two communities had not been made, Spooner points out how insular the lesbian community is: "I call myself a separatist, and I . . . haven't been involved in doing coalition political organizing."[39] At no point does the fact occur to Spooner that there might be Hispanic lesbians for whom the two identities are not a matter for coalitions but inseparable components of identity. Like Spooner, Power acknowledges that the lesbian community sees itself as separate from other com-munities, and, by default, white, noting, "I think the perceptions that I get, walking around Northampton, are of segregation. Florence Heights is somewhere out there, the Hispanic community is somewhere out there, the Black community is somewhere out there, and this is the white community."[40] Such segregation means that Northampton cannot be seen as a safe environment for lesbians of color.

Further tensions within Northampton's lesbian community can be traced along the lines of political commitments, and these have a direct impact on the financial and cultural health of the community. As will become evident below, for example, the *Calendar*'s editorial and letter pages have traditionally provided a space for explicitly lesbian/feminist views. During the Pride March controversy the *Calendar* gave regular updates of related community events and urged lesbians to participate actively in the debates. Similarly, the annual Northampton Lesbian Festival received mixed publicity following its decision in 1995 to hold it in the Northampton town center (it had previously been held on private land outside Northampton). Some lesbian commentators thought that the unavoidable presence of men in the town center would dilute the social and political feel of the women-only festival; others thought that the move would strengthen lesbians' position within Northampton, declaring that presence central to the town. The organizer of the festival believed that the negative response contributed in large part to its subsequent financial failure and demise.[41] Similarly, the drive in the 1990s to establish a Gay, Lesbian and Bisexual Community Center arises out of the conflicts over bisexual inclusion in the Lesbian and Gay Pride March and Committee, and cannot thus be seen as an initiative shared by all members of the community.[42]

Debates about pornography and sadomasochism in the late 1980s split Northampton's lesbian community in much the same way as the Pride March controversy. Rather than providing a supportive background to a thriving community, in the late 1980s Northampton became the site for irreconcilable warring factions. The May 1989 issue of *Valley Women's Voice* published a letter mourning the closing of Womonfyre Books on January 21, 1989.[43] Womonfyre operated a policy of no censorship of lesbian materials, stocking lesbian feminist texts alongside lesbian pornography and erotica. The authors, Bet Power among them, blame "anti-pornography Lesbians and ... a group of women who opened Lunaria Bookstore in Northampton, too small a geographic area to support two Lesbian-feminist bookstores" for the closure.[44] Womonfyre was allegedly the target of numerous attacks by antipornography feminist activists, closing when its owners were no longer able to meet the cost of replacing repeatedly broken windows. The debate attracted national attention when Susie Bright reported, in *On Our Backs*, "Lesbian Censors Close Women's Bookstore."[45] The next edition of *Valley Women's Voice* published a number of other letters on the closing of Womonfyre Books including a response from the owners of Lunaria who rejected the claims of Power and others. All the letters took issue with the accusation and with the editorial decision to publish the letter.[46]

From March 1989 onward there were frequent antipornography rallies in and around Northampton, culminating on April 16, 1989 in Amherst, where women publicly burned large quantities of pornographic material, opening up the floodgates of the pro- versus anticensorship debates. This event was followed up with a public lecture the next day by Andrea Dworkin, "Pornography and Civil Rights" (fig 2.3).[47] The *Calendar* refused to print the advertisement for Shelix in its listings, provoking an angry response from the anticensorship lobby. As part of the response, a lesbian sex reading was held at the New Alexandria Lesbian Library on May 7. All through the summer arguments raged, blending with the Pride March debates the following year. Those who argued against the inclusion of the term *bisexual* were commonly the same people who had been vocal in the antipornography campaigns. As is no doubt clear debates about bisexual inclusion in lesbian community take place within a space already marked by difference and tension as well as struggle and support, and cannot be separated from those differences and struggles.

One might expect—as I did—that in a town so full of lesbians and gay men, with so much to offer in the way of consumerism and community, there would also be a thriving bisexual community, a network of active, out bisexuals. When I first arrived in Northampton in Autumn 1994, I

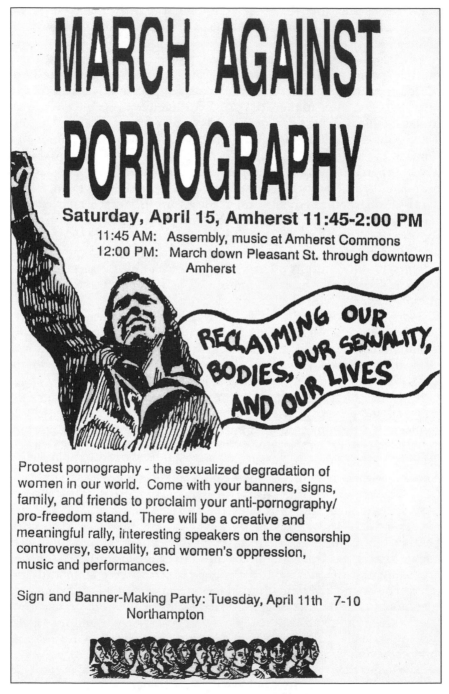

Fig. 2.3. Flyer for the March against Pornography, April 1989; The Northampton Collection, Northampton Sexual Minorities Archives.

scoured the *Calendar* for bisexual groups and activities. A bisexual women's discussion group took place on Wednesday evenings at the Haymarket. Brimming with enthusiasm and hopeful for my research, I turned up at the appointed time, anticipating several tables of bisexual women with stories to tell, and a bisexual political perspective on Northampton's lesbian and gay culture. I walked around the Haymarket a few times; there was no sign saying Bisexual Discussion Group in bold letters and the clientele of the café offered no clues. In the end I had to ask several tables of people if they were the bisexual women's discussion group—and was greeted by blank stares, or incredulous laughter—before I happened upon the right table. The bisexual women's discussion group turned out to be three women, all under twenty-five, white, middle-class, and very recently out as bisexual. All three had only moved to the area relatively recently.

A Northampton bisexual women's group had been active in the early 1990s, but had disbanded after the resolution of the Pride March controversy. The Amherst-based Valley Bisexual Network boasted over one hundred and fifty members during the controversy but also disbanded in 1992; the group was at the center of bisexual activism up until this time. The Valley Bisexual Women's Support Group was formed by newcomers to the area in Autumn 1993. This group collapsed six months later due to internal conflicts over confidentiality and political location that proved impossible to resolve. One of the group's cofacilitators felt that her needs as the only woman of color in the group were not being met. Conversely, some members of the group felt that this woman took up too much space, and was not fulfilling her role as facilitator. None of this was dealt with directly, but discussed among cliques outside the group. The bad feeling escalated until the group fell apart, not through direct confrontation, but because members of the group (unsurprisingly) simply stopped going.[48] The bisexual women's discussion group I attended at the Haymarket comprised several women from that support group. These women also organized monthly bisexual women's brunches, and advertised them in the *Calendar* so that other women could come to something more informal than a discussion or support group. These were much better attended than the discussion groups, with between five and ten regulars.

By the spring of 1995, however, the bisexual women's discussion group had ceased to meet, and a new fortnightly bisexual women's support group was organized, attracting between seven and fifteen people to each meeting.[49] This group's relative success was, I think, due to the fact that most group members had only recently begun to acknowledge their desire for people of more than one sex, and needed a safe social (rather than political or theoretical) space to explore what bisexual desire might mean. The only requirement to be a part of the group was that the woman be questioning her desire (for one sex exclusively) whether or not she identified as bisexual. Of course, the word *bisexual* in the name of the group meant that the majority of women who came were considering such an identity. Most of the women were struggling to understand their desire within the framework of Northampton's lesbian community, which had been their home for a long time. Those women in relationships with lesbians felt that there was no space for their bisexual desire (whether or not they identified as bisexual) to be acknowledged within the lesbian community. Yet they also expressed fears that the "bisexual community" would not be able to offer the level of support that they were used to. This group did not last long either. Women who were comfortable with their bisexual desire or identity found they no longer needed a support group, and the frequent changeover of participants created too much instability. By January 1996 the group had faded away. As far as I know, no other formal bisexual groups have been established since then.

General information on bisexuality is equally hard to locate. The NSMA has only a couple of books and some out-of-date newsletters from U.S. cities (e.g. Seattle, Boston, and San Francisco) with large bisexual groups. Pride and Joy stocks a couple of U.S. bisexual anthologies, in addition to a "humorous" postcard suggesting that lesbians take out "bisexual insurance." The idea is that a lesbian can use this insurance to gain compensation for being heartbroken when her fickle bisexual lover (inevitably) leaves her for a man. None of Northampton's lesbian-friendly businesses have "dyke *and* bi discounts." At the 1995 Northampton Lesbian Festival, I was the only and first ever person to facilitate a workshop on bisexuality (there were several hundred workshops over three days). Additionally, while academic interest in bisexuality has grown within the Five College area in the last few years. Nevertheless, syllabi and course outlines do not conceive of bisexuality as anything other than a last-minute addition to a women's studies or lesbian and gay studies curriculum.

Yet the evidence is contradictory. Sitting in Bart's coffee shop one day, reading the *Valley Advocate*, one of the local free newspapers, I was struck by the women's personal advertisements, approximately 60 percent of which included the word "bi:" "bi woman seeks . . . ," "bi femme looking for . . . ," "lesbian looking for bisexual experience with nonsexist man." These women were clearly marking out their bisexual desire and seeking a lover, partner, or friend on the basis of that desire. The disparity between the six or seven people making up the core of the bisexual women's group and the dozens and dozens of women anonymously proclaiming their bisexual desire does seem marked. They were prepared to advertise for it, but not to join a group of other women identifying as bisexual. At the time I thought this mismatch an anomaly, but in fact it turns out to reflect a larger mismatch among bisexual desire, identity, and community in Northampton more generally.

The above introduction to Northampton's lesbian (and bisexual) community, above, is intended to provide a framework within which to read my engagement with the Northampton Pride March controversy and to highlight the fact that lesbian community in Northampton has a history both of consolidation and of irresoluble difference. The lesbian and gay community of Northampton was further divided from 1990 to 1993 between those who favored inclusion of the term *bisexual* in the name of Lesbian and Gay Pride March and those who did not. The debates concerned the nature of sexual politics and the boundaries of lesbian community, as well as specific issues attending named inclusion of bisexuals.

In early 1988, two members of the Valley Bisexual Network approached the Northampton Lesbian and Gay Pride March Committee (PMC) requesting that the name be changed to the Lesbian, Gay and Bisexual Pride March for that summer's march. The response was negative; the reason for the decision was given as time constraints.[50] In October 1988, a unanimous vote was taken by members of the committee (five or six people, including members of the Valley Bisexual Network) to change the 1989 march's name to include the term *bisexual.* The meeting saw an influx of bisexuals and allies for the voting process, most of whom did not continue to be a part of the committee or working groups after the motion was passed successfully.[51] The 1989 PMC sent out a memo to political groups in the area announcing without preamble, "It's that time again—we're getting ready to hold the Eighth Annual Lesbian, Gay and Bisexual Pride March."[52]

A proposal to revert to the former name was made at the first meeting of the 1990 PMC, on December 13, 1989.[53] This time the vote went in favor of the original name, by one vote.[54] Several participants at that meeting did not consider the vote binding, however, and called for another, more formal, vote. The editor of the *Calendar* announced a "COMMUNITY ALERT," arguing that the lesbians who had attended the December 13 meeting had "tried to express [their] concerns, but were met with hostility and condescension."[55] Angry at the fact that the initial vote was ignored, the *Calendar* called for as many lesbians as possible to attend the next PMC meeting on January 10, 1990, and to meet the week before for a strategy meeting. Northampton Center for the Arts was also booked for a "meeting of the entire Lesbian community" on January 23.[56] The announcement makes it clear that one is expected to choose between the lesbian "we" who have "created a community we care deeply about, and are in danger of seeing . . . made invisible" and the bisexual interlopers. At the January 10 meeting attended by between forty and fifty, people a clear majority confirmed the decision to revert to the name Lesbian and Gay Pride March.[57]

The primary reason given for hostility to the change in name to include bisexuals was that it reflected a move away from lesbian visibility and politics. Among the speakers at the Seventh Annual Lesbian and

Gay Pride March in 1988 were a gay man with AIDS and black lesbian keynote speaker Barbara Smith.[58] At the Lesbian, Gay, and Bisexual March in 1989 a white bisexual man spoke on bisexuality, and a white heterosexual woman spoke about the recent Massachusetts gay and lesbian civil rights bill.[59] The absence of any lesbian speakers confirmed many people's suspicions that bisexual inclusion equaled lesbian exclusion.[60] In their defense the ten committee members—five lesbians, three bisexuals, and two gay men—argued that they had chosen to prioritize issues over identities in their selection of speakers, and that any absence of lesbian speakers were due to last minute cancellations. Most of the entertainment was lesbian, both ASL interpreters were lesbian, and the emcees were lesbian and gay. The gay men and bisexuals who had been on the committee resigned, and instead, the all-lesbian committee invited "[b]isexuals and other politically sympathetic groups to march as our allies."[61]

A community-wide meeting was called on March 15, 1990, as a "chance to discuss differing perspectives on who is a part of our 'community' ... [and] how we can model dealing with conflict in a progressive way."[62] The meeting was called by the Program for Gay, Lesbian and Bisexual Concerns at the University of Massachusetts at Amherst,[63] and was facilitated by Felice Yeskel, the lesbian coordinator of the program. As the editor of the *Calendar* notes, and as the name of the program suggests, the organizers of the meeting were in favor of bisexual inclusion.[64] Over three hundred people attended the meeting, many of whom aired their discomfort with the January 10 decision.[65] The feeling at the March 15 meeting was overwhelmingly in favor of explicit bisexual inclusion. An informal agreement was made to schedule another meeting for the fall, to continue the dialogue, and to establish a clear way of deciding who was to be explicitly included in the march's title and organization, although in fact this meeting never materialized.

In March 1990, Micki Seigel began what became known as the "newspaper wars" when she wrote a letter to the *Valley Women's Voice* protesting the exclusion of bisexuals from the PMC.[66] Seigel, a bisexual woman who had served as publicity officer on the committee the previous year, resigned after the return to the original name. According to Seigel, "[b]isexuals had been working on the march for years, without official acknowledgment. . . . Now I am the one who is invisible."[67] In their letter responding to Seigel, Sarah Dreher and Lis Brook denied the allegation that she was forced to resign as publicity officer, though they did not attempt to hide their vehement antibisexual feeling.[68] So began the parade of feelings for and against bisexual inclusion, published in local Northampton papers and the national gay and feminist presses, which lasted until mid-1991.

In 1991, the Lesbian and Gay Pride March and Committee's name remained unchanged. One month before the 1991 march, four lesbians who had secured the permit for the march and formed its steering committee called a public planning meeting. The issue of bisexual inclusion was met with a "stubborn refusal to discuss the issues and emotions surrounding the march."[69] When criticized for this refusal, members of the committee homed in on the lack of interest on the part of those requesting the name change, arguing that "the current group stepped in when no other group formed to help take responsibility for organizing the march."[70] The Committee further announced their decision to name the march "Claiming Our Identity: Protecting Our Lives," suggesting that the refusal to allow bisexuals named inclusion was a matter of lesbian and gay safety rather than a question of differences within community. In response, an alternative march committee, calling itself the Committee for an All-Inclusive Pride March, met twice weekly in the month leading up to the march. The alternative theme was announced as "Unity is Our Power, Diversity Our Strength" (fig. 2.4). The alternative committee issued a statement, saying, "The issue has become larger than just the name change. [The committee's] stance symbolizes a refusal to acknowledge and embrace the diversity of sexual identity (whether it be Bisexual, S/M, Drag Queen, and/or outside of a narrow definition of what it means to have a homosexual identity) in our community."[71] Sarah Dreher also acknowledges the significance of the issue in her speech at the 1991 Lesbian and Gay Pride March Rally, echoing these sentiments: "Something's going on here, and it's bigger than a name."[72] Dreher was booed and shouted down throughout her speech, which damned "inclusion" and "diversity" as "pretty words" designed to "guilt-trip" and which emphasized the importance of a political

Fig. 2.4. Author's photographs of alternative T-shirts for the 1990 and 1991 Northampton Pride Marches in the Northampton Collection, Northampton Sexual Minorities Archives.

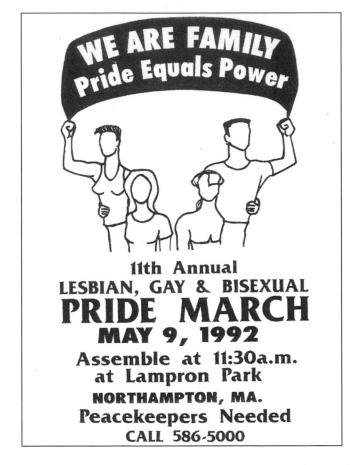

Fig. 2.5. Flyer with theme of 1992 Northampton Pride March; Northampton Collection, Northampton Sexual Minorities Archives.

lesbian identity.[73] Since the same women who were vocal in the antipornography/SM arguments in 1989 spoke most publicly in favor of maintaining the Pride March as Lesbian and Gay, their position began to be seen as advocating a homogeneous lesbian community. From this point on, the anti-bisexual inclusion advocates were damned as antidiversity and even "fascist," as well as biphobic.

After a series of long and drawn-out community meetings in 1991, a lesbian, gay, and bisexual community-wide ballot was held to determine the majority view. On February 2, 1992 voters decided in favor of a Lesbian, Gay and Bisexual PMC comprising three lesbians, three bisexuals, and three gay men. The Lesbian, Gay and Bisexual Pride March, with the theme "We Are Family: Pride Equals Power," took place on May 9, 1992 (fig. 2.5). Finally, it seemed, bisexuals had achieved the inclusion and vis-

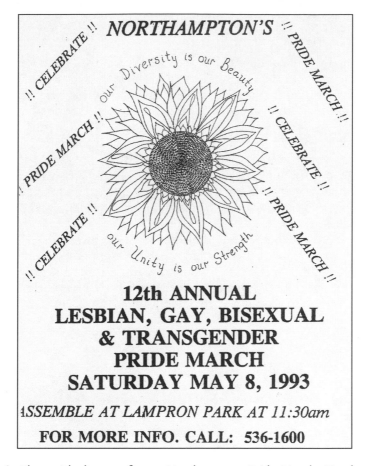

Fig. 2.6. Flyer with theme of 1993 Northampton Pride March; Northampton Collection, Northampton Sexual Minorities Archives.

ibility they sought. The title of the 1993 Pride March was similarly amended to become the Lesbian, Gay, Bisexual and Transgender Pride March" (fig. 2.6), although without the same level of discussion. Reflecting many other local and national contexts, by the year 2000 Northampton's Pride March had been renamed simply "Northampton Pride." The subtitle of Northampton Pride 2001 retains the history of addition, however, running "One of the first gay/lesbian bisexual/transgender and allied marches of the new millenium."[74]

To begin with, I want to highlight the fact that the debates about the inclusion of the term *Bisexual* in the Northampton Pride March and Committee emerged as a result of conflict within the lesbian and gay community, not outside it. The 1988 Pride March's full-page advertisement in the *Daily Hampshire Gazette* states, "Tomorrow, thousands of gay men, lesbians and bisexuals will march with their friends through the streets of Northampton proclaiming who they are within the safety of the crowd."[75] At this point, bisexuals are considered part of the core of lesbian and gay community, in need of allies rather than being allies, despite the fact that they are not named in the march. By 1990, however, the bisexual position in the lesbian and gay community has changed to one of "political affiliation."[76] Responding to accusations of bisexual exclusion, the 1990 March committee argues, "We can work together and march together; but we cannot be pressured into decisions which change the shape of our own political identities."[77] The "we" being potentially pressured here is clearly not lesbians, gay men, and bisexuals. The Northampton Pride March debates, then, foreground the question of whether bisexuals are included in lesbian and gay spaces, or whether they should be if they are not.

For lesbian discourse that aims to exclude bisexuals, one tactic employed to this end is a persistent focus on the perceived differences between lesbians and bisexual women, leading to a vilification of the latter, then, for claiming lesbian space that is (now) not theirs. Brook's comment is typical in this regard: "We lesbians have worked long and hard to create safe communities for ourselves. Bisexuals are welcome to, and should, do the same. But do not try to grab what we have created."[78] This assertion moves easily into the accusation that bisexual women are unwilling or unable to create their own community: "For reasons [the Lesbian and Gay Steering Committee] cannot comprehend, some bisexual women seem to feel they cannot create their own community, but must attach themselves to the Lesbian community."[79] Boston bisexual activist Robyn Ochs responds to such accusations of parasitic bisexual behavior thus: "I say to . . . all the . . . people who still don't get why I and other bisexuals insist on 'attaching' ourselves to the lesbian community: I do so because it is my community."[80]

Initially, then, those arguing for the inclusion of *bisexual* in the title of the Pride March do so on the basis of "group unity inclusion"[81] rather than through a desire to create a bisexual community separate from the lesbian and gay community. The rhetoric of bisexual separation or inclusion remains ambivalent throughout the debates, however. For example, committee member Sue Krause suggested after the 1990 march, "The lesbian and gay community gets on very well with the rest of the community."[82] It is not clear here whether bisexuals form part of "the rest of the community" or are included in "the lesbian and gay community." In the former case recent controversy would scarcely warrant saying that the two get on "very well"; in the latter, the "bisexual inclusion" arguments become figured once again as internal wrangles within the lesbian and gay community. Similarly, Brook's statement that: "[s]ome people were confused because [bisexual inclusion] had never been a factor before and they wanted to remain in keeping with the historical significance of using 'lesbian and gay',"[83] could be read as a lack of desire to address the issue of bisexuality, an assumption of preexistent bisexual inclusion within "lesbian and gay," or a combination of the two. Likewise, the renaming of the Pride March to include bisexuals provokes several readings. On the one hand, bisexual inclusion is sought as a way of acknowledging the history of bisexual work—personal, political and historical—within the lesbian and gay community. It is an attempt to make bisexuality visible, and to prevent its continuing to be a secondary consideration subsumed within "lesbian and gay." On the other hand, this naming signals a move toward a separate bisexual identity, and a way of making bisexuality visible in its own right, which could be read as confirmation of the view that bisexuals are not necessarily part of lesbian and gay community after all. The Northampton debates can thus be seen as a materialization of the theoretical move to rewrite history from the perspective of bisexual identity that I critiqued in chapter 1.

The Pride March controversy takes place within this contradictory framework of inclusion and exclusion. The struggle to establish the positions of bisexuality and lesbianism in relation to one another structures the controversy as I discuss below. One effect of this is that the debates surrounding bisexual and lesbian identity, desire and community become more polarized than might otherwise be the case. Bet Power reports that at the March 15th community meeting in 1990 many lesbians were angry and confused over the rift between lesbians and bisexual women, because "1. they are lovers or friends of Bisexuals; 2. they are themselves Lesbians coming out as Bisexuals."[84] Power highlights the indivisible nature of lesbian and bisexual identities rather than focusing on the separate merits of either one. The terms of the discursive rift between bisexual and lesbian, however, mean that there is little documentation that pursues this line, other than to make the case for bisexual inclusion (still separately defined) within the lesbian community.

I want now to turn to an exploration of the mechanisms used to establish bisexual women's and lesbian identity as related to different communities and desires, as, effectively, different from one another. Often this relationship is established as an antagonistic and hierarchical one when bisexuals or lesbians claim their "difference" as evidence of individual and cultural superiority.

Lesbian/ Bisexual Struggle

One of the primary ways in which the distinction between bisexuality and lesbianism becomes marked in the Pride March controversy is through oppositional use of the terms *political* and *sexual*. This is anything but an uncommon distinction. In their different studies, both

Amber Ault and Paula Rust's lesbian interviewees see bisexual women as uncontrollable and untrustworthy because of their presumed sexual behavior.[85] And Sheila Jeffreys rejects bisexuality as a valuable location within feminism on the same grounds resting her argument on the assumption that lesbian feminism is about love and care, while bisexuality is simply a set of politically and emotionally uninvested practices.[86] Such views also find material form in feminist bookstores, where bisexual texts are frequently shelved in sex and/or sexuality sections, rather than sexual politics sections.[87]

The *Calendar* emphasizes its arguments against bisexual inclusion by using a capital *L* for "Lesbian" and a lower-case *b* for "bisexual." This capitalization marks the difference between what is perceived as a political identity—Lesbian—and a sexual identity—bisexual. This same strategy of capitalizing "Lesbian" and not "bisexual" or "bi-sexual", is used sixteen years earlier in the C.L.I.T. (Collective Lesbian International Terrors) papers of 1976—"many of the women of the Black Left are Lesbians or bi-sexual."[88] Note, too, the use of the hyphen to construct bisexuality as orientation rather than identity, isolating "sexual" and making it a question of numbers (the desire for two). Of course, the danger posed by bi-sexuals to the lesbian community is that their inclusion may mean a dilution of lesbian community, such that all desire becomes like bi-sexuality, a question of taste rather than politics, or desire rather than commitment. Thus, Pamela Kimmel insists, "Some of the non-lesbian members of the committee appeared determined to define our lifestyles in purely bedroom, not political, terms."[89] The "personal" nature of bisexual sexual choice is contrasted with the continued need for a strong political lesbian identity and community, because of "societal homophobia, job security, foster care, woman-hating and violence against women."[90] Rather than focusing on "sexual preference" alone, the 1990 March Committee argue that "the abbreviated title is aimed at focusing on the broader spectrum of gay issues."[91] These "broader" issues are cited as "child-rearing, foster care and marriage."[92] These three areas of concern initially seem a curious choice to juxtapose against bisexuality, which would surely have a significant contribution to make to a discussion on children and marriage, by the committee's own admission. What is being asserted, however, is that for lesbians—who cannot legally get married in the United States, are frequently not allowed to foster children, and risk losing parental charge of their own children in court judgements—these issues are political. The implication is that for bisexuals these issues are simply matters of sexual choice or heterosexual privilege.

There is only one way for bisexuals to become more political within this discourse, and that is to acknowledge that what bisexuals and lesbians share is experience of homophobia. It is this shared ground that should be the basis for political identity. Ara Wilson argues, "It seems irrelevant to create a distinct bisexual identity—what bisexuals have in common with lesbians and gays is their experiences as homosexuals."[93] Similarly, Lesley Mountain, a bisexual woman, proposes that it is only "when we express the lesbian or gay part of our sexuality that we will suffer [from oppression]."[94] Oppression and political identity are seen as coextensive here, and should lead a woman who experiences same-sex desire to be a lesbian, or else to be frivolous. In this context, it is easy to see how bisexual women come to position themselves as the oppressed half of a monosexism binary, in order to lay claim to political identity credentials without having to relinquish their sense of themselves as bisexual, as I discussed in chapter 1.

Bisexuals' responses to the accusation that they are "watering down" lesbian politics fail to challenge this opposition of sex and politics. First, bisexuals downplay the extent to which sexual behavior is formative of a bisexual identity. Michele Moore's response is typical. She stresses that just as "'lesbianism is a way of life, not just something we do in bed' . . . bisexuals are not vaginas or clitorises or penises, we are whole human beings."[95] Second, bisexuals emphasize their political closeness to lesbians and their shared community. Hence, in response to Dreher and Brook's March 1990 letter, Ochs insists, "Gay liberation is my liberation. When out with my girlfriend, I would not get just halfway beat up by a gay basher. . . . I would not be fired from only half of my job by a homophobic boss . . . If I had children I would not lose only half of them in a custody battle. . . . I wouldn't lose half of my apartment if I were living with a woman lover and my landlord didn't like that. . . . Yes, bisexuals who are not "out" will not suffer direct effects of homophobia. But neither do lesbians who are not out."[96] Ochs redefines the issue as one of political commitment (signified by being "out") as well as common sexuality (the argument would not work quite so effectively if Ochs were out with her boyfriend). She consolidates her argument by emphasizing her political credentials, citing her participation in an impressive array of lesbian, gay, and bisexual events and groups.[97] For Karin Baker and Helen Harrison (two leading figures in the Boston Bisexual Women's Network, BBWN[98]) bisexuality's primary political contribution to the lesbian, gay, and bisexual community is not its shared experience of homophobic oppression, but its gender subversion: "Bisexual liberation . . . depends on the subversion of gender categories. The same can be said of lesbian and gay liberation."[99]

In stressing their political affiliation with lesbians and gay men, however, it becomes less and less clear why Ochs, Baker, Harrison, and Moore want bisexuals named separately. In many ways their arguments mirror rather than contradict Wilson's. Their insistence on bisexuals as political rather than purely sexual beings, and their failure to engage with any possible differences—sexual or political—between bisexual women and lesbians, leaves me wondering why they do not identify as lesbians politically, or else remain unnamed as bisexuals within lesbian political community. At no point do these writers examine more closely the function of the "sexual versus political" separation, which I would argue is precisely the technique through which bisexual women and lesbians are produced as discrete subjects in this instance. Bet Power is one of the few people to articulate the sexual *as* political in this context. Power argues that unlike lesbians and gay men, bisexuals, transvestites, transsexuals, sadomasochists, and "other sexual preferences . . . [are] just beginning to find their voices."[100] Power envisages a broader Sexual and Gender Minorities Movement evolving from the Gay and Lesbian Movement.

Since the desire is clearly to maintain a bisexual/lesbian distinction at all costs once the battle lines have been drawn, it makes little difference how bisexuals figure themselves within the debate: in response, the debate itself is simply reframed. In her speech from the 1991 Lesbian and Gay Pride March rally, Sarah Dreher argues, "Some of us feel that bisexuals are a part of our community because they are oppressed for their sexual choices. Some of us feel that it takes a lot more than sexual oppression to be a community."[101] Bisexuals' best attempts to evidence their common sexual oppression with lesbians now prove fruitless. Dreher shifts the terms of the debate by defining lesbian community as in excess of that oppression, as something bisexuals cannot access for ontological reasons. In effect, Dreher is forcing the issue, refusing bisexuals' claims to being part of lesbian culture unless bisexuality is relinquished as subject position as well. Dreher's speech is peppered with references to the form that lesbian excess takes, reveling in her "Lesbian heritage" and "our special outlook on life."[102] In reference to Northampton's lesbian community, Dreher stresses, "We have been strong. We have built a center of Lesbian power that is recognized and admired across the country."[103] The closing paragraphs of Dreher's speech remember previous lesbian community spaces in Northampton, and talk of the need to "pick up the torch" again to create new spaces, such as a community center and a local lesbian newsletter: "Our overriding goal must be to create, not destroy."[104] Dreher's perspective is very much in line with that of lesbian philosopher Sarah Hoagland who writes, "What I am calling 'lesbian community' is not a specific entity; it is a ground of our be-ing."[105]

For Dreher, bisexuals' inclusion in lesbian community, signaled by their named inclusion in the Pride March, "would erase our politics, our special outlook on life, our identity. They would have you say 'We're all alike except for who we sleep with,' and thereby reduce all our issues to sexual issues."[106] The lesbian being sketched by Dreher is the subject of a uniquely "lesbian ethos" derived from her position within *lesbian difference*. This difference resides explicitly at the heart of lesbian community, and provides both the cause of bisexual difference and the explanation for the resultant bisexual exclusion. In this sense, the very call for naming is confirmation of the need to exclude bisexuals: they are already known, and know themselves to be different. If lesbian difference is a property of self, a bisexual woman can only be a part of lesbian community if she is true to her lesbian self, if she "comes out" as a lesbian. If this difference refers to the rich history of lesbian community in the United States, bisexual women are just as surely separated out from that history. In this vein, Kimmell asserts that bisexual lack of compromise in the Northampton debates shows "an extreme lack of understanding and respect of lesbian and gay history and the people who lived it."[107] Since a separate bisexual community has only become an issue in the 1990s in the United States and Britain, the insistence on lesbian and bisexual differences that are both historical and individual reproduces a linear continuum between past and present and strips bisexual women of their own genealogy within lesbian history. If bisexuals want to be subjects of their own difference, in other words, they cannot also lay claim to the lesbian history and culture that the lesbian subject is at the center of. Again, such moves highlight the very real motivation for bisexual historical reclaiming that I discussed in chapter 1. Where *lesbian difference* is understood in ontological or historical terms, bisexual women are interlopers into or challengers of that difference.

The language used by those for and against bisexual inclusion in the Pride March is thus necessarily loaded. Throughout the debates, bisexual threat is contrasted with lesbian bewilderment. Bisexuals are "self-serving,"[108] while lesbians are "alarmed and concerned."[109] Bisexuals are parasites "attach[ing] themselves to the Lesbian community,"[110] feeding off the hard work and creativity of lesbians—"It's all being done by dykes."[111] Lesbian concern and caring is consistently met with bisexual "hostility and condescension."[112] In return, bisexuals accuse the lesbians on the 1990 and 1991 March Committees of "fascism" and "conspiracy."[113] At the predominantly lesbian 1990 Pride March, keynote speaker Virginia Apuzzo asked, "I'm wondering why my dyke self feels so at home here today?"[114] This safe lesbian home needs to be vigilantly guarded against the "danger"[115] of both homophobic violence and bisexual interlopers, the separation between the two being notably and importantly unclear.

The lesbian "reclaiming" of the 1990 march is consistently viewed in terms of territorial rights, where lesbian territory is understood as a space free from men. The *Calendar*'s triumphant editorial after the return to the "Lesbian and Gay Pride March" in 1990 was entitled "Take Back the March Night."[116] A parallel is being drawn between violence against women—traditionally protested by feminists in Take Back the Night marches—and the perceived "bisexual violence" against lesbians. This link was made even more explicit in a "note to the editors" of the *Valley Women's Voice* that read, "The following statement on lesbian occupied territory was in part sparked by the recent controversy in Northampton, MA surrounding the 1990 Gay/Lesbian Pride March."[117] The authors link the Pride March debates with the rape of a woman following the Take Back the Night march in the same year. They argue that both marches will remain symbolic until the Northampton community really becomes "LESBIAN OCCUPIED TERRITORY,"[118] which is the only space that "can offer long-term protection from men, and create alternative women's culture free from the violence of heterosexuality."[119] Lesbian freedom from the "violence of heterosexuality" is placed in the context of the antipornography debates as well as the Northampton Pride March debates. The authors state, "We see the fight against pornography as central to this politics, central to the struggle to reclaim our lives and to make Lesbian community more than mere safe space for Lesbians."[120] The threat posed to lesbian territory by bisexual women is likewise their relationship, or potential relationship, to men. This is why bisexual insistence that lesbian space is also bisexual space is so problematic and difficult for many lesbians to hear. The bisexual woman's male lover lurks in the shadows; she is his phallic envoy into uncharted territory.[121] Amber Ault discovers a similar discourse when interviewing lesbians about their feelings about bisexual women. Ault states that "bisexuals become territory markers" through the "metaphor of 'the fence' . . . [which] represents a line of demarcation between lesbian territory and the heterosexual world, and it is upon this fence that lesbian discourse accuses bisexual women of sitting."[122] This bisexual positioning between straight male and lesbian spaces is presumed rather than explored, even in texts that do not see this middle ground of bisexuality as cause for alarm.

One way of securing bisexual women's location on this epistemologically shaky fence, despite their own assertions that their experiences do not locate them there, is through the fixing of bisexual women as irrefutably subjects of heterosexual privilege.[123] Thus, bisexual women's protestations are understood as wish fulfillment—wanting to maintain the benefits of heterosexuality while distancing themselves from it in order to enjoy lesbian space as well. Brook and Dreher report that at one of the PMC meetings they were scorned for pointing out that lesbian and gay issues differ from bisexual issues "because bisexuals continue to enjoy heterosexual privilege," and told that they too could "pass" if they "dressed differently."[124] Dreher and Brook continue by saying that "Mrs. Seigel announced that she could speak for the Lesbian community 'because I have always felt like a man in a woman's body.' And so on. The horror continued."[125]

The "bisexual voice" in Dreher and Brook's letter confirms their initial accusation of heterosexual privilege and so represents the absolute antithesis of lesbian desire and identity. First, there is no doubt that Seigel is one of those bisexuals exercising her heterosexual privilege given

Dreher and Brook's pointed referencing of her as "Mrs. Seigel" throughout their letter. Second, the suggestion that Dreher and Brook could (and by implication, *should*) "pass" as heterosexual stands in opposition to the pride of being "out" as a lesbian. Finally, "Mrs. Seigel" claims to identify with and be able to represent lesbians on the grounds that she has always felt like a man in a woman's body, articulating precisely the sexological view of lesbianism as inversion that lesbian feminism strives to displace. What appear in Dreher and Brook's text as examples of bisexual difference from lesbianism are used by Seigel as reasons *for* being able to speak for the lesbian community, a further sign of Seigel's inauthenticity. At no point is there any discussion of differing forms of heterosexual privilege, passing, and male identification. That "lesbian" is the antithesis of these three "bisexual blunders" is also assumed to be self-evident, and Dreher and Brook's "horror" is cast as a natural lesbian reaction in need of no elaboration. To question that horror is to ask more precisely which acts, and which behaviors really do signify lesbian and which do not; to elaborate would be to open up lesbian culture and history to scrutiny, which is precisely the opposite of the desire effect of this discourse.

Dreher and Brook are not unusual in their understanding of lesbianism. In many respects it is an assumed distance from men that marks out a particular strand of lesbian/feminism in contemporary U.S. and U.K. culture. As the C.L.I.T. Collective argue in 1976: "the initial and continuing power of the Women's Movement flows from our actual separation from men to form a movement of women dissatisfied with men."[126] Monique Wittig's work on the lesbian as not woman relies on a similar separation of the lesbian world and other worlds. A lesbian is not a woman because she is socially and politically positioned outside heterosexual patriarchy: her desire cannot be made sense of in hierarchical relationship to men.[127] Brook continues this lesbian/feminist tradition in her letter to *Sojourner,* "Lesbians Don't Fuck Men." Brook poses her questions—"How can you call yourself a lesbian when you have sex with men? How can you have sex with men when you believe yourself to be a lesbian?"[128]—in disbelieving terms. For Brook, women who have sex with women and men are bisexuals, "period";[129] sexual behavior and identity are supposed to mirror one another. Yet, in asking her questions, Brook is unwittingly forced to discuss lesbians who do have sex with men, and bisexuals who do not. The debate in the pages of *Out/Look* sparked by Jan Clausen's article "My Interesting Condition," in which the well-known lesbian author "confesses" to sex with, indeed being in love with, a man, followed a similar pattern.[130] Also in 1990, Clausen's piece provoked an unprecedented wave of responses, the majority of which were from outraged lesbians. This response, cited in Rust, was typical: "I don't consider any women a 'dyke' who sleeps with a man. Period."[131] According to Rust, Clausen posed a particular threat because of perceived "dilution and pollution" of lesbianism, whereas bisexuals who responded argued in line with early assertions within the Northampton Pride March debates that bisexuals should be considered as insiders of lesbian community rather than interlopers.[132]

Once the incontrovertibility of *lesbian difference* from bisexual women falters, a space is created to ask these questions in a different way. Greta Christina is, thus, able to inquire, "Is a lesbian . . . a woman who only fucks other women?"[133] Here the incredulity of Brook's question is replaced by another rhetorical turn of phrase, only Christina's assumes the answer "No." Christina continues:

> That would include bi women who're monogamously involved with other women. A woman who doesn't fuck men? That would include celibate straight women. A woman who would never get seriously involved with men? Rules out lesbians who've been married in the past. A woman who never has sexual thoughts about men? That excludes dykes who are into heavy and complex gender play, who get off on gay men's porn, or who are maybe just curious. Do you have to be 100 percent directed at women and away from men in thought, feeling, word, and deed from birth to qualify as a "real" lesbian? That would rule out all but about two women on the planet. I hope they can find each other."[134]

Christina mentions a range of practices, identities, experiences, and histories, including but not restricted to bisexuality, that cannot be accounted for by the separation of "lesbian" from "sex with men." In a similar vein Pat Califia argues that denial of the extent to which lesbian and male lives are intertwined in a number of ways, directly or indirectly, poses a far greater threat to the safety of lesbian space (given the increased likelihood of HIV transmission) than any particular sexual practices might.[135]

It becomes increasingly clear why many of the arguments made against bisexual inclusion in the Pride March link bisexual women with lesbian sadomasochists and lesbians who oppose the censorship of pornography. Each of these positions is seen as increasing the likelihood of male infiltration into the lesbian community. One can add to this the increase in numbers of lesbians in Northampton coming to identify as transsexual men, and the stability of the assumption not only that a lesbian does not have sex with men, which provides a further threat to the boundaries of lesbian community. In her 1990 letter, Power asserts that many of the lesbians at the March 15th meeting were unhappy with the decision to revert to the form name of "Lesbian and Gay pride" because of their own transvestite or transsexual feelings.[136] but that she is not herself a man is threatened. Similarly, the Northampton Lesbians Fighting Pornography link SM and heterosexuality—"How many dykes can truly say that the eroticism of s/m differs in any significant way from what every tract of compulsory heterosexuality from Freud and Havelock Ellis to Harlequin has force-fed us since infancy?"[137]

These connections between "risky behaviors" are by no means restricted to the Northampton Pride March debates. In a larger U.S. context, Elizabeth Armstrong cites an anonymous writer for the *San Francisco Bay Times*, who argues that bisexuals who claim lesbians sleep with men and who call themselves "'bi-dykes' [oppress] lesbians as surely as straight male pornography."[138] In a U.K. context, Susan Ardill and Sue O'Sullivan connect a number of behaviors and identities as potentially "other" to lesbianism, in their discussion of the banning of lesbian sadomasochists from the London Lesbian and Gay Centre in 1985: "Bisexuality, paedophilia, sadomasochism, transsexuality, dress codes—all came up in the MC [management committee] discussions about who could or should be welcome in the centre."[139] The strategic positioning of sadomasochists as "other" to lesbian identity within the Northampton debates is not consistent however. As a key figure within Northampton's antipornography lobby, one might expect Sarah Dreher to denounce lesbian sadomasochism as not "real" lesbian behavior. In her 1991 Pride March speech, however, Dreher counters claims that SM lesbians are honorary bisexuals, saying that they "sure seem like 'real Lesbians' to me."[140] In a strategic move, Dreher claims SM lesbians as "same" in order to ensure that the greater threat of bisexual women remains "other."

Brook tries to circumvent the problem of lesbian desire for men by an appeal to oppression and guilt. She says, "Occasionally a lesbian may find herself having sex with a man because she is tired of fighting a homophobic society, because she is tired of hiding, because of her own internalized self-hatred or homophobia. But this is not bisexuality, this is pain."[141] Brook does admit that lesbians do have sex with men, then. Or, more precisely, a lesbian who finds herself having sex with a man (notice the passivity implied—a lesbian would never *choose* this sexual behavior) can only remain a lesbian in Brook's terms if she is a "guilty lesbian," or a "lesbian in pain."[142] Unusually, Brook distinguishes between the "lesbian in pain" and "true bisexuals," whom she identifies as those who enter "into healthy unions with both sexes."[143] Authentic bisexual subjects are not, in effect, the concern of lesbians, or of lesbian culture and history, although they may look the same at first glance. Brook thus seeks to ensure that lesbians, whether or not they mistakenly have sex with men, remain distinct from bisexuals.

Colleen Urban displays similar slippage in her article "Lesbians are not Bisexuals" when she argues that to include bisexual women in the word *lesbian* is dangerous, "because it does not recognize that there are women out there whose primary emotional, social, sexual, and spiritual connections are with women, exclusively."[144] Like Brook, Urban's emphasis on the fact that some lesbians are exclusively committed to women does not put a final barrier between bisexuals and lesbians, but rather between "complete lesbians" and those lesbians and bisexuals with sexual or emotional commitments to men. Brook's lapsed lesbian is by no means a lost cause. She can still purge herself of her nonlesbian error: "The lesbians I know who find themselves attracted to men are disturbed by this, expend a lot of time and energy soul-searching, and try to get down to the root of the problem."[145] Even for Brook the meaning of "lesbian" has shifted; being a lesbian now seems to be more about occupying a particular personal and political position in relation to men, rather than a simple refusal of attraction to men. The discursive territorial markers have already begun to shift in order to explain apparent similarities between bisexual women and lesbians that can no longer be ignored. Lesbian space is refigured, then, as a site of struggle between lesbians and bisexuals, but also between lesbians and transsexuals, and among lesbians. It is clear thus far that the Northampton Pride March debates highlight the fact that lesbian territory, far from being occupied by a single, recognizable lesbian subject, is instead a site of difference and contest between multiple subjects within very different relationships to the space that they share.

Part Two: Divided Loyalties

Lesbian and Bisexual Visibilities

Dreher's statement, "I am a lesbian and I see the world through lesbian eyes,"[146] which came at the end of her speech to the 1991 Lesbian and Gay Pride March rally, foregrounds the key context of "visibility" that structures the Northampton debates about bisexual inclusion in lesbian territory. Throughout the controversy, increased visibility is unquestioningly desired by both lesbians and bisexuals, is grasped for as a sign of political power and credibility. As with the strategic polarization of the "sexual" and the "political," the mobilization of tropes of visibility informs the way participants of the controversy understand such concepts as "self," "community," and "identity."

As I mentioned earlier, one of the main reasons why some people were opposed to bisexual inclusion was because increased bisexual visibility was understood as producing increased lesbian invisibility. The January 1990 edition of the *Calendar* reports, "We have created a community we care deeply about, and are in danger of seeing that community made invisible."[147] In the same edition the terms of the debates are established as forcing a choice between "the bisexual or the Lesbian community."[148]

Brook and Dreher's letter to *Gay Community News* picks up on the theme of visibility more explicitly with its title, "Visibility? Whose Visibility?" Advocates of the Pride March and Committee remaining "Lesbian and Gay" argue not that bisexual and lesbian visibility are in inverse proportion to one another, but rather that bisexual inclusion equals lesbian invisibility. Any increased visibility affording bisexuals (specifically, here, their named inclusion in the march) is seen as erasing lesbian visibility. In her letter that sparked the newspaper debates, Micki Seigel uses similar language to argue in favor of bisexual inclusion. Her rationale for specific bisexual naming is that bisexuals "had been working on the march for years, without official acknowledgment."[149] And in reference to the defeat of the motion to include bisexuals, Seigel adds: "Now I am the one who is 'invisible.' "[150]

Presumably, the inclusion of *bisexual* in the march's name cannot actually result in the erasure of a lesbian identity. Lesbians still exist, take part in the march, and understand themselves in relation to the lesbian (and gay and bisexual) community. Nor can the lack of bisexual acknowledgment in name mean that bisexual involvement in the Pride March is a fantasy. Bisexuals may not be visible *as* bisexuals in that context, but one assumes that they might be highly visible in other respects—as members of the lesbian and gay community, or as workers on the march committee, for example. For both lesbians and bisexuals, however, visibility is about being seen as, and being able to see one's sexual practices as given meaning through a distinct political identity. The association of bisexuality with the sexual accounts to some extent for the fears that the lesbian community as a political community will be compromised by bisexual inclusion. And that same association fuels bisexuals' determination to be valued as part of that political community. Further than this, though, bisexual visibility as part of the lesbian community does indeed mean the disappearance of the proverbial *lesbian difference*; if bisexual and lesbian women march together and both are named, one never quite knows who is who.

The relationship between sexual identity and community needs to be consolidated through another form of naming, too. Not only must community embrace you and name you, individuals must also provide validation of sexual identity, whether shouting your/their name in the street or whispering it in your ear. One of the organizers of the 1991 march explains, "I find it hard to imagine that someone who's been in a heterosexual marriage for 20 years, and goes out and has a fling with [someone] of the same sex should be setting the political agenda for me. That person can't speak for me."[151] What is implied is that while the married woman cannot speak or set the political agenda for the author, someone else could. Since the author's argument is being made in defense of not including "Bisexual" in the Pride March's name, we presume the woman who can speak for the author must be a lesbian, rather than a bisexual or heterosexual woman. But that is to presuppose a seamless visibility politics. We do not actually know the sexual identity of the author's ideal advocate. We only know about her behavior, and more precisely, what her behavior does not include. The woman the author assumes can speak for her, and set the political agenda, is described only in terms of experience and behavior: unmarried and not merely "flirting" with same-sex desire. The organizer's advocate could therefore be lesbian or bisexual. Ironically, the author assumes that sexual behavior and identity go hand in hand, even though this is precisely what is at issue during the Pride March controversy. For the author, and for visibility politics, there can be no gaps among behavior, identity, and community.

This visibility discourse, then, assumes not only a separation between terms (*lesbian* can be seen, and sees itself, as different from *bisexual*), but also a reflexive relationship among individual lesbians and among individual bisexuals that vouchsafes who they are and affirms that difference. Visibility functions as a way both of creating and maintaining self and of obtaining external political validation. Community reflects the individual, and the individual can see herself reflected in both community and other similarly formed selves. In this respect, the visibility discourse is both a way of presenting sexual identity to the world and a way of confirming what constitutes that identity. The different subjects residing within a given site must make claims for representation with others who are the same as them, then, rather than on the basis of historical or cultural shared participation. Instead of sexual identity being understood as the result of dissonance and difference (in relation to both self and others), it is its (community and individual) reflection that carries the weight. For this reason, "bisexual rights" will only ever be claimed through a false separation of bisexuals from the different cultural and historical contexts that they have forged and participated in.

The "Stay Out: Stay Proud" theme for the 1990 Pride March is, of course, highly appropriate. Not only should you "come out," you should also "stay out." What is required is repetition of the act of making oneself visible. The theme itself reads more like a demand than an invitation. Coming out as bisexual in the context of the Pride March has already been precluded (other than as ally); the theme is thus addressed only to lesbians and gay men. Hence, the statement "Stay Out: Stay Proud" is not finished—it is a demand to stay out as lesbian or gay or find another community to represent your interests. The associated issues of remaining closeted are interesting in this context. For those people in the process of coming out as bisexual (as many people did during the controversy), obeying the invocation to stay out as lesbian would be to remain closeted, although also to repeat a dissonant history of refusal and "inauthenticity."

The theme "Stay Out: Stay Proud" suggests a kind of refusal to accede to change. The reflection that confirms your identity only ever reflects who you are now, not who you might become, or even who you have been. It is a reflection that feeds off the object it confirms, in an endless but static circle. There is no room for the change of heart that bisexuals represent. Jo Eadie argues that: "Coming out appeals to the narcissistic pleasure of presenting to another a finished image of ourselves, which they return to us in exactly the same form."[152] This is the circle that needs to be endlessly repeated, projected back into the past (this is who you always were), and endlessly into the future (this is, and always will be, your true self). One could argue, then, that in this context the "Stay Out: Stay Proud" theme is primarily motivated by the fear of change represented by the acknowledgment of historical as well as contemporary bisexual inclusion. The theme of the 1991 Lesbian and Gay Pride March was "Claiming Our Identity: Protecting Our Lives." Once more, sexual identity is produced through territorial allusion. Before the march, Brook encouraged "as many people as possible to 'come out,' or reveal their sexual identity."[153] Ordinarily, this invocation would be read as asking people to "reveal" the preexistent truth of who they are. But in relation to the visibility discourse, her comment reads as asking people to become who they are through revealing it, and seeing themselves reflected back, to choose a present and a past.

The terms of the visibility discourse do, of course, mean that within the "bisexuality debates" exclusion does come to equal invisibility in a range of ways. A number of bisexuals and their allies did not attend the 1990 march because they had not been explicitly named. In addition to not participating in the 1990 march, Bet Power herself remarked that "many more Lesbians, Gay men, S/Mers, TVs and TSs, will also choose to refuse the terms of this year's discriminating Lesbian/Gay March."[154] In an exchange of letters, Bet Power and Steve Boal (a founding member of the Amherst-based Valley Bisexual Network) discussed the relative merits of staying away from the march versus participating in it as visibly as possible. Boal expressed concern at Power's decision to withdraw her support from the march, arguing that this merely played into the hands of those who would deny bisexual visibility—"no voice, no visibility."[155] Boal's response to bisexual exclusion was to try and co-opt the march's theme "Stay Out: Stay Proud" by marching "loudly and visibly"[156] and distributing armbands and balloons proclaiming their possessor to be bisexual or a bisexual ally. In her reply, Power reiterated her decision not to attend the march, adding that she would continue to "speak out" in articles.[157] Power added that she would return to the Northampton Pride March once it included "all sexual minorities."[158]

As I have argued above, the aim of bisexual inclusion was initially to represent bisexuals within their lesbian and gay community. The challenge was leveled not on the basis of difference, but of sameness. Given that the response was to redefine lesbian identity in terms of its separation from bisexual women, both sides utilize the notion of bisexual distinctness albeit in different ways and to different ends. And so, as the Pride March debates continue, . . . bisexual identity becomes increasingly associated with an independent bisexual community. In response to assertions that bisexual women are incapable of forming their own community—"some bisexual women seem to feel they cannot create their own community, but must attach themselves to the Lesbian community"[159]—bisexuals also begin to emphasize the importance of a bisexual community related to, but not coextensive with, lesbian and gay community. From Ochs's statement that the lesbian community "*is* my own community,"[160] and Jodi Lew's that "Bisexuals certainly will be invisible if they are explicitly excluded,"[161] we move to stronger assertions of bisexual community. Karen Baker and Helen Harrison argue that a "[v]isible and active bisexual community is critical to the success of the movement as a whole,"[162] and Brad Robinson of the Valley Bisexual Network speaks of a "bisexual population" that is alienated and excluded from the 1990 march.[163] This "bisexual population," or community, now claims to be "critical to" and unethically excluded from the lesbian and gay community on the grounds of the common interests and shared concerns of discrete bisexual, lesbian, and gay bodies. Cynthia Van Ness asserts, "Bisexuals are indeed participating in gay and lesbian events . . . but that doesn't mean that we aren't simultaneously building our own community. *GCN* covered last spring's East Coast Bisexual Conference, and I'm looking forward to this year's first annual National Bisexual Conference in San Francisco in June."[164] It is not clear from the documentation generally whether this growing bisexual community is conceived as a subset of the lesbian and gay community, or as an overlapping community. This lack of specificity perpetuates the confusion over bisexual inclusion and exclusion. The language is a rather vague one of coalition politics, where different, distinguishable groups are either all part of one big, if not happy, family or are allied in order to maximize their shared interests. It is no coincidence that the themes for the 1992–1994 Pride Marches are, respectively, "We Are Family: Pride Equals Power," "Diversity is Our Beauty: Our Unity Is Our Strength," and "Breaking Down Walls: Building a Community" (fig. 2.6). All three themes emphasize a common bond across difference, though all three can be interpreted in both ways.

Similar rhetoric is used by proponents of the umbrella term *queer* in Northampton. "Unity" and "diversity" are used interchangeably to present a vision of an all-inclusive queer community, where everyone is acknowledged separately, but is seen as part of a diverse whole. For all the language of unity, visibility as a particular identity is still seen as a political necessity, as can be seen in a Queer Nation pamphlet of the time, which read, "We are all diminished if any one of us remains invisible—whether it is the lack of lesbians and gay men as speakers at last year's March or the decision this year to remove 'Bisexual' from the title

Fig. 2.7. Author's photograph of 1994 Pride Northampton March T-shirt in the Northampton Collection, Northampton Sexual Minorities Archives.

and exclude bisexuals and heterosexual allies from the march Steering Committee. We also all remain invisible if those of us with privilege accept it without question or action—whether that privilege be heterosexual, white, class, gender, age, and so on."[165] Yet such queer notions of inclusion and naming are always doomed to failure, in part because it is never possible to name everyone, in which case, in this rubric, we must all be "diminished." In the Northampton context, the queer endeavor seems to end up amounting to little more than an expansive liberal pluralism, where if only we could tolerate each other's differences we would be able to live in harmony and strength. This tendency toward a "different but equal" view is satirized in the *Calendar* as an "April Fool," in an announcement for "the Bisexual, Trisexual, Transvestite, Transexual [*sic*], Asexual, Oversexual, Ultrasexual, Heterosexual, Non-sexual Pride March Committee."[166] The list is expanded to the point where even the initial inclusion of "Bisexual" appears ridiculous. The *Gay Community*

News April 1 edition of the same year—*Gay Community Nudes*—also provides a satire on the Northampton debates in its article "Dyke and Bi Factions Sling It Out," interviewing participants in a mock mud-wrestling contest between lesbians and bisexuals: "'There's been so much mudslinging already we decided we might as well go for the real thing,'" said Mac Truque, spokesdyke for one of the groups, Butches Offended by Bi's [*sic*] (BOB)."[167] As a result of facilitation the bisexual and lesbian groups find common ground in their anger at "'self-identified femme lesbians who are sleeping with men.'"[168] Everyone knows who she is, how she relates to other identities, and who the enemy is; everyone is "mud-wrestling" for her own particular patch of territory, as well as for recognition within a "larger whole."

Continuing in the queer pluralist vein Marcia Deihl, in another *Gay Community News* article, emphasizes that she "[s]trongly support[s] lesbian separatist events and spaces, and I personally would never intrude as a bisexual woman. I support the right . . . of any minority to meet alone. . . . But a Queer Pride Rally is another event entirely. Historically, it has been a coalition event.[169] Deihl is preempted by a contributor to *Sojourner* who argues that "bisexual inclusion" does not "homogenize lesbians into invisibility, but . . . [adds] our diverse voices and strengths to a community of incredible breadth and vision."[170] The bisexual/lesbian dispute is thus "resolved" in Northampton by a form of coalition politics, an additive politics. What begins as a dispute about who is able to call themselves "lesbian"—becomes a question of who can create identity and community along the same lines. Yet such views of an endlessly expansive community is not only historically inaccurate and oversimplified in structural terms, it also assumes that we can distinguish among our commonalities and differences without difficulty, while leaving the terms of identity politics intact.

Ginny Lermann unwittingly highlights one of the further problems with this political model of inclusion/exlcusion when she proclaims, "To step from the safety of the lesbian community into new territory is no mean feat. I am proud of my courage."[171] Lermann continues by saying, "I still participate in non-biphobic activities within the gay community, for this is my community too."[172] The tension, for Lermann, arises from being part of lesbian community on the one hand, and striking out to find new territory that could be safe for bisexuals on the other. Not only is it difficult to identify the boundaries of community such that one can legitimately say that this and not that space is bisexual and not lesbian, but the new identity equals, new territory conflation puts subjects of that identity at risk. While one is not likely to be physically attacked for being bisexual in lesbian space, this is of course not true of all spaces. There are a number of questions raised in my mind by Lermann's story about the nature of the hard-won "bisexual territory" that bisexual subjects are now presumed to occupy, that are reminiscent of those I asked in relation to Joan Nestle's delineation of a specific lesbian space in chapter 1. All of these questions concern the difficulty of delineating a distinct bisexual space to become a subject of, and engage Lermann's historical location in lesbian community as well as her ambivalence:

1. Does bisexual territory overlap with lesbian territory, or is it separate?
2. How will identities be negotiated within that "common ground"?
3. Is bisexual women's involvement in the lesbian community to be restricted to those "places of commonality"?
4. Are lesbians expected to "give up" some of their territory to share with bisexual women?
5. Will lesbians be welcomed in bisexual territory?
6. Will bisexual women's space be women-only some/all of the time?

To my mind, what is interesting is that the progression of the Northampton Pride March debates means that where bisexual space might be in relation to lesbian space can be posed as a direct and pertinent question that offers potential for resolution within that context, rather than outside of it. Yet detailed questions such as the above are never in fact asked, in part, I want to suggest, because of the return to abstract notions of community, space, and subjectivity in resolving whether to name bisexuals.

Thus, returning to Lermann above, while she imagines separate as well as common space, she does not flesh this vision out at any point to give a sense of what "nonbiphobic activities" might be, for example. In a similar vein, Michele Moore suggests, "Bisexual women and men are creating our own community. But building a community takes time, and all communities borrow elements from those that have preceded them. The gay rights movement borrowed from the women's movement, which borrowed from the Black civil rights movement; and so the bisexual movement borrows from the gay and lesbian movement. I'm sad some lesbians and gay men feel threatened rather than flattered that bisexuals find their movement and culture admirable enough that we want to borrow elements from it."[173] Aside from the more obvious point about her reinscription of an oversimplified linear view of political history, Moore is also abstract in relation to the community bisexuals are building here. She does not specify what it might be that bisexuals are "borrowing," relying instead on a transcendent understanding of commonality, which is precisely what was in dispute in the Northampton debates in the first place. The nature of bisexual territory, its limits, accessibility, or ethical standing, is never explored other than rhetorically and thus simply returns to being an empty signifier of inclusion more generally. In my reading, then, it is inevitable rather than surprising that bisexual community does not flourish in Northampton after the inclusion of "Bisexual" in the Pride March's name, since there is no sustained attempt to explore or delineate the forms, functions, or relationships that might define that community. I hope it is clear that a history of women's bisexuality in Northampton is inseparable from the town's lesbian history. While I acknowledge the need for bisexuals to be validated and for their work to be acknowledged, I do not necessary believe that that has to take the form of a separate naming made meaningful through the entrenched rubric of identity politics. And indeed, in Northampton, bisexual naming could be said to have resulted in near complete bisexual invisibility.

Bisexual/Lesbian Experiences

In this final section of the chapter I want to provide several examples of the ways in which the polarization of bisexual and lesbian in the Northampton Pride March controversy oversimplifies the experiences of both bisexuals and lesbians in Northampton. Consequently, the unsettled nature of sexual identity and its relationship to what Marjorie Garber terms "apolitical" desires, behaviors, and experiences tends to be minimized in relationship to the poles of the debate.[174] Part of my desire to map this dissonance is in order to highlight different threads of location and understanding that can be traced in relation to the dominant discursive formations I have discussed thus far, and to assert that these are every bit as important for a bisexual genealogy.

In May 1989, Sharon Gonsalves wrote an article for *Sojourner* in favor of "greater acceptance [of bisexuals] in the lesbian and gay communities."[175] What is most interesting to me about Gonsalves's article, however, is her representation of the relationship among her own desire, identity, and understanding of community. Initially, Gonsalves speaks of her difficulty in coming out as bisexual. She describes the sense of "loss of our community" both for her personally, and for other lesbians who have come out as bisexual." That Gonsalves chooses not to modify the term *lesbian* to "ex-lesbian" or "women who thought they were lesbian" is highly significant. Gonsalves is not speaking here of bisexual women who were previously hiding in the lesbian community, masquerading as lesbians; Gonsalves presents herself and those like her as lesbians who have taken a bisexual identity. This subtle, but important, distinction is underscored later in the same paragraph, when Gonsalves tells us, "Although being seen with a man may make me look like a straight woman (and afford me heterosexual privilege), I feel like a lesbian who's seeing a man."[176] Gonsalves experiences her desire as lesbian, even though she is in a relationship with a man. Or perhaps I should say, Gonsalves experiences her desire as lesbian and is in a relationship with a man; the two are not presented as mutually exclusive here. For Gonsalves, her lesbian desire comes not from sexual object choice but from her experience of self, and from the lesbian community, which provides the context for her desire.

One might expect Gonsalves to continue to identify as a lesbian who has sex with men, her lesbian desire relating to a lesbian identity still, irrespective of sexual object choice. After all, Gonsalves herself sees the lesbian community as "a place where I belong,"[177] and she acknowledges that in some instances she does come out as lesbian: "I'm much more likely to refer to myself as a lesbian when I'm with straight people than when I'm among lesbians."[178] Yet among lesbians Gonsalves feels "like an imposter," "invisible," and "dishonest" if she feels unable to come out as bisexual. Gonsalves says that she needs to be seen as bisexual, in order for her "true self" (the self that desires men as well as women) to be acknowledged, understood, and appreciated. And she affirms the Northampton controversy visibility discourse when she avows, "Getting rid of labels makes our differences invisible."[179] Gonsalves believes that the label *bisexual* allows her to be read as who she is, proclaiming, "I am bisexual all the time, not straight among straights and gay among gays."[180]

And yet, Gonsalves's own story is much more complex and contradictory than her "pride-in-self-identity" suggests. Gonsalves is clear that the self referred to in both gay and straight contexts is bisexual—"I am bisexual all the time"—but this self is not necessarily best signified by the corresponding label *bisexual*. Presumably, it is not through a desire willfully to misrepresent herself that Gonsalves refers to herself as a lesbian in some heterosexual contexts, but because she feels that offers a more accurate image of herself than the term *bisexual* does. In heterosexual contexts, calling oneself bisexual can give an inaccurate indication of cultural or political location, and Gonsalves may well not wish to confirm assumptions that she is "half straight." In lesbian contexts, however, Gonsalves feels that referring to herself as bisexual offers a better view of who she is, and here it may be that she wishes to mark a bisexual difference that is significant to her experience of sexual location. Gonsalves's shifting self-description suggests that one's publicly proclaimed identity does not always match one's self-perception, although she does consider her self-identity to be constant. This sits rather bizarrely with her stress on the importance of accurate labels, since her own experience brings into focus the ways in which label and self do not always precisely correspond.

The relationship between desire and identity is similarly called into question through Gonsalves's narrative. As I mentioned earlier, Gonsalves terms her own desire lesbian, and considers that this desire can be directed to a man or a woman.[181] Already, this is problematic, given the usual assumption that lesbian desire can only be directed toward women.[182] Still more unlikely, the "end result" of her desire is bisexual, not lesbian, identity. Gonsalves's desire for men could perhaps be written as a mistake, as false consciousness or even as a queer perversion, if she continued to identify as lesbian in all contexts. What her experience suggests, however, is that lesbian desire can lead to and confirm a bisexual identity. She elaborates: "[As] a lesbian, I've learned a lot about myself; the patriarchy; ways male and female children are socialized; and about ... oppression.... I've also learned what relationships can and cannot be. I relate to individuals, not penises or breasts. I am capable of loving men and women, and they are capable of loving me."[183] Gonsalves's lesbian desire does not stand in contradiction to her bisexual identity, but is a product of it. In contrast to the conventional coming out narrative, then, Gonsalves does not need to rewrite her lesbian desire as bisexual desire, nor does she need an endlessly cited set of lovers of more than one sex, in order to retrospectively endorse her bisexual identity. Gonsalves's narrative thus disrupts the time-identity relation of narrative structure that usually serves to make sense of sexual experience.

This narrative also challenges the accepted relationship between community and identity, whereby community acceptance of a particular desire eases the way into an identity reflective of that community. Thus, in Northampton, lesbian desire can become lesbian identity with the aid of a supportive and well-established community context in which to express itself. This partly constitutes the lesbian cultural history that Dreher invokes in her account of *lesbian difference*. If the expression of a certain desire—lesbian sadomasochism, or Gonsalves's lesbian desire for women and men—is unacceptable to that community, a subsidiary or alternative identity, such as sadomasochist or bisexual, may be the result. When desire and the resultant identity do not match, community may fail to provide a space for the recognition of that identity. So, the lack of support for sadomasochistic desire within Northampton's lesbian and gay community has given rise to a separate SM community both within and at points separate from lesbian community. And Henry Rubin argues that the creation of a separate transsexual identity and community emerges in the 1970s in the United States, after it was made repeatedly clear that butch lesbians were no longer welcome within the lesbian feminist movement.[184] Clearly the Northampton lesbian community does not easily provide a context for bisexual women's identity. But in terms of the structures of sexual communities, although Gonsalves argues in favor of coming out as bisexual, there is no guarantee that a bisexual community would provide the full support for her lesbian desire, either.

In attempting to resolve the tension between lesbian desire and bisexual identity in their own sexual narratives, Gonsalves and others become members of a community explicitly intended to mediate and reflect the relationship between these apparently contradictory forces. As she explains, "I have gained a lot of strength from meeting with other lesbians who have come out as bi. My support group (the Hasbians) has helped me get back out into the lesbian community—a place where I belong."[185] For Gonsalves, here, the Hasbian community acts as a kind of interim community, serving the functions (supporting and strengthening) that the larger community cannot. Supported by this Hasbian community, lesbian desire can be integrated into bisexual identity. Where lesbian community serves to blur the distinction between lesbian desire and lesbian community so that it becomes difficult to see which came first, Gonsalves's Hasbian community is self-consciously constructed to meet the needs of those for whom the disjuncture between desire and community has resulted in a bisexual identity. The form of this sexual narrative is progressive rather than circular, and importantly, does not need its past to conform to its present and thus indicate its single future; in fact, its past is required to be nonidentical. Such a sexual narrative formation may offer interesting possibilities for bisexual coming-out stories that do not repeat lesbian and gay structures within which a bisexual always runs the risk of emerging as inauthentic or unfinished.

In June 1990, May Wolf wrote a letter to *Gay Community News* in which she bravely risked ostracism from the lesbian community by asking whether or not bisexual desire can in turn lead to lesbian identity. Wolf relates the Northampton Pride March debates directly to her own experience, indicating that "[The furor] has come at a time when I have been reevaluating how I define my sexuality."[186] In her next paragraph, which is worth quoting in full, Wolf raises two key issues in relation to lesbian identity. "I know that there are many women who feel as though they have been lesbian from birth or at least a young age," she notes. "I am not one of those women. In fact I identified as heterosexual and was interested in boys all of my growing years. I had close friends of both genders. But in my 16th year, my emotionally abusive father added sexual abuse to his repertoire of efforts to injure my soul. After that certain body parts, sounds, touches and smells became triggers not to excitement or pleasure but fear and anxiety."[187] In the first couple of sentences, Wolf challenges the lesbian coming-out narrative that requires lesbian desire to have always been present in some form. In the second half of the paragraph, Wolf describes and claims her personal relationship to her father's abuse, and the influence this has had on her sexual experience. In the face of homophobic discourses that attribute lesbianism to a response to abuse and, therefore, as pathological and curable, Wolf's declaration is highly politically charged. In addition, Wolf's narrative could be used as confirming the stereotype of lesbians as women who fear or hate men, and hence she risks the wrath of a lesbian community in Northampton that has established itself as a positive woman-loving-woman community.

Wolf has been sexually and emotionally involved with a woman for more than ten years. Ordinarily, this would provide her with near mythical status in a still-young community. Yet Wolf says that she "cannot honestly call [her]self a lesbian,"[188] because, while her experience of abuse means she cannot act on it, she has a continuing sexual attraction to men. Wolf has been an active member of Northampton's lesbian community for a long time and, until now, has always marched in the Lesbian and Gay Pride March. In addition, she speaks of a complex and politicized relationship with her female partner, noting, "My partner and I live our lives, debate whether or not to have children, bemoan the fact that we can't be on each other's health insurance, make daily decisions about whether to be out to whom and to what degree."[189] In light of her relationship, it is tempting to write Wolf's experience as that of a woman who finds a home for her bisexual desire in the lesbian community, a place of harmony after the violence of the heterosexual world. It is clear, however, that Wolf does not find the lesbian community to be such a place. Wolf relates that she did not march in the 1990 Pride March because she did not feel "full belonging."[190] The need to define who counts as lesbian in the face of the Pride March debates about bisexuality results in Wolf interrogating her own place in the lesbian community. In the face of the stark polarization of bisexual and lesbian during the Northampton debates, Wolf is forced to choose, redefining as nearer to bisexual than lesbian. This reading is confirmed by the way Wolf closes her letter: "Since I haven't yet found a label which fits me, bisexual is as close as I can come. And when the march includes bisexuals, so too will I come."[191] Although in "the early years [she] identified fiercely as a lesbian,"[192] Wolf has to renegotiate her sense of self once more when she discovers that the lesbian community cannot support her (un-demonstrated) desire for men.

Wolf's narrative of desire and identity resists such an easy reading, however. Her final uncomfortable coming out as bisexual effectively undercuts itself. Wolf can not find a "label which fits" her, and so will grudgingly adopt *bisexual*. But in finally positioning herself as bisexual ally—"when the march includes bisexuals, so too will I come"—Wolf distances herself from the term she appeared to have accepted. Earlier in her letter, Wolf remarks that "I'm not even sure that the label bisexual quite explains my experience."[193] Wolf further declares that despite her sexual and emotional relationship with her female partner, the "reality is that I feel heterosexual. The reality is that I am grateful that I am also comfortable with the sexual and emotional love of my woman partner, because that means I have love and I might not have had love."[194] The problem with the relationships I have been examining among desire, community, and identity is that a "resultant" sexual identity is usually anticipated, even if that identity changes later. Wolf attempts to resist this solidification of her desire, though of course the debates about bisexual inclusion that precipitate her article make this very difficult. Wolf says, "Sexuality is a complex phenomenon; labels perhaps offer a way to generalize across great numbers of people. But if we really pause and talk with one another, the complexity and heart defy easy lines of demarcation between in and out. I am out, I am out as a woman whose sexuality has been interrupted and interfered with by incest, a woman who feels sexual feelings for men, but who lives a primary emotional and sexual life with another woman."[195] Wolf's moving passage (which just precedes the final paragraph in which she almost comes out as bisexual) complicates the relationships among desire, community, and identity within the conventional coming-out narrative. Wolf comes out, not as a lesbian, not as a complete and finished sexual package, but as a woman whose complex experiences and desires bring her to living with another woman. To insist Wolf is lesbian or bisexual, or indeed to situate the two identities as opposed and force her to choose, would be to deny her history and to violently invalidate her story.

If we can speak of Sharon Gonsalves as experiencing lesbian desire for men and women, could we also conceive of May Wolf as experiencing heterosexual desire for men and women? The latter feels much more difficult to assert, because the two conclusions have very different implications in the current political climate. One can all too easily imagine a homophobic argument being made that since heterosexual desire can be directed to both men and women, no one need now identify as anything other than heterosexual. But Wolf never asserts a heterosexual identity, and her experience of opposite-sex sex was scarcely one of privilege or power. I also think it is important to point out that Wolf's partner is fully aware of Wolf's feelings about her sexuality: "A measure of our love is that we are able to talk about everything, even the issues I raise here."[196] If Wolf's partner does not see Wolf's sense of herself and her desire as an impediment to their sexual relationship, then it seems reasonable to conclude that a woman's heterosexual desire can, indeed, be directed to women as well as men. In Wolf's case, her heterosexual desire for men is not acted upon, which may be why she never identifies as heterosexual, only as emphatically lesbian or almost bisexual. Given the model of dissonance in sexual narratives I am developing here, there would be no necessary problem with Wolf's partner identifying as lesbian. This is not to say that desire, identity, and community are voluntaristically entered into, or indeed that the relationships among these terms can be simply read off an individual's expression of their relationship. But to return to Sedgwick's epistemological challenges to sexual identity formation, one must also ask what is at stake in ignoring these expressions of and reflections upon experience, in reinscribing dominant community models despite evidence of what they preclude or disallow. The examples I have given are anything but voluntaristic, too, in that they represent the effect of politically and culturally conscious decisions that challenge the repudiative base of sexual and gender identity formation but not the political importance of those identities.

The final example of discontinuity among desires, identities, and communities I want to discuss in this chapter draws on my own experience of living in a Northampton household in 1994 and 1995. The house itself is a rented, three-story, detached clapboard Massachusetts house, with front and back porches, near the center of Northampton. To me, fresh from England, it definitely looked as if an old woman in a shawl on a front porch swing would complete the picture. The house is owned by a dyke landlady, and my room advertised as such in the *Calendar*: "woman wanted for dyke household." This is no novelty in Northampton. I replied to the advertisement not sure whether I qualified as a potential or desirable part of a "dyke household." In fact, it emerged that none of the other people living there directly met that requirement either. The landlady was a different matter: she had been living there since the 1970s, had the ubiquitous Northampton dyke haircut—short and spiky on top, long at the back—wore jeans and flannel shirts, never wore makeup, and looked faintly bemused when she visited to collect the rent or mend the boiler.

My housemate identified as a femme dyke (although she now sees herself as bisexual) was previously in a long-term relationship with a woman named Molly, and fully endorsed the recognition claims of bisexuals, sadomasochists, and transsexuals. Our friendship was cemented over hastily prepared meals and sharing our experiences of being femme women in relationships with transsexual men. The apartment above was occupied by a lesbian couple, one of whom was expecting a child through artificial insemination. Though they did not identify strongly in this way, their styles allowed them to be read as butch and femme, and their division of domestic and emotional labor followed traditional gender lines. The top floor was occupied by a butch/femme couple and their twelve-year-old son, who was the biological child of the butch dyke. The femme was already a friend of mine from bisexual groups, and is also strongly SM-identified. In the course of my time there, her butch lover began to consider identifying as a transsexual man. In racial and class terms we were mixed working- and middle-class, white English, American, and Cuban.

All seven householders were on friendly terms, sharing a beaten up car, meeting for breakfast at Sylvester's on Sunday mornings, watching videos as a group. The most regular visitors to the household were my lover and my roommate's two gay male friends, who were also friends of the other members of the household. It could be argued that this was not really a dyke household at all: too many male-female relationships; too many bisexuals; too many femmes and butches; too many male visitors. Yet all of us saw ourselves as part of the lesbian community of Northampton, and all of us saw ourselves as part of a dyke household, culturally if not in terms of object choice. The different subject locations were always understood in relation to lesbian culture, often as critical reflections upon it, rather than as outside of that culture.

One aspect of this experience that I returned to a number of times is the fact that it seems to move in such a different direction to the story of bisexual experience I have told about Northampton as a whole during this particular time frame. Throughout this chapter my concern has been with the ways bisexual women are included and excluded from lesbian community. The narrative ostensibly traces the shift from what I identify as initial bisexual inclusion within lesbian community to the separation of bisexual identity through naming. In a direct mirroring of this trajectory I initially wandered the streets of Northampton as an outsider searching for bisexual community—in vain—and ended up with a sense of my own inclusion within a miniature lesbian community. At the close of the chapter there remains a contradiction between the "resolution" of the Pride March controversy through bisexual naming, and the apparent lack of bisexual visibility during my stay in Northampton. Yet my own movement toward rather than away from inclusion within lesbian community could perhaps be seen as providing alternative closure, suggesting different bisexual locations within that narrative, and highlighting the difference between dominant and localized discourses of desire, identity, and community, as well as the relationships among them.

Chapter 3

Representing
the Middle Ground

How can I reconcile the contradictions of sex and gender, in my experience and my politics, in my body? We are all offered a chance to escape this puzzle at one time or another. We are offered the True or False correct answer . . . But the boxes that we check . . . do not contain the complexity of sex and gender for any of us.

—Minnie Bruce Pratt, *S/HE*

Whereas in chapter 2, I traced the production and development of bisexual meanings in the lesbian/feminist space of Northampton, Massachusetts, in this chapter I am concerned with how bisexuality is produced in relation to transsexuality. How are both bisexuality and transsexuality constructed within and for the contemporary fields of sexuality and gender studies in U.S. and U.K. contexts? I am interested in mapping the discursive spaces carved out for bisexual and transsexual bodies within these fields, and in exploring the possibility of imagining alternative bisexual and transsexual spaces of representation. I examine bisexuality and transsexuality together in this chapter because there are a number of similarities in the ways that bisexuality and transsexuality are given and give meaning within queer and feminist studies currently, and in addition because of their overlapping locations within sexological and psychoanalytic accounts of gender and sexual subject formation through the twentieth century. In contemporary contexts bisexuality and transsexuality become each other, and each other's alibis, in part due to a past that is assumed to be the cause of their contemporary locations. Their contemporary meaning, location, and histories are difficult to disentangle. Interestingly, even if I desired to separate out bisexual and transsexual locations, cartographic inquiry into queer feminist terrain will not allow me to do so.

As I outline below, and throughout this chapter, bisexuality and transsexuality are both abstracted as the middle ground of sexual and gender culture. I have highlighted the construction and reproduction of bisexuality as the middle ground of sexual and gendered culture throughout this project thus far. What has also proven significant in my research is that transsexuality is likewise positioned as middle ground, though not in exactly the same ways as bisexuality. Within contemporary queer and feminist terrain, however, both are understood by turns to consolidate or transcend sexed, gendered, or sexual oppositions, to embody by turns the worst aspects of heterosexuality, and the best of queerness. One could argue, too, that it is no coincidence that the beginning of a separation of bisexual meaning from sexed or gendered merging occurs as transsexuals gain prominence within queer theory as either fixing or transcending those same oppositions.

In one strand of thought, both transsexuals and bisexuals are seen as traitors, as not feminist or queer enough to be considered viable political subjects in their own right. Hence, for Bernice Hausman, writing in 1995, as well as for the hugely influential Janice Raymond, writing originally in 1979, transsexuals become subjects only through surgical and medical patriarchal intervention, which has as its true aim maintaining the status quo.[1] And for Ara Wilson and Elizabeth Wilson writing in the 1990s, political bisexuality shakes the firm ground of lesbian and gay identity and community by fetishizing heterosexuality as sexually transgressive,[2] a position that is not so far removed from the Collective Lesbian International Terrors (C.L.I.T.) Collective's view in 1975–76 that "bisexuality" only benefits straight women who "want a little excitement in . . . their sex lives" with men.[3] Transsexuality and bisexuality are also positioned at the cutting edge of debates about gender, sexuality, and political meaning. In the former case, it is a focus on transgenderism, in particular, that becomes *de rigueur* within queer theory up to the mid-1990s. *Transgender* is defined as "an umbrella term to include everyone who challenges the boundaries of sex and gender. It is also used to draw a distinction between those who reassign the sex they were labeled at birth, and those of us whose gender expression is considered inappropriate for our sex."[4] Richard Ekins and Dave King note that "[c]onceptualising gender in terms of 'performance' (Butler, 1990)—as opposed to category or identity—places cross-dressing and sex-changing (now theorized as transgenderism) at the forefront of contemporary challenges to gender oppression. . . ."[5] In some queer accounts of "trans" theory and culture, transgender and transsexual locations are melded, or separated out in quite stark ways in order for the former to be produced as distinctly queerer than the latter. I discuss this "splitting" of trans location later in this chapter. Similarly placing bisexuality as a leader in the process of transgressing dualisms, Marjorie Garber asks, rhetorically, "Is bisexuality a 'third kind' of sexual identity, between or beyond homosexuality and heterosexuality? Or is it something that puts in question the very concept of sexual identity in the first place?"[6] Both bisexuality and transsexuality are thus located in between or outside of discursive sexual and gendered polarization.

Even from the brief account above it is clear that bisexual and transsexual identities and experiences carry a number of different anxieties about the nature of sex, gender, and sexuality within queer and feminist terrain. I will be arguing throughout this chapter that transsexual and bisexual subjects emerge in feminist and queer texts in order to mark the limits of ontological inquiry and epistemological ground within that terrain.[7] I hope to show that bisexual and transsexual subjects, particularly when considered together, highlight the structural and political problems with a repudiative model of sexuality and gender, as well as offering an example of the usefulness of cultural repudiation as an enabling, cartographic rather than psychoanalytic, alternative to this model.

Part 1 of this chapter, "Bisexual/ Transsexual Textualities," situates bisexual and transsexual meaning as it is generated in contemporary feminist and queer texts, particularly in terms of how this construction reflects older mergings within sexology, and affords more recent political and personal connections among bisexual and transsexual subjects. I begin by identifying some of these disparate connections before interrogating the desires of queer and feminist theorists to reinforce bisexual and transsexual subjects' occupation of the middle ground of sexed, gendered, and sexual spaces. I am especially interested in the way that heterosexual femininity is often invoked as the link between bisexuality and transsexuality, as well as evidence of their normativity, and conversely an emphasis on queer masculinity as evidence of their subversion. This approach maps onto a larger concern of mine, which this is not the place to fully explore, of the acceptance within queer and feminist culture of the privileging of masculinity. Masculinity and femininity become identified as respectively the signs of queer and heterosexual culture—further evidence, I believe, of the limits of a repudiative model of gender and sexual identity that finds a feminine queer subject (of whatever sex) difficult to embrace.[8] I discuss the value of transsexual and bisexual knowledges and locations within, rather than outside of, queer culture for signaling a move away from the epistemological and ontological fusion of queer with lesbian and gay subjects. Part 2, "Transsexual/Bisexual Representations," returns to my questions concerning time and sexual narrative posed in chapters 1 and 2. I examine attempts to represent bisexuality visually, without reproducing univocal bisexual meaning of "in between-ness," insatiability, or disloyalty. I ask whether there might be other ways of forming bisexual narrative that consider its location within other sexual and gendered spaces, without reframing this as a sign of inauthenticity. Here I utilize the work of photographer Stephanie Device, whose work has been published in *The Bisexual Imaginary*.[9] I consider transsexual representation in a similar vein, opening this part of the chapter with a reading of a Loren Cameron self-portrait in terms of a specific transsexual male narrative.[10] I hope here too to consider the problems and possibilities afforded by a linking of bisexual and transsexual readings/representations, in order to continue what I perceive to be a productive political, cultural, and theoretical closeness between bisexual and transsexual subjects and narratives, and to consciously develop an ethical nontranssexual theorizing about transsexuals."[11]

Part 1: Bisexual/ Transsexual Textualities

Here on the gender borders at the close of the twentieth century, with the faltering of phallocratic hegemony and the bumptious appearance of heteroglossic origin accounts, we find the epistemologies of white male medical practice, the rage of radical feminist theories and the chaos of lived gendered experience meeting on the battlefield of the transsexual body: a hotly contested site of cultural inscription, a meaning machine for the production of ideal type.

—Sandy Stone, "The Empire Strikes Back: a
Posttranssexual Manifesto"

Within U.S. and U.K. lesbian, gay, bisexual, and transgender communities the distinctions between transsexuality, bisexuality, and homosexuality are only now beginning to be charted.[12] Historically bisexuality has been read as physical or psychical hermaphroditism (Sigmund Freud),[13] or as psychical androgyny (Magnus Hirschfeld and Otto Weininger).[14] Other sexological authors conceive of bisexuality as the "ground" from which heterosexual or homosexual adult sexual orientation evolves (Wilhelm von Krafft-Ebing and Havelock Ellis),[15] or as the "co-existence of characteristics of both sexes in human (or animal) bodies."[16] Thus, in her article "The Sexual Reproduction of 'Race': Bisexuality, History and Racialisation," Merl Storr cites Ellis, who suggests, "We can probably grasp the nature of abnormality better if we reflect on the development of the sexes and on the latent organic bi-sexuality in each sex. At an early stage of development the sexes are indistinguishable ... it may be said that at conception the organism is provided with about 50 per cent of male germs and about 50 per cent of female germs."[17] Storr also quotes Krafft-Ebing, who suggests that the "primary stage [of evolution] undoubtedly was bi-sexuality, such as still exists in ... the first months of fetal existence in man."[18] Physical hermaphroditism (bi-sexuality) is used by both Ellis and Krafft-Ebing as an explanation for later gender and sexual inversion. Importantly, in all of these accounts, bisexuality is a state (either sexed, gendered, or sexual) rather than a subjectivity. Transsexuality has similarly been read as inversion (Ellis), or hermaphroditism and intersexuality (Allen).[19] Unsurprisingly, then, there are points where bisexuality and transsexuality are also used interchangeably, and as Jay Prosser and Storr note, this slippage in meaning continues today.[20] Bisexuality and transsexuality may be read for one another, then, through their common association with hermaphroditism, gendered inversion, and sexual ambivalence. As with bisexuality, transsexual location as "in between" is read as a merging of two poles, but also as universal incorporation or transcending of those poles. Thus, again, Prosser and Storr note that within early twentieth century sexology "all subjects are to varying degrees transgendered and/or bisexual."[21] Male nipples and female facial hair are considered evidence of both a persistent physical bisexuality and cross-gender characteristics. To underline the extent to which transsexuality and bisexuality lie at the center of dominant sexual and gendered discourse, Prosser and Storr emphasize that "no category in sexology takes its meaning without at least implicit reference to their layered and broad significance."[22]

Understandably, recent energy from bisexual and transsexual communities has been expended in trying to wrest those merged meanings apart, and to reassign historical personages as one thing or another. Transgender activists (such as the group Transsexual Menace in New York) have been concerned with reclaiming such canonical figures as Gertrude Stein, Radclyffe Hall, and Billy Tipton from lesbian and gay history as transgendered if not transsexual—"queer, but not gay."[23] Prosser argues convincingly that "female" inverts are the predecessors of a contemporary transsexual subjectivity rather than lesbian subjectivity (sexual perversion being a subset of inversion in Ellis, and not necessarily coextensive with it).[24] And as discussed in chapter 1, bisexual activists have insisted that Sappho and Oscar Wilde, for example, were really bisexual rather than lesbian and gay. As I have been arguing, to insist that these characters were really bisexual or transsexual is often politically counterproductive as well as historically oversimplified, telling us far more about contemporary concerns than about the past. Similarly, my desire to connect rather than separate bisexual and transsexual histories has everything to do with what I perceive to be the theoretical and political value of considering bisexual and transsexual subjects as linked within current queer and feminist terrains. In this aim, I have no wish simply to recreate pre-1930s conditions whereby bisexuality, trans-sexuality, and homosexuality are viewed as subsets of one another, even if such a move were possible. But I would attempt to steer a slightly different course than the contemporary political one within lesbian, gay, bisexual, and transgender communities, which seem bent on negating historical overlaps in the search for the discrete bisexual or transsexual, lesbian or gay, body and identity. My refusal to interrogate the boundaries between bisexual and transsexual subjects, but instead to focus on the overlaps and continued slippages among understandings of those subjects, aims to reflect cultural uncertainties about who is who, and which couplings equal which sexualities. This approach is of course similar to the one I pursued in considering bisexual women as inseparable from lesbian identity and community in chapter 2, and reflects a continued commitment to valuing bisexual subjectivity in its *partiality*. And this approach is also pragmatic, allowing me to concentrate on the mechanisms, functions, and effects of continuing to produce bisexuality and transsexuality as *similar to* or *different from* (one another, and from lesbian and gay or queer identities) rather than struggling primarily to disentangle them. Interestingly, bisexual activism has been its least universalizing and most dynamic in those moments where it has forged and embraced coalitions with transsexual community in the United States, where its focus is on shared experiences of marginalization and narrative shifts in sexuality and gender rather than on bisexual difference from "monosexuals."[25]

In addition to the political and theoretical links between bisexuality and transsexuality, I am specifically concerned with the relationship between bisexual femme and female-to-male, or FTM, subjectivities.[26] I want to look at some of the ways in which these two subjectivities' histories and experiences relate to, mirror, and problematize one another. I emphasize bisexual femme, rather than bisexual woman, and FTM, rather than MTF (male to female), not because I think this conjunction is more widespread or more significant in terms of the discourses of gender and sexuality I am concerned with, but precisely because neither bisexual nor transsexual experience can be generalized. Many bisexual women learn the expression of their desires in lesbian communities. Many FTMs also learn the expression of their desires in lesbian communities, often as butches. Both bisexuals and FTMs may maintain and negotiate their ties to the lesbian community, whether or not they consider themselves to be an active part of that community. And like the anxiety surrounding bisexual women's open presence in the lesbian community that I documented in chapter 2, FTM presence in the lesbian community is often a cause of controversy. As in the Northampton context, the fear of transsexuality is partly structured by issues of inclusion and exclusion. Trans or bisexual people can be included in a Pride March as additions to a community without too much disruption, but problems occur the moment a lesbian expresses bisexual or transsexual experience within "her" own subjectivity.

My choice here is also partly influenced by a sexual relationship that I had with an FTM, which means that I am more familiar with FTM community than I am with MTF community, and because I am interested in the theoretical and political challenge to current modes of queer inquiry that this particular coupling offers. Later in this chapter I highlight the ways in which I believe that bisexual femme and FTM pose difficulties for queer theory's desire to maintain parody as the preserve of lesbian and gay subjects. What happens, I ask, when the difference between heterosexuality and homosexuality cannot be presumed, or when you cannot tell just by looking which gender performances counter or reinscribe normative sexual discourse? As I discuss below, transsexual men and bisexual femmes provide a coupling that current queer theory can only transform or reject if the terms of its own debate are to remain intact.   .

Transsexual/Bisexual Femininities

Transsexuality has been a subject of contention within feminism ever since Janice Raymond published *The Transsexual Empire*, her condemnation of transsexual subjectivity and medical technological intervention as always and necessarily patriarchal, in 1979. For Raymond, transsexuals—and in particular male-to-female transsexuals— are the horrific result of men's womb envy, the material form of the desire to leave women no integrity in a coercive and patriarchal society.[27] While for Raymond transsexual women ("male-to-constructed-females") are malicious men who sap female energy, transsexual men ("female-to-constructed-males") are women seduced by the desire for patriarchal power.[28] For many writers Raymond's work was one of the factors preventing adequate theorization of transsexual subjectivity within feminist theory until very recently. Thus Sandy Stone writes at the time of publication of "The Empire Strikes Back" that "here in 1991 . . . [*The Transsexual Empire*] is still the definitive statement on transsexualism by a genetic female academic."[29] And Stephen Whittle reiterates that *The Transsexual Empire* "discredited for a long time any academic voice that [transsexuals] might have [had . . .] with feminist theorists. As a result of [Raymond's] work, feminists saw transsexuals as misguided and mistaken men seeking surgery to fulfil some imagined notion of femininity, and furthermore, upholding the gendered sex-role structure inherent in the patriarchal hegemony which sought to discredit feminist work."[30] Here Whittle touches on an issue that strikes me as central to any discussion of Raymond's argument—her intense dislike of femininity. Existing work tends to focus on Raymond's transphobia for understandable reasons, critiquing her for stereotyping MTF embodiments of gender rather than interrogating Raymond's own feminophobia. Throughout *The Transsexual Empire* Raymond argues that only by embracing stereotyped femininity can an MTF transsexual gain access to hormones and surgery: "the male-to-constructed-female transsexual exhibits the attempt to possess women in a bodily sense while acting out the images into which men have molded women."[31] In addition, lesbian-feminist transsexuals seek to "possess women at a deeper level, this time under the guise of challenging rather than conforming to the role and behavior of stereotyped women."[32] In other words, male-to-female transsexuals confirm femininity as a projected male fantasy whether through displaying classically feminine behavior and garb, or through possessing women by guile (and hence behaving in a traditionally male/masculine way).

Raymond's belief that femininity per se is an irredeemable ill (not just when displayed by transsexuals), and further that femininity and heterosexuality cannot be ontologically or epistemologically uncoupled, is confirmed in her more recent work. For Raymond femininity can only ever be a subset of masculinity, derived from maleness and "the patriarchal order," and therefore the opposite of liberatory gender practice. As part of her argument that male impersonation by a woman (as distinct from transgender or transsexual subterfuge) does not rely on an investment in male privilege, and so is fundamentally different from female impersonation by a man, Raymond states that "[t]he reason that women wear pants is mainly comfort and convenience. Pants are practical in all types of weather and don't make women physically vulnerable or encourage sexual harassment, as certain styles of feminine clothing do."[33] This is a quite startling assertion. Raymond vilifies transsexuals with the excuse of protecting feminist culture, yet here accuses women who wear "certain styles of feminine clothing" of making themselves vulnerable to, or even encouraging, sexual attack. This could hardly be considered a feminist approach to issues of violence against women and indeed is precisely the kind of argument that feminist theorists of sexual violence have spent years countering. Raymond's profound dislike of femininity has precedents, of course, and draws on a long tradition of ambivalence within feminist philosophy concerning women's passivity, frivolity, and vanity. I am reminded in particular of Simone de Beauvoir's long and vitriolic passages in *The Second Sex* detailing every conceivable pointless attention to appearance and ennui that women (of the upper middle classes) pay, which read not unlike the male litanies against women's narcissism that Beauvoir otherwise seeks to counter.[34]

For other radical feminists, androgyny offers an alternative to the ills of femininity or masculinity within a heteronormative structure. Thus, for Del Martin and Phyllis Lyon androgyny offers women physical freedoms more often afforded men, although their depiction of that androgyny seems strikingly similar to Raymond's woman in her "practical pants." Martin and Lyon's androgynous woman thus wears pants, not skirts, as "they give you much more freedom of movement than skirts, and they are warmer,"[35] while she continues to wear lipstick.[36] Raymond, however, despite agreement with the relative physical freedoms of different clothing, perceives androgyny to be a merging of the two gendered opposites that nevertheless remain unchallenged, "and so androgynous humanism replaces feminist politics."[37] Raymond ends her article by insisting that a "real sexual politics says yes to a view and reality of transgender that transforms, instead of conforming to, gender."[38] Yet what "a real sexual politics" might be remains singularly unaddressed: she is certain that heterosexual femininity in genetic women and transsexuals, or the "gender blending" she reduces transgenderism to, do not offer this real sexual politics, but the political subject she imagines appears to be one formed primarily through refusal. Judith Butler identifies one of the central problems with such conceptions of "the feminine" in a remark she makes about gender theory, which she says "would misidentify the construction of the feminine within a masculinist economy with the feminine itself."[39] Raymond certainly never considers ways in which femininity could be figured as anything other than masculinity's closest relation, despite the volume of feminist material that has done so,[40] while also failing to offer a clear sense of what she imagines to be a viable alternative.

Bernice Hausman, writing in 1995, might seem an unlikely successor to Raymond's comprehensive antitranssexual position, given that her perspective is influenced more by Michel Foucault and Judith Butler than by Janice Raymond. Hausman charts the importance of the historical and medical separation of "gender identity" from "sex" and the body in the production of contemporary transsexual subjectivity. Following Roland Barthes, she argues for a perception of contemporary gender identity as the "mythic" signifier that has displaced sex and the body in the primary semiotic chain naturalizing heterosexual reproduction.[41] Hausman conflates these two main strands of her argument by presenting the transsexual subject as wholly (and often willingly) produced through technology and therefore as the personification of that regulatory "myth" of gender identity. For Hausman as for Raymond, gender is an unquestionably bad thing, and transsexuals are the most gender invested of all contemporary subjects. There have been a number of critiques of Hausman's work on the basis of her exploitation of transsexual experiences and bodies for her own theoretical ends, and I will return to this issue later in this chapter.[42] In relationship to "gender as the sign of the duped subject" Prosser takes issue with Hausman's "gender chronology," which fixes the emergence of gender identity as a category of self firmly in the 1930s and onward. He writes, "Such a precise historical fixing of a category as complex and elusive as gender begs to be excepted. To suggest only one instance: Is not Freud's theory of sexual development a theory of gender, one which, moreover, proposes masculinity and femininity as achieved and thus non-essential states? Arguably, in Freudian psychoanalysis, which preceded the medical technologies subject to Hausman's focus, gender is already in excess of corporeal sex."[43] I would suggest that Hausman's "error" is needed to fix the simultaneity of gender identity's emergence and transsexual subjectivity, in order to underwrite her premise that transsexual agency is wholly circumscribed by medical technology.

Feminist writers have similarly rejected bisexuality as a political or personal challenge to patriarchy through its association with an oppressive femininity. To return to Martin and Lyon, they note, in commenting on lesbian roles and styles of the early 1970s, that "[w]e have found some interesting anomalies in the butch-femme pattern over the years. One which crops up rather consistently is women—usually divorced and, we suspect, not Lesbian at all—who pair up with butch Lesbians. In these partnerships the entire male-female dichotomy is acted out to the nth degree. The femmes insist that their butches wear only male clothing and that they appear and act as nearly like the stereotyped male as possible. . . . Most of these femmes have been divorced more than once. It appears that they have been so badly treated by men that they can't bear the thought of re-marrying."[44] Martin's and Lyon's two references to "divorce" in this passage emphasize these femmes' behavioral bisexuality. The bisexual/femme makes real the fear that (heterosexual) femininity craves heterosexual masculinity for its fulfillment, settling for a butch only when "a real man" is unavailable or has disappointed her. The figure of the bisexual woman thus confirms the link between femininity and heterosexuality and shores up the assumption that femininity is always and only ever defined in hierarchical relation to masculinity. Bisexual and feminine behavior, are conflated to locate femmes at the middle ground between heterosexuality and homosexuality. This "not Lesbian" femme is depicted here as an interestingly manipulative and powerful figure, in that familiar femme fatale way. She is the one who insists on heterosexual masculine behavior, forcing her male stand-in to perform in ways that Lyon and Martin are apparently convinced she would otherwise resist most fervently. While clearly hoping their construction of gender relations will lay the blame for heterosexual aping at the door of femmes, making femininity rather than masculinity the link between heterosexual and lesbian worlds, the effect of the scenario is rather different, positioning butches here as passive, easily lead and content to be second best.

Writing in 1995, Minnie Bruce Pratt describes the political and personal motivations for conceiving of masculinity and femininity in wholly negative terms. She writes, "As women and as lesbians we wanted to step outside traps set for us as people sexed as woman, to evade negative values gendered to us. We didn't want to be women as defined by the larger culture, so we had to get rid of femininity. We didn't want to be oppressed by men, so we had to get rid of masculinity. And we wanted to end enforced desire, so we had to get rid of heterosexuality."[45]

In this narrative, lesbianism figures as the primary challenge to heteropatriarchy because of its rejection of both femininity and sex with men. Although Pratt is writing here about her memory of lesbian politics in the 1970s, the narrative she traces is not one consigned to the past. Julia Penelope, writing in a radical feminist volume in 1996, argues similarly that embracing femininity is always about passing as heterosexual, is always about being a closeted lesbian. Again, the links with bisexuality are central but not explicit. She writes, "We may or may not choose whether we will love women or men, but we do choose whether or not we will act on our desire. Many lesbians still choose to behave heterosexually, to marry men, and to bear them sons. Eventually, some find their way to acting on their love for a woman, but not all, and they frequently bring their acquired heterosexual behaviors with them when they enter the Lesbian community. Apparently, it does not occur to most of them that unlearning femininity might be a good idea. Others, the hasbeans, choose to love women for a while and then marry men and bear them sons."[46] Femininity, marrying men, bearing sons, behaving heterosexually while being lesbian; these are combined as part of Penelope's attack on the bisexual women she can never quite bring herself to name, except as once having been lesbian. Even in the title of her article, Penelope conflates "passing" and "femininity" as one and the same thing, implicitly insisting that real lesbians are never feminine, even if masculinity in a lesbian is always also problematic. Mirroring Raymond's abhorrence of the femininity of transsexual women, Penelope concludes her article, "Femininity is a choice I won't respect."[47] Penelope echoes Martin and Lyon's portrait of the controlling bisexual femme forcing her butch to conform to heterosexual stereotyped behavior, arguing that passing (feminine/bisexual) lesbians are one of many sources of real lesbians' oppression, in particular that of working-class fat lesbians. Penelope directly associates femininity with having money (being able to buy all those accessories), with having access to money (through better job prospects and male attention),[48] and with being thin.[49] Clearly, not all femmes and butches are working class, as Sheila Jeffreys points out,[50] but to claim, as Penelope does, that lesbian femininity only ever denotes class privilege is inaccurate to say the least. Penelope's argument stands in direct contradiction to the testimony of femme theorists Joan Nestle, Madeline Davis, Elizabeth Lapovsky Kennedy, Dorothy Allison, and Amber Hollibaugh, all of whom have documented the importance of femme-butch identities in working-class lesbian communities as well as the struggles of becoming femme against the odds. In these accounts lesbian femininity daily risks its challenges to heterosexuality; it is a sign of alterity, not capitulation.[51]

The negative association of bisexuality and femininity is directly linked to anti-transsexual feeling in Sheila Jeffreys's work on the legacy of the 1960s "sexual revolution." Jeffreys picks up where the C.L.I.T. papers left off, arguing that bisexuality is a way of straight/feminine housewives pleasing their husbands.[52] In the same volume Jeffreys also critiques transsexuality in terms of what she perceives to be its structural homophobia, noting that transsexuals "are people who have grown up in a homophobic society but are attracted to others of their own sex. Such is their aversion to homosexuality that these men and women are unable to accept that they are simply gay. In order to relate to people of their own sex they need to transform their bodies so that they can convince themselves that they are really heterosexual."[53] The same passage can easily be reread substituting "bisexual/femme" for "transsexual." Bisexuals are commonly accused of being unable or unwilling to relinquish heterosexual privilege, or of suffering from internalized homophobia. With a slight twist reminiscent of Martin and Lyon, the third sentence could read, "[bisexual/femmes] need to transform their [same-sex lovers'] bodies [from lesbian to butch/male] so that they can convince themselves that they are really heterosexual." The melding of femininity with heterosexuality, and of heterosexuality with heteropatriarchy, allows theorists as disparate as Raymond, Hausman, Penelope, and Jeffreys to dismiss bisexuality and/or transsexuality as apolitical and reductive without further consideration of bisexual and transsexual experience.

These productions of bisexuality and transsexuality as politically reductive and therefore incompatible with feminism and lesbianism occur because there is so much at stake. To disagree with the assumption that lesbianism is always the most effective challenge to patriarchal heterosexuality, or that femininity is always and only ever circumscribed by oppressive masculinity, is to question some of the central tenets of feminist thought. Flawed though those tenets may be, the threat of their disappearance is nevertheless disconcerting. I argue through this chapter that this association of femininity and women's bisexuality with heterosexuality finds echoes within contemporary queer studies in its privileging of masculine subjects and its inability to sustain cultural models of subject formation within both feminist and queer studies.

Bisexual/Transsexual Subversions

The aims of queer theory might usefully be summarized in the following way. First, queer theory seeks to expose the difference and opposition between heterosexual and homosexual identities as fictional histories and epistemologies in order to challenge heterosexuality's normative status. Heteronormativity is typically addressed through a focus on its reliance on homosexuality as both closeted and ever present in the formation of modern knowledges,[54] or through accounts that historicize and particularize rather than universalize same- and opposite-sex meaning.[55] Second, queer theorists challenge the a priori relationships among sex, gender, and sexuality in the formation of contemporary and historical queer subjectivity. The importance of the latter approach is its insistence that "other" aspects of identity, such as race, class or body size, are as significant in the formation of the sexual self as sex and gender.[56] In this insistence queer theory also offers a useful challenge to feminist analyses that subsume (hetero)sexuality under gender as one of its normative effects. This second approach, certainly not separate from the first historical and epistemological one, explores the errors in the heteronormative chain of repetition, seeking thus "to denaturalize gender, to loosen its tie from sex, gender's bodily referent."[57]

Bisexuality and transsexuality might well be presumed to be ideal locations from which to queer dominant understandings of the relationship among sex, gender, and sexuality in all of the above ways. Thus bisexuality might be said to problematize the assumed relationship between the gender of object choice and resultant sexual identity, as well as the linear progress of sexual narrative, and transsexuality might be said to problematize the assumed relationship between genetic sexed body and gender identity, and frequently linear sexuality as well. Indeed, Diana Fuss suggests as much when considering those identities and locations that cannot be easily subsumed within a heterosexual/ homosexual logic, asking, "What gets left out of the inside/outside, heterosexual/homosexual opposition, an opposition which could at least plausibly be said to secure its seemingly inviolable dialectical structure only by assimilating and internalizing other sexualities (bisexuality, transvestism, transsexualism ...) to its own rigid bipolar logic?"[58] Setting aside the contentious assumption that transvestism and trans-sexuality are sexualities per se, for Fuss, bisexuality, transvestism, and transsexualism are positioned together as "outside" the dialectical structures that they are said to shed light on. Fuss's lack of further attention to these three categories only confirms the impression she gives that they provide the same critique and occupy the same outsider position as one another. Marjorie Garber, too, conflates transgenderism, cross-dressing and bisexuality, and does not address transsexuality at all. In *Vested Interests*, Garber argues that transvestism and transgender provide "a space of possibility structuring and confounding culture." They are "the disruptive element that intervenes, not just a category of crisis of male and female, but a crisis of category itself."[59] In her 1995 book *Vice Versa*, Garber makes almost identical claims about bisexuality's capacity to force a "crisis of category" as those she had made about transvestism: "Bisexuality is that upon the repression of which society depends for its laws, codes, boundaries, social organization—everything that defines 'civilization' as we know it."[60] The interest that the idea of bisexual and transgendered behavior (not identities) generates is rarely sustained in terms of close attention to these categories, except as a foil through which to consider the vagaries of the human condition (in Garber's case), or the limits or potentials of gay and lesbian subjectivity. In the following section, I address the ways in which I perceive gay/lesbian and bisexual/ transsexual separation to be maintained.

Bisexual Pleasures

If bisexuality as identity has not been embraced within queer theory and culture, bisexual behavior certainly has. Queer community throughout the 1990s and into this decade has in effect been preoccupied with lesbian desire for men, and gay male desire for women, whether acted upon or not.[61] Importantly, however, this desire is consciously positioned as having nothing to do with bisexual identity. In Nic Williams's erotic short story "The Boy at the Bar," for example, the gay male protagonist is picked up in an SM leather bar by a tough, menacing stranger. His humiliation (and queer pleasure) is complete when the stranger reveals herself as other than the male leather daddy the protagonist had thought he was responding to.[62] Heterosexual behavior is not antithetical to queer in this fictional scenario. The discovery of the "true" sex of the leather daddy provides precisely the desired queer disjunctures among sexed body, gendered role, and sexual identity. But as the story develops it becomes clear that the "heterosexual" act and the queer sexual identity must remain distinct and in oppositional tension. The protagonist, Phil, realizes that his "leather daddy," Chris, is a woman through the following exchange:

"That's for staring at my girlfriend."

Jesus! What now? Did he mean he's straight? What the fuck?

"Some of us like cocks," he continued evenly. "We just don't need the guy attached." Oh my god, what a set up. Tony's [the barman's] friends with all the dykes, he must have known . . . Jesus, a woman, a dyke at that, fucking me![63]

Phil moves swiftly from imagining his "daddy" to be a straight man (signaled by the reference to the girlfriend), to realizing "he" is a "she" and unquestionably a dyke (because of her dislike of men). At no point—even before her revelation that she just likes "cocks," not men—does Phil consider bisexuality as a viable identity for his "assailant," even though this would actually make more immediate sense in terms of the protagonist's train of thought. Chris's dislike of men precludes bisexuality once again within the narrative, so that both Phil and Chris can be united in their refusal of bisexuality. Only through this refusal can they remain unambiguously gay and lesbian within this queer narrative.

In *Public Sex*, Pat Califia ruminates on the reasons she does not call herself bisexual, even though she has opposite-sex sexual partners. She writes, "Why not simply identify as bi? That's a complicated question . . . A self-identified bisexual is saying, 'Men and women are of equal importance to me.' That's simply not true of me. I'm a Kinsey Five, and when I turn on to a man it's because he shares some aspect of my sexuality (like S/M or fisting) that turns me on despite his biological sex."[64] Here Califia's opposite-sex desire is coded as queer because of its S/M context. She continues, "I know that a gay man who has sex with me is making an exception and that he's still gay after we come and clean up. In return I can make an exception for him because I know he isn't trying to convert me to heterosexuality."[65] Califia "eroticize[s] queerness, gayness, homosexuality," and argues, "It is very odd that sexual orientation is defined solely in terms of the sex of one's partners."[66] Califia, unlike so many queer writers, explicitly locates her discussion of opposite-sex practices in relation to bisexuality. However, in the process of marking her own sexuality as not bisexual, Califia makes two key assumptions. First, she presupposes that a bisexual could not be a Kinsey 5, but must instead be a Kinsey 3, equally attracted to men and women. In fact, a good deal of attention within bisexual writing has been paid to debunking this particular myth, emphasizing the importance of the qualitative value rather than the quantity of attraction to differently-sexed partners. Second, Califia never considers the fact that while she may not identify as bisexual, her male sex-partner very well might: his presence within a queer SM space does not mean he must identify as gay. In Califia's nonbisexual narrative it is important that both participants in the scene are located such that they both have to "make an exception." Califia's partner needs to "still [be] gay after we come and clean up" in order for the primary aim to be securely sadomasochistic rather than based in object choice. In other words, if biological sex were not something to be overcome for either of them, the queerness of the scenario would, for Califia, be compromised.

In both of the above examples, the "heterosexual" act and gay or lesbian identity must remain separable, and indeed opposed, for "queer pleasure" to be the resultant effect. Heterosexual behavior operates as one form of queer behavior, then, as long as it remains behavior. Where bisexuality is present at all it is somewhere else (i.e. not a part of this particular scene) or relocated as the middle ground that would enable the transgressive behavior to take place. Sadomasochism can replace the "normal aim" precisely because humans "are bisexual, really," just not here, and not now. Jo Eadie makes a similar point when discussing the following comment made by Graham McKerrow in the British magazine *Gay Times*: "Sex between gay men and lesbians is . . . coming out of the closet . . . Now people talk openly of their opposite-sex-same-sexuality lovers and at the party after the SM Pride March a gay man and a lesbian had sex on the dance floor, but it wasn't heterosexuality. You can tell."[67] The telling phrase in the above passage is "opposite-sex-same-sexuality"; "What is being collapsed here under the words 'same-sexuality'?" Eadie asks.[68] For Califia and Williams, the pleasures of opposite-sex desire can be acknowledged, acted upon, and even witnessed in a queer context as long as one "can tell" it is not heterosexuality. Being able to tell that an opposite-sex act is not heterosexuality never seems to open up a space for bisexual queerness, which leads me to conclude that in fact what you need to be able to tell is that the act is not *not* lesbian and gay.

The closer bisexuality (as behavior or as identity) comes to being the same as queer, the more subversive it is deemed to be. Hence Carol Queen writes, rather defensively, "When I strap on a dildo and fuck my male partner, we are engaging in 'heterosexual' behavior, but I can tell you that it feels altogether queer, and I'm sure my grandmother and Jesse Helms would say the same."[69] Although this passage could be read as an attempt to break down the division between heterosexual and queer acts, its appeal to external arbiters and the scare quotes around the word *heterosexual* suggest a desire for the heterosexual act to be simultaneously acknowledged and erased through queer feeling.[70]

It seems to me that what is occurring in these gay and lesbian stories of opposite-sex pleasure is a reversal of the coming-out narrative. Where in the latter opposite-sex behavior is consigned to a past that has been overcome, in the queer revision, the same behavior is acted out in the present and evacuated of heterosexual, and heterosexist, meaning. Where in conventional sexual narrative coming out marks the end of one set of desires and the beginning of another on the basis of object choice, the queer narrative allows for a far greater range of sexual behaviors, as long as the sexuality of all individuals concerned remains identical and constant—that is, lesbian or gay. Thus, in Williams's story above, narrative uncertainty resides in the gap between the narrator's assumption that his sexual partner is gay and the realization that she is a dyke. Once he realizes that her sexuality, though not her gender, is the same as his, uncertainty can give way to queer pleasure. And for Califia, common sexuality frames an encounter that might otherwise suggest conversion. Queer narrative, then, does indeed dispute the relationship between sexual object choice and sexual identity; however, in this reversal sexual identity becomes the privileged sign of queerness, within which it is the sexuality rather than the gender of who one has sex with that is primary. Sexuality, not object choice, comes first. Thus, when Eve Kosofsky Sedgwick argues that *queer* challenges "the decisiveness of gender-of-object-choice" in ways that bisexuality can not do since the latter reaffirms the fact that there are two sexes and genders,[71] I believe that she misrecognizes bisexuality's unforgivable error: that bisexuals will have sex not so much with *any body* as any sexuality. Sedgwick admits the possibility that the term *bisexual* could function as "one sexually dissident self-description among others,"[72] but only within terms already laid out by queerness. In this sense, bisexuality is a problem for queer theory and culture precisely because once sexual object choice is destabilized as the ground of sexual identity, it is important that you be able to tell what sexuality your partner or player is simply by looking.

The production or restriction of bisexual meaning in accordance with queer theory's allegiance to the lesbian and gay subject also occurs in the context of the butch/femme couple. As I discussed in the introduction, Judith Butler heralds the butch/femme couple as bringing into relief "the utterly constructed status of the so-called heterosexual original. Thus, gay is to straight not as copy is to original, but, rather, as copy is to copy."[73] Bisexuality is necessary to Butler's framework only as middle ground between heterosexuality and homosexuality, the potential that structures both object choice and incorporation of the lost and unmournable object.[74] In the introduction, then, I highlighted the ways in which bisexuality clearly cannot be understood to have a subject, since this would challenge the psychoanalytic framework on which the notion of repudiation in the formation of the gendered and sexual self relies. But my argument there did not examine the central factor here: that the parodic, and thus transformative subject, needs to begin and end as lesbian or gay. As with Graham McKerrow's comment, above, this reinscription of a heterosexual/homosexual opposition works through a visibility mode, where heteronormativity is only thrown into relief when the reiterative gaps in gender identity formation are recognizable. Transgender and opposite-sex behavior need to remain behavior, in order that the a priori ground of sexual opposition remain untouched.

As suggested, for Butler, what makes butch/femme and drag potentially so subversive is their very closeness to heterosexuality, the way in which their "performance" makes conscious the mechanism of repudiation in sustaining our identities, though this is clearer in a butch than a femme.[75] The point for Butler is that gender subversion lies in the closeness, the mirroring of heterosexuality, and at the same time in the underwriting of difference from heterosexuality. If just the former is in place, the result is not parody but approximation; if just the latter, an overdetermination of the boundary between normative and subversive. If both are in place, that difference from heterosexuality must be visible in order to be recognized by all parties in the scene. Butch/femme as masquerade is exemplary in this regard because it comes close to heterosexual roles and gender oppositions—indeed, it marks their rigidity as learned not natural—yet remains distinct: butch/femme is finally seen not to be heterosexuality. This necessity for visibility explains why, for Butler as for so many queer theorists, femininity remains so chronically undertheorized. The femme is only visible as close to but distinct from heterosexuality when clearly coupled with a butch; her history is mythically marked by heterosexual suspicion. Without that distinctness, the clearly *lesbian* underpinning of the masquerade, femme closeness to heterosexuality might well be sameness. Thus, as Carole-Anne Tyler notes, in the Butlerian scenario "mimicry functions as an index of [the 'real'], gesturing toward it, and maintaining a certain contiguity with it."[76] Yet in the end mimickry must be seen not to be the "real."

Pat Califia's femme-butch poetry foregrounds the tension generated by femme closeness to heterosexual femininity,[77] making it legible as part of lesbian and therefore queer masquerade:

> And you can tell she's a femme
> Because she makes you cry
> When you can't give her everything
> You imagine she wants
> That a man could give her[78]

The butch lover imagines herself lacking in relation to a man; it is her femme (who is, of course, accustomed to this scenario, structured as she is by its confines) who "makes her cry," not by leaving her but by chiding her lover for her foolishness. Califia is the femme's champion, acknowledging her bravery and the taunts she receives for her brilliant heterosexual parody, yet also her ambivalent and dependent distinctness:

> Being a successful femme
> Means making a butch desire you
> And then enduring when that lust
> Turns into suspicion.
> "If you want me," she sneers,
> "You must really want a man."
> Nobody knows how much it hurts
> When you go out on the street
> And straight men tell you
> The same damned thing.[79]

The "successful femme" (the femme who does not fall into heterosexuality), endures her butch's suspicion, rather than deflecting or circumventing it, presumably because she knows that to be impossible. The poignancy of the poem lies in Califia's astute perception that both straight male and butch readings of the femme must necessarily coexist. The shadow of Tyler's grammatical structuring—the femme as not quite not straight[80]—lurks between these lines, echoing Califia's earlier sentiment in the same poem that she's "a sucker" for "women who can never have what they want / Because the world will not allow them / To be complete human beings—that is, men.[81] The structure of this sentiment allows multiple readings. Men are "the world," are that which prevents women having "what they want"; or, what those women want is men, but the loss of human status attending such desire is too high a price to pay for heterosexual privilege.

In Califia's poetry, the structuring myth of the femme's imminent abandonment (her femininity calling into question her final repudiation of man/masculinity as lost sexual object) is made conscious, becomes part of the social and erotic dynamic of the butch/femme play. The specter of straightness that has always structured the femme is thus transformed in these poems into an "operative myth" that makes her visible as refusing to be absorbed (back) into heterosexuality. In other words, the femme's visibility lies in the parodic reiteration of the terms of her very invisibility: her potential straightness is worn on her sleeve as conscious refusal. Small wonder then that what the femme must disavow above all else is the suggestion of bisexuality, since her queerness cannot be signified other than through persistent refusal of opposite-sex desire. To underline my point here, Califia's representation of butch desire for (the occasional) man can be allowed within queer parody, because her difference from straight femininity is visibly incorporated in her gender performance. Thus, "You can tell she's a butch / Because she's one of the boys / (And fucks one of them occasionally / To prove it).[82] A butch's prior (homo)sexuality is writ large on her body as absolute loss, and so she can afford a little more clearly ironic closeness to heterosexual behavior. At the close of "Bisexual/Transsexual Textualities," I will take up the butch/femme couple again, only this time examining what difference it makes if we conceive of that couple as FTM/bisexual femme. I will suggest some of the questions such a coupling raises in terms of Butler's "close yet distinct" performative model, given that the difference from heterosexuality is precisely not visible, and thus the closeness cannot finally be rescued. My aim in this is to consider what other kinds of performativites might be imagined if visible lesbian or gay sexuality is not a precondition for queer behavior. In the meantime, however, I return to the question of transsexual location within queer theories, paying particular attention to the ontological and epistemological load that transsexuality is forced to carry.

Transgender Performance

Just as bisexuality can be contained within queer discourse through its consignment to the middle ground of behavior or potential, transsexuality has commonly appeared in queer contexts as all that is subversive of gender norms when figured as transgenderism, as gendered surface rather than depth. And just as bisexuality is understood as normative when configured as identity, transsexuality becomes problematic when insisted upon as real, a property of the self, because of a perceived reinscription of dominant (i.e. heterosexist) gender and/or sexual discourse. I will be arguing in this section that queer theory displaces its own a priori assumptions about the subject and object of queer knowledge onto and in the production of transsexual and transgendered subjects. Queer discussions of transsexuality and transgenderism are far more developed than those of bisexuality, emerging more centrally and consistently as part of queer debate. Thus Susan Stryker, Sandy Stone, Judith Halberstam, Jay Prosser, and C. Jacob Hale, to name but a few, are frequently cited and discussed authors who are all concerned in one form or another with the development of what has become known as transgender studies.[83] And while there has only been one special edition of a nonbisexual academic journal focusing on bisexuality, there have been a number on transsexuality and trans-genderism, and in journals with wider dissemination. In addition, the co-opting of transgenderism over and above transsexuality by queer theorists has been directly addressed within transgender studies, in particular through the debate between Halberstam and Prosser, which I discuss below.

Transgender performance assumed an almost mythical position within queer theory and politics in the early 1990s as *the* manifestation of discontinuity between sexed body and gender role or identity. As with the notion of bisexual transcendence that I critiqued in chapter 1, transgenderism is similarly positioned as the middle ground of sexed and gendered poles. Its transgression thus purportedly resides in its inability to be reduced to one or the other pole, exposing the binary system as power imbued and imbuing rather than natural. Both nontransgendered and transgendered writers have taken this line. In this vein, we can recall Marjorie Garber's enthusiasm for the transgendered deconstruction of category, as well as Kate Bornstein's; Bornstein argues that "the transgendered person [is] a gender outlaw [causing] the destruction of the gendered system of reality on which most people base major aspects of their lives."[84] And writers such as Gilbert Herdt and Leslie Feinberg celebrate transgenderism as a "third sex," or as a space in-between male and female.[85] Transgendered blurring or highlighting of the structures of sex, gender, and sexuality is also seen by some theorists as posing a challenge to the often unspoken "raced" nature of that relationship. For example, Garber elaborates her assertion that transvestism causes "category-crisis," noting, "I mean a failure of definitional distinction, a borderline that becomes permeable, that permits of border crossings from one (apparently distinct) category to another: black/white, master/servant, master/slave."[86] Garber expands on her assertion when she discusses the function of transvestism in slave narratives. She looks at instances where African male slaves cross-dressed in order to escape captivity: "a black man sees that he can pass as a woman because he is, in white eyes, already a woman."[87] Garber suggests that such forms of cross-dressing make strategic use of race and gender constructions in an imperialist, patriarchal society. Readers may be reminded of similar claims for the transgressive location of bisexuality as a site not only of sexed, gendered, and sexual melding, but also of raced blurring or incorporation. To my mind, such abstract claims of transferable transcendence or merging obscure more than they reveal. They are unhelpful precisely because they reproduce as distinct the opposites that they then proclaim are reunited, and rely on that middle ground as unifying and static.

Jennie Livingston's *Paris Is Burning*, a documentary of African-American and Latino drag balls in New York participated in by gay men, drag queens, transgendered and transsexual subjects, has been the subject of an overwhelming number of critiques in terms of its presentation of the intersections of gender and race, and of the successes or failures of a transgendered model of gender performativity.[88] Judith Halberstam argues that the film offers its audiences "lessons about how to read gender and race ... as not only artificial but highly elaborate and ritualistic significations,"[89] and Jacqueline Zita reflects on her own preoccupation with its stylized and moving camp affect.[90] Jackie Goldsby's declaration that "never has speech, as performance and oral text, been so irresistible to my eyes and ears,"[91] expresses sentiments that resonate with the majority of the documentary's critical queer audience. What interests me about the readings of *Paris Is Burning* within queer studies, however, is that they emphatically mark the boundary between subversive and normative performances in general, and this difference is mapped onto gay/transgender and transsexual bodies respectively. As discussed above, queer transgression of heterosexual presumption is marked by its visible closeness to and difference from the dominant, and thus in readings of *Paris Is Burning* is signaled by failing or refusing to pass as straight or white. Thus, queer subversion occurs only when passing is incomplete, when the drag performances can in effect be read as gay drag performances. This is not necessarily a move that occurs beneath the surface: several writers simply assume that they are self-evidently discussing gay men, even though several of the most central protagonists quite clearly identify themselves as transsexual. For example, Halberstam states unequivocally that the documentary "focused questions of race, class, and gender and their intersections with the drag performances of poor, gay men of color,"[92] mirroring bell hooks's less celebratory interpolation of the characters as "unfortunate poor gay men of color."[93]

Venus Xtravaganza, one of the film's transsexual Latina protagonists who can pass successfully as a white woman, and who has been the focus of much queer critical attention, is murdered during the making of the documentary. The documentary itself moves from a celebratory, playful representation of the participants in the balls, gradually telling the story of the demise of their transgressive authenticity through the commodification of voguing by mainstream pop culture.[94] Venus's death is narrated toward the end of the film, associating passing as a straight white woman with that mainstream commodification. Just as voguing ceases to be subversive of dominant norms, so too the move from visible drag to transsexual passing marks the end of the balls' subversive era.

Butler similarly uses the example of Venus to correct earlier readings of her work as being overinvested in the subversiveness of transgendered parody, saying, "Venus, and *Paris Is Burning* more generally, calls into question whether parodying the dominant norms is enough to displace them; indeed, whether the denaturalization of gender cannot be the very vehicle for a reconsolidation of hegemonic norms. . . . I want to underscore that there is no necessary relation between drag and subversion, and that drag may well be used in the service of both the denaturalization and reidealization of hyperbolic heterosexual gender norms."[95] Butler's turn here is interesting. She uses the figure of Venus to highlight the fact that drag and subversion do not necessarily correspond. In effect, then, Butler splits passing transsexuals and transgendered subjects off from one another, so that when drag does fail, it is because it has ceased to be visible as parody, i.e. has actually ceased to be drag. If we combine this splitting with my prior noting of Halberstam and hooks' unquestioned faith that the film is about poor gay men of color, transgender subversion becomes firmly allied with gay rather than transsexual subjectivity. In other words, transgender and transsexual are split so that transgender/gay can remain a subversive coupling. The implication of this line of argument is that the denaturalization of white heteronormativity would have been secured had Venus performed her subjectivity exclusively within visible queer frames. What seems extraordinary to me is that the evidence that straight, white culture quite clearly finds Venus troubling, to the extent that her very closeness to that culture may have resulted in her death, is never dealt with in queer texts. Prosser makes a similar point in insisting that "Venus is killed for her transsexuality, for inhabiting a body which . . . is not coherently female."[96] In the context of Brandon Teena's death in Nebraska, C. Jacob Hale cites a headline that noted that Teena was "killed for carrying it off."[97] As a passing man who was born female, Teena's "subversion," like Venus's, may reside in the fact that her difference is *not* visible. To rewrite these acts of violence as simply homophobic, arising in the moment where the perpetrators realize that the heterosexual subject is homosexual after all, is not only to deny validity to the transsexual subject but also to skip an important stage. The realization of difference in both cases significantly follows an earlier belief in their sameness: violence surely follows the recognition in the heterosexual subjects that they *could not tell* by looking.

Through her sleight of hand, which dismisses passing as a strategy that might offer up different readings of transgressive performance, Butler effectively distances herself from the scene she surveys to position herself behind Livingston's lens. In her critique of *Paris Is Burning*, hooks argues that Livingston, "a white Jewish lesbian from Yale,"[98] takes on the role of detached white observer who offers fame and fortune to unfortunate poor gay men of color, but who takes the accolades for herself.[99] Butler counters hooks by reading Livingston's position as lesbian desire for a different femininity, clearly identifying with Livingston when she remarks that hooks's comment is "an interpolation which also implicates this author in its sweep."[100] Butler asks, "What would it mean to say that Octavia [a black male-to-female transsexual] is Jennie Livingston's kind of girl? Is the category or, indeed, "the position" of white lesbian disrupted by such a claim? If this is the production of the black transsexual for an eroticizing white gaze, is it not also the transsexualization of lesbian desire?"[101] Through her use of the term *transsexualization,* Butler turns transsexual lives into verbs for the queering of gay/lesbian objects. Transsexual and raced passing in themselves may mark the limits of lesbian and gay queer subversion, but can be reconfigured as queer in a different way through the queering of the lesbian gaze. This requeering process allows Livingston's white eroticizing gaze to become lesbian (and therefore, for Butler, not white?) while Octavia's location as both black and transsexual is overwritten.[102] I presume that only in returning Livingston's transsexualized lesbian gaze might Octavia herself lay claim to a visibly subversive subject location.

Coco Fusco provides a further critique of Butler and Livingston that sets them in the context of cultural appropriation and an ethnographic documentary tradition. Fusco asks, "If subversion occurs because of ambiguity, for whom does it occur?"[103] Interpreting the director's relationship to her transsexual subjects in *Paris Is Burning* as subversive does not consider whether subversion is even a question that is relevant to the balls. Interpreting the voguers' self-made, nonnuclear families as undermining the traditional heterosexual family unit assumes a white Western family as the norm to be subverted, and sees the voguers only in that context. As Fusco indicates, "To suppose that the voguers reinvented the white American middle-class family also implies that subaltern lives are purposely organized to subvert white heterosexual American norms, which is hardly the case, though whites may read them as such. To assume so, as Butler would seem to do, is surprisingly, if not alarmingly, ethnocentric."[104]

As highlighted throughout this section, one way of maintaining a lesbian or gay subject of queer is to separate transsexual and transgendered identities and behaviors, identifying the former with the consolidation of heterosexist norms and the latter with a challenge to those norms. In the process transgenderism becomes the mark of visible performativity, while transsexuality is moved too close to heteronormativity for its own comfort. Judith Halberstam's controversial article "F2M: The Making of Female Masculinity" provides a now notorious model for this process. She writes that, "within a more general fragmentation of the concept of sexual identity, the specificity of the transsexual disappears. In a way, I claim, we are all transsexuals. . . . We all pass or we don't, we all wear our drag, and we all derive a different degree of pleasure—sexual or otherwise—from our costumes. It is just that for some of us our costumes are made of fabric or material, while for others they are made of skin; for some an outfit can be changed; for others skin must be resewn. There are no transsexuals."[105] Viewed only as transgressive spectacle, transgender performance fails to mark the difference between material and skin as anything other than arbitrary form, and characteristically for queer approaches views the difference only in terms of a continuum of pleasure. Transsexuals who claim that their desire for sex changes is meaningful in different ways to drag risk in this framework being accused of essentialism, of upholding rather than dismantling a static concept of gendered or sexual identity. In her analysis of Linda/Les and Annie, a documentary of Les Nicols's transition from female to male, and his relationship with "postporn" star Annie Sprinkle, Halberstam indeed insists that "[b]y apparently understanding his gender performance as no performance at all and his gender fiction as the straight-up truth, Les Nicols takes the trans out of transsexualism. There is no movement, or only a very limited and fleeting movement, in crossing from a stable female identity to a stable male identity, and Les seems not to challenge notions of natural gender at all."[106] Here transsexuality is understood as failing to deconstruct an oppositional sexed system, indeed shoring it up, insofar as a visible queering of sexed, gendered and sexual oppositions—"Les *seems* not to challenge notions of natural gender" (my emphasis)—is not the primary effect of his subject location. In an interview for the British transgender journal *Radical Deviance* Butler directly acknowledges this queer desire for transsexuality to signify disruption, arguing, "I would so much prefer that transsexuality be a radical epistemic challenge to reigning biological descriptions, than an acceptance of received biological descriptions."[107]

Halberstam's article provoked a good deal of hostility from the transsexual community because of its perceived erasure of transsexual specificity, and its collapsing of transgender experience into a queer concern with undoing gender's dependency upon sex for its meaning. Jay Prosser's article "No Place Like Home" accused Halberstam of a dual violence in appropriating transgendered experience as centrally queer and voluntaristically accessible to all, and in dismissing and trivializing transsexual experience as not matching up to that standard. Instead, Prosser suggests that transsexual narratives have an independent trajectory, and should not be judged lacking by externally imposed measures. Prosser argues that while queerness requires the deconstruction of gendered meaning, in transsexual autobiography "gender is not so much *undone* as queerness would have it as redone, that is, done up differently."[108] Halberstam directly addresses the reception of "F2M" in her book *Female Masculinity*, suggesting that a misunderstanding of her writing had occurred. Far from subsuming transsexual and transgendered experience under the rubric *queer*, Halberstam argues, " 'F2M' was actually trying to carve out a subject position that we might usefully call transgender butch to signify the transition that the identity requires from female identity to masculine embodiment."[109] I remain unconvinced by Halberstam's indication that her generalizing of transgender and transsexual experiences in "F2M" was her way of "creating a theoretical and cultural space for the transgender butch that did not presume transsexuality as its epistemological frame."[110] The insistence in "F2M" on all gender *except* transsexual gender as effectively "trans" undoes that retrospective claim. In addition, my resistance finds validation in the language Halberstam uses to discuss critics who either defend or attack her work. In discussing Jordy Jones's defense of her work as an acknowledgment of the range of transgendered expression, Halberstam writes glowingly that Jones is "eloquent and forceful,"[111] where Prosser's work is "polemic" and theoretically "shaky."[112] Since Halberstam does not provide a sustained critical reading of Prosser's failings, simply insisting that his work produces an unhelpful and slippery division between transsexual and transgendered narratives, the difference in Halberstam's descriptors for Jones and Prosser's writing emerges as a further celebration of *transgender* itself as "eloquent and forceful," and *transsexuality* as "polemic" and "shaky," associations that of course mirror Halberstam's difference between them in "F2M" in the first place.

In line with this queer desire for a finally lesbian or gay transgendered but not transsexual subject, it is common to read Sandy Stone's "The Empire Strikes Back: a Posttranssexual Manifesto" as underscoring the queer argument for the transgressively transgendered self. Stone argues that it is the disruptions to the smooth linear narrative of self that make transsexuality so disturbing to heteropatriarchy. She writes, "In the transsexual as text we may find the potential to map the refigured body onto conventional gender discourse and thereby disrupt it, to take advantage of the dissonances created by such a juxtaposition to fragment and reconstitute the elements of gender in new and unexpected geometries. . . . In order to effect this, the genre of visible transsexuals must grow by recruiting members from the class of invisible ones, from those who have disappeared into their 'plausible histories.'"[113] Stone concludes by directly addressing "passing transsexuals," invoking them to "re-vision" their lives, to lay "the ground work for the next transformation."[114] On an initial reading, Stone's words do not seem very different from Halberstam or Butler's, with their focus on incongruity and fractured narratives. Indeed, Hausman pits Stone against her transsexual contemporaries as evidence of her agreement with her own critique of fixed nature of transsexual gender identity.[115] Hausman cites Stone's request that transsexuals become "posttranssexuals,"[116] continuing, "Stone asks for this in order to alleviate the compromises of silence that she believes regulate transsexual subjectivity and keep an alternative, multi-faceted, and potentially subversive story of gender, sex, and the body from surfacing in and through culture at large."[117] I see this as a reading of Stone's words. Stone certainly does not believe that transsexual subjectivity is regulated through "compromises of silence." Stone does not see transsexuals and medical discourse as complicit with one another, as Hausman suggests, but existing within an unequal relationship of power controlled by medical discourse. While Stone seeks to imagine a transgressive transsexual subject and politics, this cannot be reduced to a queer fantasy of gender performativity, since her emphasis remains consistently on the transsexual body. It is not transgendered/gay visible difference that Stone wants made visible, but a specifically transsexual visibility whose contours are unlikely to map so clearly onto a queer visibility. It is Stone's fight for a viable *transsexual subjectivity* that motivates and permeates her presentation of the transsexual body as text, whereas for Halberstam, Butler, and Hausman, transgendered performance is a tool for validating and prioritizing a queer discontinuity that ultimately resides in a lesbian or gay, but not transsexual, body.

One effect of such a separation around the subversive queer subject is that the transsexual body is continuously reproduced as heterosexual: it is highly significant that the lamented passing identified is always a heterosexual passing, as in Venus's case. In other words, the transsexual betrayal of transgendered (lesbian or gay) subversive potential is identified as a gendered betrayal, but is always marked by a return to heterosexuality, and is thus more fundamentally a betrayal of queer sexuality. It is impossible to imagine Butler or Halberstam positioning a passing transsexual *lesbian* femme at the limit of queer performativity, for example, precisely because, despite being understood to consolidate sexed and gendered norms within a queer schema, her sexuality can still be made visible.

Bisexual Femme/FTM Performativities

Returning to my earlier suggestion that lesbian butch/femme parodies may not be the only butch/femme couplings that challenge hetero-normativity, I return to my earlier queries about the different parodies that an FTM/bisexual femme couple might make. Unlike Butler and Califia's lesbian butch/femme performances, the closeness of both bisexuality and transsexuality in the FTM/bisexual femme couple cannot necessarily be refused through making visible that lesbian difference. The specter of straightness materializes; the closeness cannot be deferred in the making of an evidentially queer happy ending.

The anxiety that such closeness gives rise to can be evidenced in the writings of lesbian femmes in the 1990s, responding to the increasingly visible transitions to FTM of partners they previously understood as butch. Heather Findlay pinpoints the source of this anxiety when she notes that in the same moment that a butch lover acknowledges transsexual subjectivity, becomes a man, the lesbian femme's sexuality is also called into question.[118] Findlay wryly suggests that the fear in such a scenario is less that one might now be heterosexual or bisexual, but that one might always have been so: Butler's refused loss come home to roost.[119] Butches and femmes, as we have seen, have historically and symbolically been identified as wanting to *be* and wanting to *have* a man respectively. A butch's transition to FTM, considered over years, propels an equally symbolically loaded "transition" in a femme lover, one she may well not have anticipated or desired. Debra Bercuvitz similarly discusses the tension between her desire for her increasingly transgendered lover Kris and her own identity as lesbian, associating the latter with the visibility that her partner's passing sometimes erases.[120] In response to men's anger at discovering Kris was "really a woman" Bercuvitz stops correcting the interpolation of her lover as "sir." She explains, "I became more protective of Kris and more invisible myself. *Invisible* is an odd word to associate with me because I am assertive and have such a powerful presence, sexually, intellectually, and just generally. I am very strong and very in-your-face with people, especially about being a dyke. But sometimes I do become invisible."[121] Bercuvitz battles with two prescriptions of femme subjectivity here: first, that she is invisible as lesbian without the presence of a butch, and second, that heterosexuality must be consistently and visibly disavowed. Bercuvitz insists that the dynamic between her and Kris is not heterosexual, however, despite her expressions of sexual invisibility: "One clear dynamic was my need to give, hers to take. But, of course, not in the straight way."[122] Thus, Bercuvitz quite clearly self-identifies as lesbian and designates her desire very specifically for "passing women," not men born male,[123] and she is highly articulate about the historical presence within lesbian community lovers like herself and Kris. One could, of course, read Bercuvitz's words here as wish fulfillment, but to do so one would have to ignore all instances of non-heterosexuality except the visible. But while the closeness to heterosexuality of Findlay and Bercuvitz's couplings are the source of anxiety, both are clear that the evidence of their lesbianism (or lack of it) cannot be restricted to visible differences from heterosexuality, but is instead a question of the meaning of experiences and their cultural and community location.[124]

As I hope is clear from the discussion above, a butch/femme relationship that cannot be fully signaled or read as lesbian is not an unproblematic parody of heterosexuality but an ongoing struggle to articulate the terms of a range of sexual and gendered boundary markers. Closeness to heterosexuality, particularly perhaps where both partners in the butch/femme dynamic are not lesbian, cannot distance itself from the risk of heteronormativity. Thus, Marcy Sheiner writes about her relationship with Rob, an FTM; her ambivalence, her curiosity, and her own desire are more the subject of discussion than Rob himself. Of sex, she writes,

"It was as if his whole body became one giant cock, and I simply became cunt, opening up to receive the energy . . . Ironically, I felt more female with Rob than I had ever felt with a genetic male. Maybe it was because I was more trusting of a he-who-had-been-she, and could therefore drop my survival skills, allowing myself to become pure, primeval woman. It felt liberating—for awhile. Eventually, of course, there was a price to pay."125

The "price" Sheiner pays is her transition from capable independent feminist of dubious sexuality to heterosexualized, complementary vessel. Such an account makes for distressing reading, and seems to confirm the feminist rejections of a bisexual or transsexual femininity that I discussed in *Bisexual/Transsexual Femininities* earlier in this chapter. Sheiner's representation of her experiences surely reinforces Raymond's worst fears about the predatory nature of transsexuals, and the dangers of being seduced by masculinity.126 Worse still, Sheiner's "transitions" are not alien to me. I have a journal full of dull and repetitive entries about my own femininity being brought out through my relationship with an FTM, my own calls mirroring Sheiner's "hysterical phone calls at 7:00 AM."127 I do not believe that such experiences should be taken as absolute in any way, however, not because I want FTM/bisexual pairings to be assured subversive status, but because it seems unlikely that any particular relationship form could carry such weight. I am reminded of Sue O'Sullivan's insights into the terrible expectation that butch/femme relationships not repeat heterosexual norms, creating a silence around the ways in which all relationships are bound to do so, butch/femme no less than any others.128 Rather than denying the often *highly unparodic* closeness to heterosexuality that all gender and sexual performances reproduce, it would seem more generous and indeed politically productive to pay attention to the ironies such closeness produces within sexual and gendered narratives over time.

In the context of my own relationship, then, I would want to ask not, "Is this or that behavior subversive or normative?" but, for example, "How are closeness and difference from *both* heterosexuality and homosexuality negotiated?" In asking the former question, passing as a straight couple would be understood as normative, and being read as nonheterosexual subversive. Yet in the context of the relationship, it was not passing as straight that was a concern, but more passing as lesbian butch/femme: it was in the latter context that my lover felt his transsexuality to be erased. In early transition, passing as heterosexual was a sign of success, passing as lesbian a failure of gender expression. In this light, too, my bisexuality was conceived of as highly problematic, since my desire for him could be interpreted as the desire not for his maleness, but for the "ultimate" dual-gendered bisexual object choice. And indeed, Annie Sprinkle thus rejoices in her lover's "mismatch": "a female-to-male transsexual/hermaphrodite—the perfect playmate for bi-sex!"[129] Because I do not exclusively desire men, my lover was unsure I was not responding to his masculinity as butch rather than male. The fact that I was able to eroticize his body/gender mismatch, while enabling on one level, was unsettling to him on another. I did not mind what he clearly minded so much.

In asking questions that do not presume that subversion and normativity map inevitably onto queer or bisexual/transsexual experiences, or indeed that subversion/normativity is a valid paradigm to measure all sexual or gendered contexts and subject formations, the specificities of transsexual and bisexual constrained experiences may better be analyzed. The specter of straightness informs these negotiations directly, and cannot be banished from our culturally learned butch/femme performances.

Part 2: Transsexual/Bisexual Representations

If bisexuality and transsexuality are located within queer and feminist theory predominantly as figures of difference, or as boundary markers, how then might alternative representation occur? My aim in this part of the chapter is not to find truer representations of bisexuality and transsexuality, but to look at how transsexual and bisexual photographers have interrogated the problem of representation and the gaze in each case. Transsexual writers have commonly responded to the hostile, universalizing gaze that would render transsexual subjectivity and experience normative or monstrous by turning the question back upon the possessor of the gaze: From where do you look? What do you hope to see? How do you position yourself in relation to me, and to what ends? In her preface to *The Transsexual Empire* Raymond proposes, "While various individuals have looked at the issue of transsexualism very few have ever really seen it. Transsexuals see themselves as women. . . . Doctors fixate on hormonal techniques. . . . Therapists view transsexualism as a humane solution. . . . The public sees the media's image of the talk-show transsexual. . . . Many women see the transsexual . . . as the man who has paid the ultimate price of manhood in a patriarchal society.[130] The implication is that Raymond herself does not need to look at what she sees because she sets herself up as the observer, as the one who does not view but the one who knows, a position very much in accordance with the extensively critiqued masculinist empiricism of natural and social science. Raymond positions herself as the holder of common sense, rather like the speaker who can tell who is heterosexual and who is queer just by looking. Her purpose is to "depict the wider environment in which transsexualism is created and to do a truly ecological analysis."[131] In response, mirroring Donna Haraway's call for knowledge claims to be transparently and accountably located,[132] Carol Riddell writes, "I want to know where Janice Raymond is coming from about transsexuals. . . . If Ms. Raymond sorted out her projections about transsexuals it might lead her to want to write in a different way."[133] Again drawing implicitly on feminist work on reflexivity, Riddell's suggestion is that Raymond would produce different kinds of knowledge if she located her own interests in theorizing transsexuality. And in relation to transsexual representation in visual culture, Susan Stryker underlines her direct, challenging gaze at the camera with the question, "I know why I let myself be photographed. Do you know why you look?"[134] Stryker links this issue of perspective to the queer desire for transsexuals to provide liberation from gender oppression, which then turns to anger when "we don't offer a way out they've been looking for but haven't found."[135] She concludes, ardently, "I'm tired of being a scapegoat for the gender trouble of everyone else. Ask yourself—why do you look when we transsexuals make spectacles of ourselves? Is it the curiosity of the freak show, the same voyeuristic desire mixed with dread and titilation [sic] that makes you scan the asphalt for gobs of red as you drive slowly past the accident scene? Or is it some fantasy of transcending material limits to behold the sex of angels? And ask yourself, too, what it is that you see. Monsters, mutants, cyborgs, perverts, exotic objects of queer lust? Or just men and women by other means?"[136] Echoing Stryker's response to the objectifying gaze of the nontranssexual, rule 11 of C. Jacob Hale's "Suggested Rules for Non-Transsexuals" advises, "Focus on: What does looking at transsexuals, transsexuality, transsexualism, or transsexual _____ tell you about **yourself, not** what does it tell you about trans."[137] I have already mentioned the critical response to Hausman's work from within transgender theory and politics, and want to return here to an analysis of her "fascination" with transsexualism. Hausman ends her book by saying that she has no desire to "condemn transsexuals themselves,"[138] locating herself as objectively interested in transsexuality rather than implicated in or responsible for the kinds of knowledges that she produces. Yet, inevitably enough perhaps, Hausman's reading of transsexual meaning and subjectivity emerges through the book as profoundly invested and located, and her fascination with transsexuality seems to spring less from benign curiosity and more from its other meaning of "terror or awe."[139] Hausman's "terror" in respect to transsexual bodies is first evidenced when she writes, "I am perhaps one of the few expectant mothers who worry that they will give birth to a hermaphrodite. At four months, I sat in front of my computer rewriting my chapter on intersexuality, thinking that I knew more about congenital abnormalities of sex than any pregnant woman should know. Rachel waited until I sent the manuscript off to Duke before making her way into this world; I thank her for her patience."[140]

God forbid that Hausman should give birth to one of those "abnormally sexed" beings that are the object of her scrutiny. Hausman presents herself as an Eve-like innocent, where knowledge of intersexuality could, like the original sin it has historically represented, harm her unborn child. Prosser remarks that the same passage confirms beyond any doubt that Hausman "views the unclearly sexed body with anxiety and alarm because she imagines her own body in a clean, unambivalently sexed location."[141] Rosi Braidotti usefully analyses the genealogy of the "monstrous body" in her article "Signs of Wonder and Traces of Doubt"; she recounts, "Pare describes the monstrous birth as a sinister sign ('mauvais augure') that expresses the not the truth of the infant, but the guilt or sin of the parents."[142] Hausman's insistence on transsexual "monstrosity" could be read as part of Braidotti's teratological genealogy, as a way of Hausman maintaining a distance between self and other. Certainly Hausman's story expresses more about her own subjectivity than it does about transsexuals. To conceive of a positive intersexual or transsexual agency after setting the direction of the gaze so firmly would be difficult indeed. Throughout the book, Hausman's "terror" simmers under the surface of the text, containing her intractability on the subject of transsexual agency, bubbling up in her insistence that transsexuals should tell the true "horror" of their physical experience of transition, and finally being reduced to her concluding warning that taking hormones should not be done "without proper medical treatment and supervision,"[143] thereby reinforcing the medical-transsexual relationship she has been so critical of.

Transsexual Gazing

Bearing in mind the framework of self-location in reading transsexual representations I have discussed above, I want now to locate myself in the process of gazing at Loren Cameron's *Self-Portrait Nude #46A* (fig. 3.1).[144] In the same article that discusses the importance of "the gaze" in transsexual representation and reading cited above, Stryker says of Cameron, "So far, [he] is the only photographer familiar enough with the nuances of transgender desire and transsexual embodiment to do the kind of work I wanted to be a part of."[145] Cameron is particularly well known for his self-portraits, in which he confronts the viewer of his work with the specificities of transsexual embodiment and with the problems of both transsexual self-representation and the constrained meanings transsexuals are forced to operate within. "Triptych," a series of three self-portraits framed by medical, queer and feminist interpolations of the transsexual subject, makes this latter concern crystal clear.[146] In addition to his book of female-to-male transsexual portraits, *Body Alchemy*, and

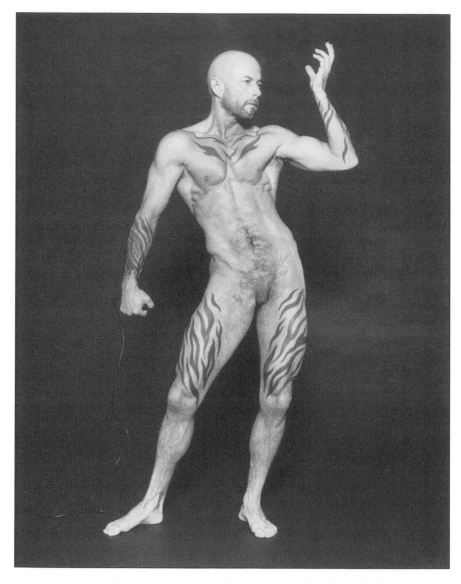

Fig. 3.1. Loren Cameron, *Self-Portrait Nude #46A* (2000), from his *Photo Gallery*.

the *Photo Gallery* on Cameron's web site, his work has been published in Leslie Feinberg's *Transgender Warrior*.[147] Cameron's newest project documenting female-to-male surgery has also recently been published.

In terms of reading Cameron's self-representation, I want, as a non-transsexual, to focus on the process and narrative of my own reading here. I am interested in what nontranssexual readers of Cameron's text might want that text to tell us, and how we make that text meaningful. I would like any nontranssexual readers of this chapter to open themselves up to that kind of self-scrutiny too, so that they can read with me. More specifically, the two guides that I offer the reader in this process are first, Stryker's inquiry, "I know why I let myself be photographed. Do you know why you look?"[148] and second, Prosser's insistence that "gender is not so much *undone* as queerness would have it as redone, that is, done up differently."[149] I take these textual fragments as enabling of a focus on representational meaning as generated in the specificity of a transsexual/nontranssexual dynamic, and of a challenge to queer authority within that dynamic.

Cameron exposes himself naked, in classical nude sculpture pose. He is strong, confident, and, you feel, looks to his left rather than at the camera, not because he cannot, but because he does not want to. But in that description I have already made a series of assumptions. He is male; he is strong; he is assured. He is a man of physical and emotional strength. Why (and perhaps more importantly, how?) do I come to make these assumptions so confidently that I present them as initial description preceding a reading?

Take One: Cameron presents ideal male elements in his self-portrait—well-defined muscles (particularly defined pectorals and flat stomach) and slim hips, positive, self-reliant stance, and appropriate masculine disinterest. Other characteristics complement or complete the picture—facial and body hair, a bald head, a discrete earring stud. His flame tattoos accentuate those chiseled surfaces, drawing attention to the surface of his body. In short, he is unequivocally male. Cameron confirms this reading for me when he says, "I used to read a lot of graphic art novels and loved looking at all those masculine archetypes. I always wanted a body like those comic book heroes with their bulging biceps and firm, hard pecs. But it wasn't just about muscles, it was about gender identity."[150] Earlier work of Cameron's reflects the comic book influence more directly, perhaps. *Transsexual Portraits* includes self-portraits of Cameron in bodybuilder pose, or with jester hat—he seems more nymphlike there, more self-consciously ironic, although combining similar visual effects.

Take Two: Twin scars just under his chest and hair on his abdomen tapering down to a hormone-enhanced clitoris-penis, rather than penis and scrotum, reveal Cameron as inhabiting a modified body, reveal his assured body as having changed over time, as other than static and self-evident. Does his pose come from that temporal narrative, or exist in spite of it? Are the flames as much a part of that modification, of the desire to inhabit a body he can live in and with? Do the scars and genitals sit at odds with the take of Cameron as unequivocally male? What is the difference between the various "modifications" that Cameron clearly displays here, and which are the more significant? Do I read Cameron as male despite his lack of a penis, or because of the predominance of male signifiers in the representation as a whole?

Take Three: Which is Cameron's narrative and which my own? In scrutinizing my own responses to this self-portrait do I distance myself from the image itself or come closer to it? I trace and retrace the representation of Cameron's body over time, trying to track my own responses accurately, wondering about the order of reading, the order through which Cameron's body emerges as meaning. I imagine the difference in meaning if Cameron were clothed, if he were only wearing pants or a shirt, did not have tattoos, looked at the camera instead of away . . . you get the idea. And I wonder about Cameron's desire for this level of scrutiny. He has photographed himself naked, of course, and relies professionally on viewers' willingness to look. But my obsessive gaze embarrasses me, such that at several points I decide not to include a reading of Cameron's self-portrait in this book at all for fear of risking too much. I am left with the knowledge that it would feel easier to stick to textual analyses of queer and feminist productions of transsexual meaning that I can figure as having "nothing to do with me" than to respond to Cameron's invitation to look properly, to sort through the signs and work out which ones produce gendered meaning for me. The only certainty for me at this point is that Cameron is male, however it is that I arrive at that point.

This narrative beginning and end for me, that Cameron is male, sits at a tangent with two other readings of an earlier, although similar, self-portrait of Cameron's. Stephen Whittle reads a self-portrait of Cameron's from 1993 as highlighting the relationship between queer and transsexuality. He suggests that Cameron's self-portrait, "shows a man who is proud to be without, because his masculinity does not come from a penis but from himself. . . . Cameron does not 'gender blend'; instead he escapes gender because it can no longer be imposed by the observer as the boundaries keep moving.[151] And Prosser reads the same image as evidence that transsexual gender is finally "profoundly unreadable," writing that "his muscular chest and shoulders and the beautiful tattoos spread across them . . . only make more visible what is excessive or absent from this picture: what doesn't pass."[152] Both Whittle and Prosser conclude that Cameron is not satisfactorily a man or a woman, since the eye is always "drawn and fixed" to the differences in bodily markers of gender, and, in that sense, can never rest). Whittle perceives this as propelling the "reader" (willing or not) "beyond gender"; Prosser perceives this as the reason transsexuality both cannot be read within and cannot escape bodily markers of gender. In the end, surely, each of our readings of Cameron marks our own narratives, and our own investments in the relationship between gendered meaning and its bodily

referents. I find Cameron's self-representation beautiful and readable as male, both within gender and its referents, and in terms of opening up different gendered endpoints—both Cameron's and my own.

I read Cameron not as "gender-fluid" but as male, despite the "female" markers. Or, possibly, I finally read him as all the more male because of them. A synthesis of all the "takes" I described earlier leads me to believe that my reading narrative works thus: (1) I immediately read Cameron as male; (2) I question that conclusion when I see that the pieces do not hang together in the coherent ways I anticipate; (3) I test out the possibility of Cameron's being a woman instead, and reject that almost straight away (it does not fit with his self-portraiture at all, or the effect of all the male signs in the portrait as a whole); (4) I return to my initial conclusion that Cameron is male/man, though this is now an elaboration after having consciously traced the signs that I assume add up to my initial reading of Cameron as male. Finally, I can describe Cameron as a transsexual man, a term available to us contemporarily, and I am suggesting that, in a way, calling Cameron a "transsexual man" also describes my own reading narrative. This narrative is not simply nontranssexual, but a reading based on the sum of those nontranssexual experiences. Perhaps because my participation in transsexual community is either as a bisexual femme, as an academic, or both, I read Cameron's self-portrait through my experience and theorization of femininity. My own reading therefore signals my experience of femininity as attained, as femme, rather than as given by virtue of being born female. Neither is it secured through psychic repudiations necessarily, but through consistent and ongoing cultural acceptances and refusals. This belief is in line with Lisa Duggan's suggestion, a kind of femme folklore, that femme is a gender transition from female to femme. I read Cameron's image, then, as a representation of gender identity as risk, and have a vested interest in understanding that identity as signaled through the amalgam of gender signs, the whole body as sign, rather than through the presence or absence of a penis, breasts, or any isolated signifier. Rather than Cameron "passing as" a man, I would argue, he effectively exposes the *passing of the penis* as the phallic signifier, and exposes not his lack, but the penis's attempt to cover up its lack of irrefutable phallic authority.

Our own readings resonate with Cameron's representation of his body and gender. If we decide that Cameron transcends, subverts, or reproduces heterosexual norms, realizes or fails to attain full maleness, we must attend to how we locate ourselves through such a reading. In exposing himself to scrutiny, Cameron exposes the assumptions that I make when I read him or anyone. Cameron thus exposes not just himself, but the mechanisms whereby we make sense of him, ourselves, and the structures we understand our selves by.

Bisexual Objects

Bisexual activists and theorists have also been consistently concerned with ways of representing both the bisexual body and bisexual sexual history. In his introduction to *RePresenting Bisexualities* Donald Hall states, "This collection takes as one of its foundational premises that BISEXUALITY cannot be definitively REPRESENTED."[153] As I argued in chapter 1, the contemporary imagination seems locked into the figuring of bisexuality and bisexuals through threes, as a result of which bisexuality is impossible to conceive of effectively as an independent sexual identity or subjectivity. Similarly, most contemporary attempts at resolving the problems of bisexual representation have used the same paradigm to create images of threes—two men and a woman; two women and a man—through which to recognize bisexual behavior or identity. The images that Garber uses in *Vice Versa*—film stills from 1931 to 1994—provide a case in point, relentlessly figuring bisexuality and bisexual narrative through multiple gendered and sexed mélanges.[154] The front cover of the U.K. bisexual anthology *Bisexual Horizons* (fig. 3.2) continues this theme, though here the sexual and gendered triangle is created through repetition of representations of recognizable couplings.[155] Interestingly, this image is taken from an HIV/AIDS safer sex campaign where lesbian, gay, and straight HIV risks are brought into focus but bisexuality is never mentioned. On the cover of a bisexual anthology, however, these same images combine to suggest a sequence of possible bisexual behaviors. Bisexuality is thus figured either as the result of all three combinations or, presumably, as that which precedes and makes possible all three specific sexual desires based on object choice. In other words, none of the bodies or behaviors here represented needs to be bisexual in itself. The cover photograph of the "bisexuality issue" of *Newsweek* from July 1995 is exemplary of this pattern of bisexual representation (fig 3.3). Two men and a woman look, confrontationally, straight at the camera. They are all young, dressed in black and white, smart and stylish. Again, bisexuality is the effect or interpretation of the representation since there is no sexual proximity among the particular individuals—no hand holding or kissing—to indicate any one's relationship to any other. Of course the component parts for bisexual behavior are present: more than one gender and more than one of each. The implication is that if the three people represented were to have sex with each other, that would denote bisexuality at one level. But in fact, even at this level, sex with each other does not signify bisexuality for all three individuals. For the woman on the *Newsweek* cover sex with the two men could in fact be a reinforcement of her heterosexuality, although the doubling of her desire here might suggest a fetishization of the normal aim, her desire being not for male objects per se, but for two objects. In a different way, bisexual meaning here may be understood to derive from

Bisexual *Horizons*

Politics
Histories
Lives

Edited by
Sharon Rose,
Cris Stevens et al

The Off Pink Collective

Fig. 3.2. The front cover of the 1996 book *Bisexual Horizons*.

Fig. 3.3. "Bisexuality," *Newsweek* cover, July 17, 1995.

the location of the viewer, rather than the viewed. The *Newsweek* cover, and bisexual representation in threes more generally, may function as the object of bisexual desire rather than a representation of it. In other words, such representations may be attempts to produce a bisexual display or commodity, to be devoured by the bisexual gaze, feasted upon with relish as part of indiscriminate bisexual lust. In the representation of bisexuality in threes, then, a tension exists between the sexual orientation of those represented, indicated by proximity not behavior, and the orientation of the presumed possessor of the bisexual gaze.

One way in which this tension between subject and object of bisexual desire is managed is by drawing on the range of bisexual meanings currently available. As suggested in relation to the front cover of *Bisexual Horizons*, bisexuality is both sexual and gendered potential preceding representation, or the identity endpoint of a variety of sexual experiences. The gaps in both meaning and interpretation thus opened up are closed down in the text itself. In the *Newsweek* article, only bisexuals are discussed or interviewed. There are no lesbian, gay, or heterosexual partners: bisexuals apparently only desire bisexuals. Problems of object choice are thus resolved by making bisexuals themselves the object of bisexual desire. To reinforce this creation of a bisexual object, meanings of bisexuality as sexed, gendered, and raced merging are brought into the picture, again in order to resolve the difficulty of the double hetero-sexuality or homosexuality arising from the isolation of one sex in the triad, as in the *Newsweek* image. Thus, not only are both sexes present, the gender of those sexes is also mixed and matched. The woman is saved from her potential heterosexuality by her "cross-dressing," and from lesbian stereotyping by remaining "feminine": the man's jacket she is wearing appears a little too large for her feminine form, and her short, but not too short, haircut is complemented by a touch of lipstick. The men, too, are feminized, through their hair and their location behind the woman. Desire for any one of the figures represented can thus be understood as bisexual desire in gendered terms, at the same time as the objects themselves can also be understood as bisexual in terms of their own cross-gendered codes. Drawing once more on the theorization of bisexuality as transcending race as well as gender, itself reflecting the earlier sexological meanings of allowing racial as well as gendered differentiation and civilization, bisexual triads commonly depict a range of racial or ethnic locations in order to associate bisexual meaning with a bisexual subject and object of the gaze. The front cover of *Bisexual Horizons* is a case in point, complementing the sense of "bisexual progression" through various partners with the refusal of single raced as well as gendered object. Bisexuality thus becomes represented as the lack of "specialization" in gazer and gazed at.

These tactics of bisexual representation are directly parodied in a series of photographs by Rachel Lanzerotti published in the winter 1996 issue of *Anything That Moves*.[156] Echoing the form of the *Newsweek* front cover, the image shows two men on either side of a woman, holding in front of them a copy of the bisexuality issue of *Newsweek* with its front cover displayed. The *Anything That Moves* front cover makes explicit the bisexual meanings that the *Newsweek* image implicitly utilizes, making them both transparent and challenging them in the process. The woman has her arms around the two men, bringing them into the picture, establishing their three-way relationship directly. This constructs a bisexual scene that is active and cultural, about touch rather than psychic merging. On the back cover of this issue of *Anything That Moves*, the last of the photographs in a strict chronological sense, but more likely to be the second one seen, the necessity for each of the individuals represented to themselves be bisexual, perhaps an implication of the front cover, is undercut. Here the two men take center stage, kissing deeply, while the woman looks on gleefully. She shares their pleasure, it seems; and her presence changes the scene even though the two men appear blissfully oblivious to her presence (their eyes are closed and the hand that holds the head of one of the men is also excluding the woman from this particular erotic act). Thus by the time the reader turns to the photographs within the magazine itself, several of the assumptions contained in the *Newsweek* image have been addressed: bisexuality is both embodied and displaced. This sets the stage for the ironic depictions of three-way bisexuality within the text, where "absolute bisexuality" is depicted as unlivable fantasy. The three are placed equidistant from one another in a perfect circle. They strain to kiss one another at the same time, tongues meeting in an ideal but clearly uncomfortable and nonintimate kiss. The picture is completed by the symbolic presence of a white picket fence in the background, both suggesting and parodying the notion of "bisexual family" that the *Newsweek* article forced on its readers.

The raced and gendered merging germane to the *Newsweek* image's readability as bisexual is also literalized in the *Anything That Moves* parody. The "woman" in the *Anything That Moves* images is recognizable as such only because her placement echoes that of the woman in the *Newsweek* image. In fact, she is coded butch or FTM, and in a different context could easily be read as male. The men, too, are markedly more feminine than in the Newsweek image, again identifiable as men as much through context as through embodiment. In other words, what the *Anything That Moves* images highlight is that bisexual meaning precedes the viewers' assignment of gender to the participants in the scene, rather than gendered difference giving rise to bisexuality, as is suggested by the *Newsweek* image. And again, the subjects of the *Anything That Moves* images make explicit the racial underpinnings of bisexual meaning—they are white, black, and Hispanic. By suggesting gendered and raced inclusivity on the front cover, only to challenge the feasibility of this model of bisexuality as livable in subsequent images, Lanzerotti begins the important task of imagining bisexual representation as critique of dominant meaning rather than as the limited search for truer bisexual representation.

Similar attempts to circumvent or address these problems of bisexual representation include the front cover of *Vice Versa*, which shows a painting by Janet Rickus called (appropriately enough) *Three Pairs*. [157] The image is of three pears that are leaned against one another. The voicing of what we see, three pears, and Rickus's title, *Three Pairs*, deflect attention away from questions of visual representation and onto textual slippages. On the cover of a book on bisexuality, Rickus's painting moves beyond punning to signify both the ménage à trois (back to the visual), and, as Garber suggests, bisexual sequential representation as suggested more literally by the *Bisexual Horizons* image. The success of Rickus's image is its ability to contain these highly gendered and raced meanings of bisexuality without visual bodily signs. The front cover of the sexual geography volume *Mapping Desire* offers a slightly different way to signal bisexual meaning without gendered or raced amalgam.[158] Here we have an image of a navel, shaded in such a way that it masquerades as an orifice. The image is ungendered and deliberately ambiguous in terms of subject or object of desire. In the context of the volume's subject matter, the image could be read as mapping out new territory for sexual identity, one where a navel is understood as a significant marker of sexual pleasure in subject or object, and where gender is less significant in determining sexual identity. Although *Mapping Desire* is not a bisexual volume as such and there is no comment on the meaning of the image within the text itself, it does open up scavenging possibilities in terms of bisexual representation that does not reproduce bisexuality as middle ground.

Many of the same issues concerning bisexual representation are raised in the photographic work of Stephanie Device. As in Lanzerotti's photographs, Device's work foregrounds the presumptions that the viewer makes in reading images as bisexual and refuses to locate bisexuality among sexed, gendered, raced and sexual oppositions. Device plays with the contemporary and historical meanings of bisexuality in an ironic and conscious way. Object of desire, gendered object choice, associations of bisexuality and nonmonogamy, narratives of partners one might have had—all these themes interweave. In addition, Device uses the temporality of bisexual experience in order to reconfigure the codes through which we understand a particular image, or set of images, as bisexual. In a manner similar to Cameron's, I think, Device does not attempt to show bisexuality in a single moment, but creates a narrative in the mind of the reader, and a relationship between reader and artist that is made explicit, and throws the gaze back onto the interpreter of the images rather than closing down their meaning. The previously unpublished series *fingerprints* (fig. 3.4) comprises four linked photographs,[159] two of which were originally published in *The Bisexual Imaginary* as *silenced 1: missing* and *silenced 2: jealousy*.[160]

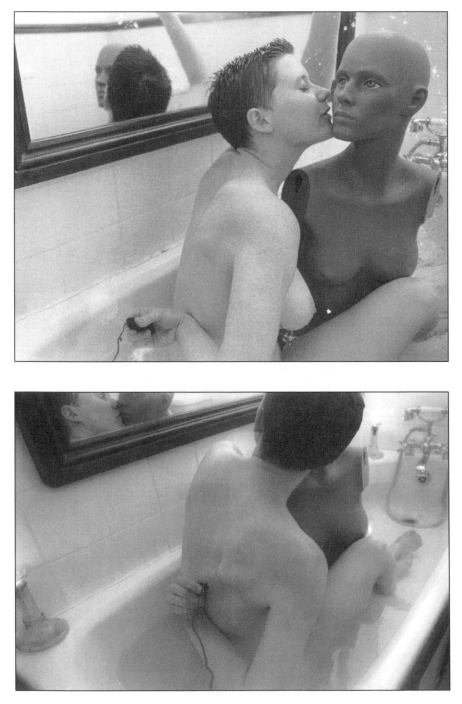

Fig. 3.4. Stephanie Device, *fingerprints*. © Stephanie Device 1997.

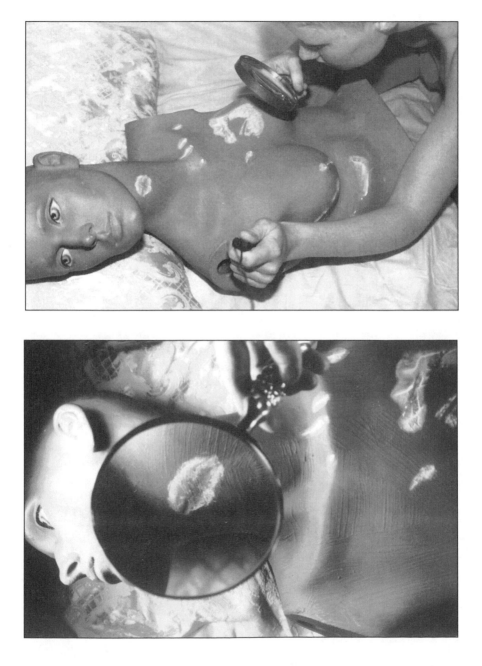

In the first image, Device sits naked in a bath with the object of her desire, and throws water, as if in blessing, over her lover's head. The effect is almost claustrophobic. They are confined in a small and somewhat unlikely space; the water falling also has the effect of seeming like bubbles floating upwards, as if Device and the object of her affection were underwater. Device's eyes are closed; she seems unaware of anything but the touch of her lover's cheek under her lips. It is a scene of intense intimacy and we are firmly cast as voyeurs. And yet, this intimacy is undercut from the start in two particular ways. First, of course, the object of Device's desire is an armless mannequin torso, an unappreciative piece of molded plastic that stares past Device, unmoved by her shower of affection. In addition, Device foregrounds a push-button camera control in her hand, so that our voyeurism is offset by the knowledge that this scene is staged for our viewing pleasure. Device writes that she was inspired to shoot this series by a Patsy Cline song, "Fingerprints":

> And when the day is through
> I dream only of you
> I sit alone and dream of all the things we didn't do
> Now I am all alone
> And when the teardrops start
> I feel the fingerprints that you left on my heart.[161]

Device's first image could be read as absolute isolation—a bisexual image that does not present bisexuals as having an endless stream of sexual partners, but rather as being forced to create an intimate fantasy with an inanimate object. Of course, the image is also playing off and with other images of bisexuals as not restricted to one gender of object choice. Does Device's placement in relation to the more female than male mannequin torso denote displaced lesbian desire, or does the mannequin function to show the limits of sexual identity being read through the gender of object choice in the first place? The mannequin is neither female nor male, and is therefore in a sense more gendered than sexed. Yet the mannequin's gender cannot tell us about Device's sexual location in the terms we culturally recognize or expect. Instead of presenting us with a range of gendered choices, then, Device's location both highlights and deflects gender as significant in terms of her desire. Indeed, the specificities of Device's desire cannot necessarily be read as substituting for a particular human, sexed as well as gendered, body. The mannequin's presence belongs as properly to the terrain of cyberfeminist inquiry as it does to queer inquiry, a terrain where flesh and plastic are not incompatible in the making of the modern subject. Perhaps, in other words, the mannequin herself is Device's object of desire. Mannequins may be Device's fetish, a replacement of the normal sexed aim with gendered plastic. Given my argument in chapter 1 that bisexual desire makes a fetish of both the homosexual and heterosexual object, such a reading of Device's relationship to the mannequin in her bath might be considered a bisexual reading. The second image in this series underscores similar points: Device's head obscures the mannequin's, so that we can only see its breasts and the shoulder where its arm would be. Again, gender does not reveal sexed truth in order to interpret Device's affection. In the corner of the mirror, almost out of the photograph's frame, we see Device kissing the mannequin. Once again, Device is fully absorbed in the scene, while the viewer and the mannequin contemplate each other, both seeming to ask the question, "What are you doing here?" By this point, I think it would be difficult to write the mannequin out of the picture as merely a stand-in for sexed and gendered realness. In these first two images, then, Device has fully shifted responsibility for answering questions of the significance of her particular object choice onto the viewer of the image; in making the mannequin more actively engaging than she is, Device confronts the viewer with their own desires for meaning. Device creates a way of representing her desire for gender as part of her bisexuality, the mannequin both signaling and displacing gender-specific lust.

The third and fourth images directly address issues of jealousy and bisexual narrative in representation. The scene has shifted to more comfortable surroundings, and Device takes the opportunity to scrutinize her lover. Again, Device is inspired by Patsy Cline:

> If you can't be all mine
> Then why am I all yours
> I wonder where a heart draws the line.[162]

Wondering where a heart draws the line again has a number of resonances here. Once again, Device raises the specter of a common bisexual stereotype, that of nonmonogamy. And again she defuses it not through disavowal, but through multiplying its effects. Here nonmonogamy is experienced unevenly, where one partner is all the others, but not vice versa. The fully possessed in Device's work is not the mannequin, as one would expect, but Device. It is Device who scrutinizes the traces of touch on the other's body. The body under scrutiny is one that bears the marks of a previous encounter—a handprint, a mark on and under the right breast, and the mark of a mouth on her lover's neck. In the next photograph Device holds her lover's head with care while examining the mouthprint in close-up. Device covers the ground of jealousy, of imagining real (and fantasy) lovers when with one lover. These images highlight a certain attention to detail, a curiosity with, as Device says, "lovers' skin as terrain which other people have travelled."[163] Those marks are not usually visible to the human eye—hence the light dusting as if fingerprinting. Perhaps it is here that Device's feelings surface—fingerprinting usually only occurs at the scene of a crime. In relation to the Patsy Cline lyrics, the crime emerges as one of passion that Device's imagination cannot erase. And once more, the crime could be the mannequin's (nonmonogamy is not always above board), Device's (does she have the right to examine the mannequin so closely?), or indeed a third party's (the mannequin as a victim of crime). She could be acknowledging her lover's past; she could be fetishizing it; she could be racked with jealousy and possessiveness. We have no way of telling.

The mannequin's narrative is made visible to Device; previous lovers reside in the present moment, in the moments of greatest intimacy. The mannequin is hereby given a narrative of its own—whose imprints are these? They cannot be gendered, and we do not know whether they were made five minutes ago or five years ago. Similarly, we cannot tell if the mannequin consented to the touch, or whether the crime scene denoted by the fingerprint dust and the magnifying glass implies a rape scene. This narrative of bodies touching, resurfacing in unexpected ways, imprints of affection or rage left on the body—the mark on Device's lover's neck could also be a love bite, a bruising—suggests a sexual narrative that never breaks but is ongoing and regenerative, potentially pleasurable, possibly harmful. One could also argue that the marks on the mannequin are Device's own marks that she examines in preparation for someone else to witness; a way of making her own lust visible for someone else to scrutinize, perhaps. In terms of bisexual narrative, Device's images suggest to me that one's sexual past does not always conform to one's sexual present or future, but that the marks of previous or simultaneous lovers (of whatever kind) are left on the body and the mind. Importantly, too, bisexual narrative here is reauthenticated; it is not a series of unimportant liaisons, unmarked by lack of loyalty or love. This is a past that is embodied and can be given new meaning in the present.

Much like Cameron, Device throws this problematic back onto the viewer and interpreter of her images, leaving us to struggle with hidden and disclosed meaning, the path we take being more indicative of our own desires than her own, about which we can never be sure. Both Cameron's and Device's images open up, I suggest, new ways of reading and representing transsexual and bisexual bodies not as transgressive or normative, not as *other,* but as salient to the ways all subjects are located.

Chapter 4

A Place
to Call Home

San Francisco is where gay fantasies come true, and the
problem the city presents is whether, after all, we wanted these
particular dreams to be fulfilled—or would we have preferred
others? Did we know what price these dreams would exact?
—Edmund White, "San Francisco: Our Town"

In this book I have thus far been concerned with how, and to what
effect, bisexuality is produced in gendered and sexual spaces where a
visible bisexual identity or community does not necessarily take center
stage, or where bisexuality is visible but not only in identity form. In this
chapter I document in more detail the bisexual fantasy of discrete identity,
community, and space that "came true" in the summer of 1990, by focusing on the history and execution of the 1990 National Bisexual
Conference (NBC) in San Francisco. I see the 1990 NBC as a peculiarly
rich example of a contemporary space where bisexual desire, identity,
and community form the core around which "other" identities are
negotiated. As the first national bisexual conference in the United States,
it was viewed as a key moment in the development of bisexual identity
and community for many individuals. The conference marked the inception of a national U.S. bisexual network, what is now known as BiNet,
and so provides an exemplary site for interrogating the relationship
between bisexual subjectivity and bisexual community formation. In a
genealogical rather than historical vein, I am particularly interested in
exploring the following questions: How is this dream (of separate
identity) made possible? In what does this dream consist?

Focusing on the NBC in San Francisco is apt for a number of
additional reasons. First, I later lived in San Francisco, in the winters of
1995 and 1997, and became well acquainted with members of the San
Francisco Bay Area bisexual community and its resources. Second, I am
interested in this particular bisexual space precisely because of its San
Francisco context. San Francisco is a mecca for gay men and shapes a gay
imaginary, much as Northampton, Massachusetts shapes a lesbian imagi-

nary.[1] It seems appropriate to the scope of this thesis to consider bisexual space in such a predominantly gay space, particularly after examining the production of bisexuality in relation to the predominantly lesbian space of Northampton and the contemporary terrains of queer and feminist theory.

In thematic terms, this chapter focuses on many of the same concerns as other chapters, and in particular develops the following threads that run throughout this book. I continue to emphasize the ways in which bisexuality is discursively produced and reproduced as a static middle ground between heterosexuality and homosexuality, and the problems that this poses for the mapping of concrete bisexual space. If bisexuality is conceived of as middle ground, the aim of those attempting to create a specific bisexual space is to fulfill the dream of sexual, gendered, and raced inclusion. This is an aim that, as I hope to show, results in additional motivation not to address the actual exclusions necessary in the formation of that space. The history of bisexuality I map in this chapter is concerned with the crosscutting of race and gender in the formation of what is now named "bisexual space." I continue to inter-rogate the slippage among gendered, raced, and sexual paradigms in the articulation of bisexual space, looking in particular at understandings of bisexual subjectivity as the embodiment of both gendered and raced mergings. In effect, then, I take popular representations of bisexuality as hermaphroditism, androgyny, or racial mixing, as exemplified in the *Newsweek*, *Bisexual Horizons*, and *Anything That Moves*, images discussed in chapter 3, and examine how these bisexual meanings are interpreted, challenged, or reinforced politically in the formation of a national bisexual movement.

This line of inquiry also reflects my persistent engagement with Judith Butler's understanding of the mechanisms of repudiation in the construc-tion of the sexual and gendered subject. My argument here, as throughout this book, is that a contemporary bisexual subject is located not through gendered disavowal, loss, and incorporation, but through political and cultural refusals that are related but not simply reducible to dominant discursive gendered and sexual meanings. In this chapter, then, I analyze the specific repudiations that allow a contemporary bisexual subject of bisexual space to emerge. I hope to show that the particular refusals that do occur are historically and culturally locatable, do not precede or determine sexual subjectivity in a linear way but exist in a mutually reinforcing dynamic through which the sexual subject makes sense of herself.

The importance of examining different narratives in the construction of histories of identity is also a concern in this chapter. In contrast to my focus in previous chapters, here I am concerned specifically with provid-ing a history to bisexual activism and community building in the United States. Although this is my final chapter, I want to stress that I do not see the spaces I have been concerned with as progressive, as inevitably leading to the creation of a separate bisexual space and identity. As I have argued throughout this book, not only are spaces where bisexuality is not named important to a genealogy of bisexual subjectivity, but longed-for bisexual inclusion may also result in a more profound erasure of the history of bisexual specificity anyway. Through a historiography of bisexual community in the United States, my interest in this chapter is in the process of making history as well as the tracing of events. I shall be asking the following in pursuit of this goal: How is the story of where we have got to, and when, told and retold? Which histories are included in this tale of bisexual emergence, and which foreclosed?

In telling the story of the the lead up to the 1990 Bisexual Conference I will also be telling the story of shifts from one phase of bisexual activism to another and the coincidence of different local and national bisexual trajectories within the United States. Part of the project in this account of bisexual space is to challenge accounts of U.S. bisexual history that locate its inception in the 1980s, tracing links instead between the contemporary form of bisexual spaces and those carved out within the sexual freedom movement of the 1960s and 1970s. I will be focusing on the desires of the writers of bisexual history, and on the way in which particular moments or facts are given paradigmatic significance. So, for example, my own desire to tease out the links between a largely non-identity-specific sexual freedom movement in San Francisco and its contemporary bisexual community is faithful to and productive of my larger project of imagining bisexuality as partial, contingent, and in process, rather than whole or completed. Other writers' failure to see bisexual history in the archival material on organized orgies in the 1970s clearly reflects their own desires to preserve a bisexual identity of a different, less disordered kind. Thus, as always, a historiographic approach here foregrounds both the importance and limits of reflexivity in research and interpretation. As I suggested in the introduction, I came to the process of mapping bisexual spaces from a position of dissatisfaction with existing ways of accounting for bisexual experience—my own and other people's. In feeling that the available representations of bisexuality did not resonate in any profound way with my sense of self, I am, of course, not voicing much more than a widespread and inevitable failure of "identity" generally to fully represent individuals' experiences. In aiming for a reflexive historiography, what I wish to trace is not simply a different trajectory that more fully represents what I perceive to be my own location both within and outside of contemporary U.S. and U.K. bisexual communities—although articulating an alternative version of bisexual identity formation is clearly one central aim of this project. These visions are not separate from one another: I am located not by a single trajectory of bisexual meaning, but by the overlaps among a range of bisexual and other meanings. My aim is not to create a revisionist bisexual history more reflective of my own sujective narrative, but to identify as carefully as possible how the conflicts and crossovers among different versions of bisexual history and meaning locate bisexual and other subjects. The question thus shifts from "How did I become positioned as I am?" to "What conflicts of meaning are overlooked if (my) ambivalent bisexual location is naturalized or deflected?" Both questions arise from the author's positioning, reflexive or otherwise. The first authorizes both the self and the trajectory one thus traces. The second, following Elspeth Probyn, focuses on the difference between ontological and epistemological location in the formation of experience,[2] understanding that experience as a nodal point of knowledge providing useful information about the relationship between subjects and the environments they inform and are informed by. I am certain that I cannot claim always to be doing the latter, but insofar as location consistently informs this and all projects, this reflexivity also cannot be avoided.

Part 1 of this chapter, "Bisexual Presence," begins by situating bisexual space in San Francisco around the time of the conference as a starting point for tracing its history. The rest of part 1 examines existing accounts of bisexual activism in the 1970s and 1980s, leading up to the establishment of a national bisexual network-in-formation and the decision to hold a National Bisexual Conference in San Francisco in 1990. The questions I ask here is which narratives gain prominence in these histories and what techniques are employed to establish these particular narratives as dominant? Part 2, "Bisexual Home," attends closely to the 1990 bisexual conference space, beginning with the decisions and debates about the formation of bisexual space from within the conference committee. Questions here are, how is a notion of bisexual inclusivity maintained, despite the decisions about bisexual specificity that have to be made? And how do these decisions play out within the conference space once the conference itself has begun? The second half of part 2 looks in depth at how bisexual space is delineated in relation to feminism and multiculturalism, suggesting that bisexual subjectivity is formed in relation to these specific cultural and political imaginaries, rather than gender or race in the abstract. In part 3 I return to the questions I asked in the introduction to this book, showing how the emergent bisexual cartography here and in the book as a whole sheds new light on the terrain of queer and feminist studies.

The sources for this chapter come mainly from the archived material from the conference organizing committee. Most of the archive material was stored in dusty boxes in the basement of one of the conference's main organizers, Lani Ka'ahumanu.[3] These boxes contained an almost complete set of minutes of the 1990 Bisexual Conference Committee Meetings from 1989–1990, flyers for fundraising events and the conference itself, financial and logistical information, personal correspondence, conference programs and statements of purpose, information on the U.S.

National Bisexual Network (NBN), conference evaluation sheets, and other miscellaneous documentation including some photographs. I supplemented this material with interviews conducted with key members of the conference committee, and was granted access to audio tapes of workshops and conference videos. These enabled me to hear the discussions that were going on during the conference, and to gain a clearer picture of what kind of bisexual space, subjectivity, and community were being experienced and formed by the conference delegates themselves. Further, they gave me a more precise sense of the ambience of the conference—how it looked and sounded. Although a number of people had described the opening conference plenary to me in some detail, it was only when I watched the video footage of this event that I began to develop a strong sense of its emotional importance for both organizers and delegates.

San Francisco's general library resources and gay and lesbian archives are second to none, and there is already a wealth of secondary material on San Francisco's queer cartography. For background information on San Francisco's lesbian and gay activism, I consulted materials at San Francisco's Public Library, including the David Lourea Archives, and the Gay and Lesbian Historical Society of Northern California (GLHSNC).[4] In particular, I consulted back issues of two bisexual publications, *Bisexual Women* and the *Bay Area Bisexual Network Newsletter*.

Part 1: Bisexual Presence

Before unraveling the specific threads of bisexual emergence I am concerned with here, I want first to create an imaginative geographical space of bisexual identity in the mind of the reader unfamiliar with San Francisco's sexual minority terrain. San Francisco's Castro district is well known as the "Gay Ghetto." The countless bars, restaurants and shops that line this always-crowded neighborhood cater specifically (although not exclusively) to San Francisco's thriving gay male community. The block on Castro between Eighteenth and Nineteenth Streets is home to A Different Light, the city's famous gay and lesbian bookstore. The bars on Eighteenth Street (between Noe and Castro Streets) are thronged day and night with gay men talking, drinking, and cruising. Gay gyms and offices on the first floors provide a further level of the gay experience, and give rise to what is known as the "Castro Clone," a "handsome, masculine-looking,"[5] white, middle-class consumer and barfly whose mirror-image can be recognized a thousand fold throughout the neighborhood. The Castro has been, and continues to be, the most important site of gay community and political activism in the San Francisco Bay Area. Harvey Milk's camera store, from which he coordinated his polit-

ical career in the late 1970s until his assassination in 1978, was opposite
the Castro Cinema between Seventeenth and Eighteenth Streets. The
Castro streetfairs, the annual Halloween street party, and the Lesbian,
Gay, Bisexual and Transgender Pride Marches, are all centered in the
Castro, and the street itself is often the site for political leafleting, demonstrations, and confrontations. San Francisco gay male politics and
identity, in particular, are formulated, contradicted, and resolidified on
the streets that make up this vibrant community landscape. Thus, the
passionate disagreements between the "old gays" and a new generation
of queer activists—"gays and the gay anarchists"[6]—took place in the
form of poster wars and heated arguments on the streets of the Castro in
the early 1990s.[7] The Castro is not an unproblematic gay male space,
however. As Alan Berubé notes, participation in the social life of the
Castro, and indeed, San Francisco generally, is predicated upon financial
access and stability, thus excluding many young and/or of color gay men.
He writes, "What I experienced most directly as a white gay man with
little money and no college degree was how the gay community reproduced class hierarchies. There were many gay restaurants, disco parties,
conferences, resorts, and bathhouses I couldn't afford. And I didn't have
the income to live in the Castro."[8] The Castro is not the only gay space
in San Francisco, of course. The South of Market district has traditionally been a more marginal gay male space, in terms of class and sexual
practice. South of Market is also more mixed in terms of color and
gender than the Castro for the reasons Berubé suggests.[9] As Pat Califia
suggests, it has long been a zone where sex workers, drug dealers, and
clients of queer sex clubs descend after dark, although not always harmo-
niously.[10] It was in the South of Market district that SM bars initially
found their place. The community spaces of the Castro and Valencia
Street, however, are defined through their sexual minority populations in
unique and significant ways, not least because their queerness is not
limited to particular times of the day.

The lesbian community in San Francisco is less demarcated and more
diffuse, but nevertheless locatable. Although San Francisco is most
known for being a gay male space, "San Francisco is one of the very few
cities where lesbians are residentially concentrated enough to be
visible."[11] In the 1990s the spinal column of the lesbian community was
Valencia Street, stretching from the women's sex shop Good Vibrations
all the way to Fourteenth Street. Pat Califia describes Valencia Street as
one of two "nascent 'lesbian ghettos,'"[12] the other being Park Slope in
Brooklyn, New York. Valencia marks the north boundary of the Mission
district, which in the 1980s and early 1990s was a low-income neighborhood populated by a mix of Mexicans, Central Americans, students,
and "radicals," and which is now almost completely gentrified (both
despite *and* because of lesbian presence there). Lesbian-friendly spaces
on or near Valencia include the impressive San Francisco Women's Build-

ing (fig. 4.1), Osento, the Women's Bathhouse, the Lexington women's bar, and the lesbian performance space, LunaSea. These and numerous other neighborhood cafés, bars, and restaurants combine to create a lesbian-friendly environment that makes Valencia one of the most desirable areas for lesbians to live in.

Fig. 4.1. Author's photographs of the San Francisco Women's Building, on Eighteenth Street.

Valencia Street is not as uniformly lesbian as the Castro is gay, however; unless you were looking for it, it would be easy to miss or ignore Valencia Street's lesbian presence. This can be attributed to the more dispersed nature of lesbian space, and to the fact that there are fewer lesbians than gay men in San Francisco. But these are not the only reasons. As I discussed in relation to Northampton in chapter 2, lesbian space is more precarious than gay male space generally. Hence the demise of San Francisco's Old Wives' Tales women's bookstore, and the women's bar, Amelia's (now the Elbo Room), in the early 1990s, both of which were located on Valencia Street. Such "early closings" may be related to the fact that lesbians (as women) earn less money as a whole than gay men (as men) and hence are unable to support a wide range of venues, or to the lesbian community's increasing awareness of alcoholism which also restricts the number of lesbian bars. Additionally, lesbian space in San Francisco is more vulnerable to interlopers and capitalist expansionism, precisely because of the scarcity of space in the city as a whole.

From a different perspective, Valencia's lesbian territory is hard to pin down because lesbian space is rarely exclusively lesbian space. On opening night at the Lexington in February 1997, several dozen men joined the hundreds of women, but at an equivalent opening night at a Castro gay bar you would be unlikely to see any women at all. And in the early 1990s, Valencia Street from Fourteenth to Eighteenth Streets was the center of heterosexual prostitution.[13] Further, as is made clear by the terms *women's bar, and women's building, women's sex shop,* lesbian space is rarely named lesbian space. Although it is part of cultural knowledge that a women's bar is effectively a lesbian bar, women's performance spaces and bookstores are historically feminist spaces that include lesbians rather than assuming a lesbian subject.[14] The San Francisco Women's Building houses (both temporarily and more permanently) numerous different identities and communities: feminist and lesbian groups, in particular feminist and lesbians of color groups; a Women's SM fair in the summer; and in 1995 the First International FTM Conference.[15] Given the gender identity of the majority of delegates to the FTM conference, the Women's Building here functions as a space of historical and theoretical conflict (FTMs in relation to "women's" space) as well as a space of newly formed identity. As Henry Rubin wryly notes of the opening night of the conference, "The buzz from the numbers of all different kinds of transsexual men in one place superceded the irony that overenrollment had forced the last minute shift of the conference to the San Francisco Women's building."[16] Spaces such as the Women's Building might best be viewed as sites of contemporary sexual, gendered, and raced negotiation rather than as any one community's home. And Valencia Street as a whole might also be viewed as a space producing and reflecting an important concentration of lesbian community that is always intervening and intervened in, and overlapping with, "other" communities.

Compared to the lesbian space of Northampton, San Francisco is uncommonly diverse, and as a result one would reasonably expect there to be a more visible bisexual presence there. Indeed, in his interview with Califia, Gordon Brent Ingram optimistically asks, "Has there been a diversification of spaces in the ghettos and sex zones to include bisexuals, transsexuals, transvestites, and sadomasochists?"[17] Califia's answer that "Those groups of people still have fairly marginal positions in gay space in San Francisco"[18] does not offer much hope of the development of permanent bisexual space in San Francisco at present, however. Yet while permanent social or political space still eludes bisexuals in San Francisco, the same cannot be said of temporary spaces.

One of the results of bisexual organizing for the 1990 NBC was that a temporary bisexual territory was indeed staked out in San Francisco in 1989 and 1990. This space, a bisexual organizers and social space, was concentrated in a narrow band around Noe, Valencia, Eighteenth, and Twentieth Streets, and overlapped with lesbian and gay spaces in San Francisco. The majority of the committee meetings for the conference were held at organizers' apartments on Guerrero, Dolores, or Noe Streets, and in the latter stages of organization, representatives from twelve committees crammed themselves at least twice weekly into one or another space. Ka'ahumanu talks of those weeks with nostalgia, remembering the "bisexual conference time line" that was pasted around the inside walls of her apartment, and notes that "we would kid because Noe was in between the lesbian Valencia and the gay Castro, and so Noe was the bisexual neighborhood."[19] The Bisexual Conference Steering Committee was concerned with practical and ideological issues of space from the outset. Twelve subcommittees were set up to negotiate areas such as logistics, media, housing, site, access, a people of color caucus, and the annual Lesbian and Gay Freedom Parade. The conference ran from Thursday, June 20 to Saturday, June 23, during San Francisco's annual Gay Pride Week.[20] Conference participants were encouraged to stay and attend the Freedom Parade on Sunday, June 24 in order to make the bisexual contingent as visible as possible (the bisexual contingent was the second largest in the parade that year.)[21] A cable car was rented for the parade so that bisexuals with disabilities could participate fully in the march. After much discussion, the steering committee made the decision not to share the cable car with any other groups, in order to maximize bisexual space and visibility.[22] The conference opened with a reception on Wenesday, June 20, at the Mission High School, an ornate, somewhat Gothic building on Eighteenth Street between Delores and Church Streets, where the majority of the conference took place.[23] On Thursday, June 21, an Evening Celebrating Bisexuality was held at the Women's Building, including a performance by members of the performance group Bisexual Diaspora.[24]

The bisexual space I have been sketching here quite literally occupies the middle ground between the gay male Castro and the lesbian and Hispanic Mission. Although only temporary, these bisexual spaces form a cluster that overlaps the borders of those other spaces. The San Francisco Women's Building is figured as a temporary home for bisexual community as well as for lesbians and transsexuals, and the organizers' homes overlook the Castro and the backbone of lesbian San Francisco. The other nongeographically located bisexual spaces I have described— the cable car, the bisexual contingent in the Freedom Parade, the attempts to provide space for difference—open up spaces within other communities, and carve out spaces within the existing bisexual community as well. I am certainly not making claims here for a bisexual space of the same duration, visibility, or infrastructure as lesbian or gay male space in San Francisco: Califia is correct in her assertion that diversity within lesbian and gay communities does not necessarily translate into bisexual visibility. But, in fact, the differences of bisexual space in relation to lesbian or gay spaces are significant precisely because of their lack of consolidation into permanent sites of bisexual visibility. What is interesting to me is that the conference organizers themselves conceived of and labeled their organizing environment "bisexual space" despite the certain knowledge that it would be temporary. And the conference itself was a particularly intense moment for bisexual spatial consolidation, temporary or otherwise, with over four hundred delegates in attendance and its focus on the founding of the National Bisexual Network.

Bisexual Tracks

I want to turn now to a detailed examination of the emergence of this contemporary bisexual cartography in San Francisco. What is its history? Has bisexual community in San Francisco always been negotiated in relation to lesbian and gay spaces?

The 1970s

BiPOL, the San Francisco bisexual community's political wing, was founded in 1983, and was the primary organizing group of the 1990 NBC. Bisexual writer Amanda Udis-Kessler suggests that until the early 1980s the bisexual community had been primarily a support network that organized social gatherings as a way of reducing individual bisexuals' isolation. She argues that in the mid- to late-1970s, during the period of "gay male utopianism and lesbian feminist construction of community norms, bisexuals were not doing much, at least not in an organized way."[25] Udis-Kessler includes the San Francisco Bisexual Center (founded in 1976) among those "social-only" groups,[26] as does Elizabeth Reba Weise, who writes that the Bisexual Center's activity was restricted to running "support groups, rap groups and social functions for a large bisexual network."[27] Udis-Kessler provides a starting point of 1980 for the contemporary bisexual movement in the United States, noting, "In 1980, the year the New York and Chicago bisexual social groups peaked in popularity, a lesbian activist in San Francisco went public with her relationship to a man and quietly initiated the process that led us to where we are today. In 1982, she ran an article in a Bay Area Women's paper calling for bisexuals to become a political force within the Women's movement."[28] Udis-Kessler suggests further that: "[p]ost-Stonewall lesbian and gay groups got along fine for more than a decade without bisexuals insisting on inclusion, and bisexuals presumably got along fine during that period without seeking it."[29] This seems a strangely uncritical view of the mechanisms of political exclusion, where not insisting on inclusion is necessarily or only an indication of contentment.

In fact, however, such a historical elision, of both the Bisexual Center and 1970s activism more generally, is possible because the bisexual history Udis-Kessler traces is one with lesbian/feminism at its center. This is certainly not an unusual approach: several of the groundbreaking bisexual texts of the early 1990s represented bisexuality and feminism as primary cultural and political allies. While I have no doubt that lesbian/feminism has had, and continues to have, an enormous influence on the contemporary bisexual movement in the U.S., I question a historical narrative of bisexuality that rejects other possible roots as simply apolitical. Udis-Kessler overlooks or denies pertinent bisexual histories, either because they do not evidence the appropriate (feminist, or lesbian and gay) political position, or because they are not prepackaged and conveniently labeled *bisexual*. As a result, I believe that she (dis)misses a series of contests over sexual space both from early periods, and contemporarily, in which bisexual behavior is central to the terms of debate.

In contrast to Udis-Kessler, Stephen Donaldson makes an equally strong case for considering the Sexual Freedom League (SFL), of which he was a part from 1967, as the single precursor to the contemporary bisexual movement, even though it did not organize under the term *bisexual*. He writes, "[b]ased in San Francisco but nationally organized, the Sexual Freedom League propagated the slogan 'If it moves, fondle it,' . . . and staged some memorable bisexual orgies."[30] As bisexual activist and writer Liz Highleyman suggests, "members of these groups were often more closely connected to heterosexual 'swinger' communities than to gay or lesbian communities"[31] Udis-Kessler may wish the situation were otherwise, but the SFL and the National Bisexual Liberation Group (founded in New York in 1972)[32] are very much part of a narrative of contemporary bisexual community despite their apparent lack of feminist politics. Udis-Kessler's fusion of bisexuality and feminism results in direct misrepresentation of, as well as silence around, those sites that were not explicitly feminist. She states that "San Francisco, which later boasted some of the earliest political activism, was content at this point [in the late 1970s] to speak of the need to recognize and value the natural androgyny of people. . . . The overwhelming theme among these early bisexual organizations was human freedom and potential, a clear recall of early gay liberation statements."[33] On one level, as Highleyman points out, Udis-Kessler is simply inaccurate here. The Bisexual Center was "from the start engaged in political activism,"[34] educating on sexual health and forming coalitions with gay and lesbian community leaders throughout the 1970s.[35] One of its board members, David Lourea, aware of the "party image" of the Bisexual Center, wryly remarks that "none of us had the time, interest,or energy to devote to an organization that was primarily a place to party."[36] On another level, Udis-Kessler also manages to dismiss early gay liberation in the same gesture, on the basis of its sexual freedom stance. Interestingly, the concept of *androgyny* is given a range of different meanings in the Bisexual Center's newsletter. Where Udis-Kessler assumes that it refers to the "natural" existence of dual-gendered characteristics in each individual, within the newsletter its significance is a subject of debate, understood as variously spiritual, utopic, or political. In the latter case, androgyny is not defined as a psychic or essential merging, but embraced as a political category that could be strategically employed in order to abolish patriarchal gender oppositions.[37]

The Bisexual Center is worth a little closer scrutiny. Its founder, Maggi Rubenstein, describes her own difficulties "coming out" as a bisexual in post-Stonewall San Francisco: "In those days I worked with gay, lesbian, transgender and heterosexual people in counseling, but not bisexual and I was troubled because I felt I was bisexual and I couldn't find anything about my orientation except what Kinsey had researched and written about. All the research has been flawed because we [bisexuals] have been left out."[38]

Rubenstein began to provide "bisexual education" herself. As one of the founding members of San Francisco Sex Information in 1972, she insisted on a core bisexual component to the information and education provided. When the Bisexual Center was founded in 1976 by a group of about twenty people,[39] its central focus was on bisexual issues and politics, but it did not attempt to split itself off from the communities it was a part of. According to Rubinstein, "We decided . . . it was going to be a bisexual center, but it wasn't going to limit itself to supporting bisexual rights only. It was going to support lesbian and gay rights, and all people's rights. There wasn't much on transgender issues then, so we weren't very sensitive to that in the early '70s, but we are much more sensitive to that now. We wanted to make this as far-reaching an organi-zation as we could. We wanted the Bi Center to be a safe harbor for people to share without getting trashed."[40] Thus, on June 30, 1977, the Bisexual Center held a press conference to speak out against Anita Bryant and Florida state senator John Briggs's Proposition 6 which, if passed, would have barred homosexuals from being employed as schoolteachers in the California school system. In this regard, the Bisexual Center's press conference "emphasized that gay concerns were also bisexual concerns."[41]

David Lourea remarks that despite such political initiatives, "[w]e were politically unaware and naive, hoping for acceptance. 'We're nonthreatening. We're nondemanding.'"[42] Rubenstein summarizes the Center's approach when she says, "We were having a good time and we were also delighted that we were offering a service."[43] The context for this political and sexual openness is a pre-HIV and AIDS San Francisco. The Bisexual Center brought together bisexual people from the group sex, heterosexual, lesbian, and gay communities at a time of sexual exploration and freedom. As David Lourea comments to Naomi Tucker, "The late '60s and early '70s were exciting times. During the sexual freedom movement, swingers were exploring their sexuality and challenging the stereotypes within the context of group sex scenes. In the process, many people began to open up to bisexuality. If you were lying down blindfolded and a number of people were touching you, you couldn't tell whether they were male or female. . . . Oh! A light bulb goes on! Maybe there isn't a difference!"[44]

Ann Kaloski makes a similar point about the 1960s in a U.K. context when she notes, "Something about the time did create new spaces for all kinds of behaviour. . . . It *was* a time which challenged notions of gender and sexual orientation, and the relationships [among] bodies, genders and sexualities."[45] Lourea connects the growth of interest in bisexuality to developments within San Francisco's SM community in the 1970s. As women made inroads into gay male SM scenes, the question shifted from "Are you gay or straight?" to "Are you a top or a bottom?"[46]

Despite this energy and activity, both Rubenstein and Lourea acknowledge that the lesbian and gay communities in San Francisco continued to marginalize bisexuals in the late 1970s, and Lourea points out, "We kept giving our lifeblood, our energy, to gay and lesbian liberation, yet we were still being discounted."[47] Lourea also notes that the local newspaper, the *Bay Area Reporter*, would frequently omit bisexual involvement in any given action or event, publishing letters of complaint from bisexuals under biased headings such as "Bis *Feel* Left Out."[48] The activists involved in the Bisexual Center were convinced that within a few years bisexuals would become accepted within the lesbian and gay and heterosexual communities, and that a widespread grassroots bisexual movement, "probably larger than the gay movement,"[49] would flourish. Lourea notes with the benefit of hindsight: "*That* was our naïveté."[50]

The 1980s

Despite the optimism of its founders, the San Francisco Bisexual Center closed in 1984, shortly after BiPOL was founded.[51] The center's demise occurred as people gradually stopped using the service; its organizers eventually decided that the need for the center no longer existed within the community.[52] There are several possible explanations for the decline in the center's use. First, at that time, San Francisco's bisexual community base may not have been broad enough to support both BiPOL and the Bisexual Center. Second, members of the center had become increasingly divided over the question of whether its function should be primarily social or political. These battles were never resolved. In contrast, BiPOL was unequivocal about its political function from its inception, describing itself as a "progressive, feminist, political organization," while it continued the Bisexual Center's dedication to supporting the sexual freedom "of all people, regardless of age, gender or different abilities to explore and define openly their own sexual styles."[53]

The central reason for the center's closure, however, was its continued emphasis on nonmonogamy, group sex, and SM as political expressions. Its closure in 1984 coincided with the peak of the early HIV and AIDS pandemic in San Francisco, when accurate sexual health information was still scarce, and AIDS was still known as gay related immuno-deficiency (GRID). The Center's borrowed slogan, "make love, not war" could no longer serve as a rallying cry in San Francisco in the early 1980s, when people were dying as a result of sexual practices that had not previously been considered dangerous. As Lourea argues, the increased "awareness of GRID and eventually AIDS [meant that we] pulled back from the Center. Suddenly there was something else; our energy *had* to shift into AIDS work. Because we had not nurtured and developed a strong group behind us, the Bi Center changed."[54] The response to AIDS changed not just the individual lives of bisexuals affected with the virus, but also the political map of bisexuality in relation to the rest of the queer community in San Francisco. "As horrible as it is, I think AIDS brought bisexuality out of the closet,"[55] notes David Lourea. Not only were bisexuals fighting for their lives in the 1980s, they were also struggling against the predominant stereotype of the bisexual as transmitter of AIDS from gay male to heterosexual or lesbian communities. The fight against AIDS remained central to the U.S. bisexual movement in the 1990s: "The main focus of the bisexual movement has been and continues to be the visibility and liberation of all people. Currently and most urgently this is in our struggle against AIDS."[56]

Although some bisexual activists from the 1970s, such as Donaldson, lament the shift away from an emphasis on the revolutionary power of a liberatory (bi)sexuality, and toward a more focused identity politics,[57] the majority of Bisexual Center activists channeled their energy into the newly formed BiPOL and, later, the Bay Area Bisexual Network (BABN), founded in 1987.⁵⁸ David Lourea, for example, was one of the 1990 NBC organizers and a keynote speaker at the opening plenary. There are, in fact, strong connections between these two phases of bisexual political activism, even though the differences between them are strongly marked. As I discuss more fully later in this chapter, the threads of "sexual freedom" politics still operate in a 1990s San Francisco bisexual imaginary, primarily through debates about inclusion and exclusion. If we write out 1970s bisexual history as apolitical or irrelevant to a contemporary bisexual movement, those connections may be lost, and the complexity of contemporary bisexual spaces oversimplified.

BiPOL was politically active around HIV and AIDS issues from its inception. In the summer of 1983, it organized one of the first AIDS demonstrations in San Francisco, protesting outside the Haitian embassy at the arrest of fifty-six gay and bisexual men in an AIDS panic in Haiti.⁵⁹ AIDS awareness programs were developed that simultaneously critiqued the stereotyping use of the term *bisexual* in the existing literature as problematic and dangerous, and raised the question of women as a potential risk group. BiPOL never lost sight of the San Francisco bisexual movement's historical participation in the sexual freedom movement, however, emphasizing sex positivity instead of silence, shame, and stigmatization of particular identity groups at a time when this was not a widely favored perspective.⁶⁰ BiPOL activists shared bisexual-focused HIV/AIDS information at conferences, on committees, and at the city's bathhouses and public crusing areas. BiPOL members contributed to the activism that defeated Proposition 102 in California, which would have made it mandatory for HIV-positive people to report this information to the state authorities.⁶¹

In 1985 BiPOL organized the first bisexual contingent to take part in the Lesbian and Gay Freedom Parade. This first attempt to carve out a separate bisexual space within the march was highly successful. Hutchins was dressed as Janis Joplin, with a sign displaying Joplin's famous quote: "'Don't compromise yourself, it's all you've got!'"⁶² Other members of the contingent carried signs such as "Bi Cuspids, Bi Focals, Bi All Means. Lani [Ka'ahumanu] was Bi and Large."⁶³ The energy of that event is typified by the humor with which antibisexual feeling from onlookers of the march was handled: "We held up wooden BiPhobia Shields to the sidewalk crowds whenever they booed us for being bold enough to proclaim ourselves bi in a gay crowd."⁶⁴

BiPOL's high profile in the mid- to late 1980s resulted in rapid growth of the San Francisco bisexual community. By 1989 there was enough support to allow several different bisexual groups to flourish in the San Francisco Bay Area, including (in addition to BiPOL) the umbrella group BABN, BiFriendly (a regular social group meeting in restaurants and cafés in San Francisco), and several university campus organizations in the Bay

Area. The political growth of the San Francisco bisexual community in the 1980s in response to the AIDS pandemic means that it saw itself as politically and socially allied to the city's lesbian and gay communities, whose population has been decimated by the virus. The San Francisco bisexual community has very little contact with the white heterosexual community. Rubenstein reasons, "Sometimes it has been easier and more comfortable to hang out with the gay and lesbian community and push for our rights there than to buck the mainstream."[65]

Despite this emphasis, however, gay and lesbian communities in San Francisco have not fully recognized the bisexual community's contribution to and investment in queer culture and politics. And despite bisexuals' high-profile role in fighting ignorance about HIV and AIDS in San Francisco and the ever-mounting death toll of bisexuals, gay and lesbian activists frequently fail to acknowledge the extent of bisexual investment in this struggle. On January 31, 1989, for example, ACT UP San Francisco organized a roadblock of the Golden Gate Bridge in protest at the apathy toward and violence against HIV-positive people and people with AIDS, handing out flyers to drivers that read, "We are gay men and lesbians who see our community being devastated by the AIDS epidemic. We are straight and bisexual people who are involved in the fight against AIDS."[66] What is notable about the language in this flyer is its alignment of straight and bisexual people as allies "involved in the fight against AIDS." There is no acknowledgement that bisexuals "see [their] community being devastated by the AIDS epidemic" too. This elision of bisexuals can be read in more than one way, indicating either a lack of belief that there is such a thing as bisexual community; an evacuation of bisexuals from lesbian and gay community, allying them instead with heterosexuals; or a refusal to acknowledge the extent of the effects of AIDS on bisexuals. Susan Stryker and Jim Van Buskirk's work in *Gay by the Bay* also reflects a characteristic lack of familiarity with bisexual issues. They include just one and one-half pages on bisexual involvement in San Francisco's lesbian and gay communities, failing to document bisexual involvement in AIDS work or the 1990 NBC. They also argue that it is only "in the late 1980s, with the organization of the Bay Area Bisexual Network (BABN) and BiPol [*sic*], a political action committee, [that] the issue of bisexuality gain[ed] widespread visibility in the 'monosexual' queer community."[67] Although bisexual visibility did increase in queer communities in the late 1980s in San Francisco, I would not say that it was ever "widespread," for the reasons given above. Stryker and Van Buskirk's ignorance is additionally evidenced by their dating of the inception of BiPOL as "the late 1980s" rather than 1983, and their fusion of BiPOL and BABN. Bisexual invisibility within queer communities is thus compounded by scarce and frequently inaccurate information.

The role of organizations like the GLHSNC in recognizing bisexual activism in local and national contexts is key. Stryker and Van Buskirk were both involved in the executive committee of the society before its name change to the Gay, Lesbian, Bisexual, Transgender (GLBT) Historical Society, when there was little access to bisexual-specific materials. Significantly, since the name change in 1999, bisexual activism has been increasingly acknowledged and even targeted, in order to address the society's new mandate. For example, a bisexual exhibit was included in the society's annual *Making a Case* exhibition in 2000, which included information on the establishment of the Bisexual Center and BiPOL. In addition, bisexual art (mostly from *The Bi-Monthly* and *Anything That Moves*) was showcased in the *Queer Folk Art* exhibition in April 2001, held at the GLBT Historical Society and the San Francisco Public Library lesbian and gay reading room. In consolidation of this heightened visibility the newsletter of the GLBT Historical Society, *Our Stories*, included details of the bisexual exhibit at the former event, and also pointed out the recent addition to the archives of materials belonging to the late Cynthia Slater, a prominent bisexual activist involved in San Francisco's SM community and one of the members of the 1990 National Bisexual conference steering committee.[68] In contradistinction to the effects of named inclusion in the Northampton Pride March, then, named inclusion in the GLBT Historical Society appears to yield tangible positive results.

Bisexual Visions

The seeds of the 1990 NBC were not just sown in San Francisco. Bisexual groups and organizing were increasing throughout the United States, and particularly but not exclusively on the coasts, during the 1980s. Weise writes, "Since the early 1980s, other bi groups, both women's and men's, have emerged across the country. Some of the strongest are in Seattle, Los Angeles, Washington D.C., Philadelphia, Santa Cruz and Chicago."[69] The Seattle Bisexual Women's Network, founded in 1986, was particularly involved in establishing the NBN,[70] and the Boston Bisexual Women's Network (BBWN) was founded in 1982.[71] By 1987, the BBWN had over fifty members, an autonomous newsletter *Bi Women,* and a mailing list of almost one thousand women in the United States, Canada, and Europe.[72] The East Coast Bisexual Network (ECBN), a regional umbrella group, was founded in 1985 to facilitate communication among various East Coast bisexual groups and individuals, and began holding regular regional conferences. In May 1987, ECBN hosted its Fourth Conference on Bisexuality in New York City, at which Rubenstein gave the keynote address; the conference attracted over 150 people from fifteen states.[73] During that conference, the need for a National Bisexual Network was established, and plans were made for ECBN to sponsor a National Bisexual Contingent to the 1987 March on Washington for Gay and Lesbian Rights.[74]

As the largest group in the area, BBWN organized the national contingent. Viewing it as an opportunity to organize bisexuals nationally, BBWN constructed the contingent as the starting point for a national bisexual movement. Before the 1987 March on Washington, BBWN distributed a flyer, "Call to Bisexuals," the last lines of which read, "Witness the birth of a national bisexual movement in Washington on October 11th! Whatever the size of the Bisexual Contingent, it will be a proud contingent. You can count on it. We'll be waiting for you."[75] During and after the march, BBWN handed out copies of a flyer—"Are You Ready for a National Bisexual Network?" (fig. 4.2) which had BiPOL San Francisco's post office box number on it.[76] Recipients of the flyer were encouraged to detach and return the bottom section of the flyer to BiPOL, state their opinion about the feasibility of a national bisexual network, and commit themselves to participating.

In an article for *Gay Community News,* one of the organizers of the National Bisexual Contingent, Liz Nania, writes retrospectively of the event as "surely one of the finest moments in bisexual history. Gutsy bisexuals [converged] from about twenty states, women and men with the courage and conviction to affirm their identity before more than half a million lesbians, gays, and gay-rights advocates."[77] It is, of course, highly appropriate that this event—widely viewed as the beginning of the formation of the NBN—took place within the context of lesbian and gay community and activism, setting the tone for the queer focus of national and regional bisexual politics through the late 1980s and the 1990s. Nania continues, "Sunday morning marked the beginning of the first ever gathering of bisexual women and men from all over the country."[78] In fact, the ECBN conference on Bisexuality held in New York City in May of the same year had also been a gathering of bisexuals from all over the country. Nania's claim is probably less an example of historical amnesia than it is the manifestation of her own—and a shared—desire for the October 11 National Bisexual Contingent in Washington, D.C. to be particularly significant as a landmark event leading to the cohesive National Bisexual Network). In her emphasis, Nania locates herself as part of a trajectory that prioritizes national over local gatherings in order to ensure the that need for a national network predominates. Nania thus persists, noting, "Although the March weekend couldn't have been more beautiful and empowering, the important question remains: *How do we use this experience? . . .* For you bisexuals out there, read your local gay papers and watch for the new and expanded gay and lesbian projects that the March generated and take part as an OUT bisexual. Participate in the formation of the new National Bisexual Network."[79] Lucy Friedland similarly marks the importance of the National Bisexual Contingent in the 1987 March on Washington in a letter written for *Sojourner* almost a year later. She writes, "You may ask 'What's so hugely important about 100 bisexuals?' . . . I sense that in order for these 100 people to participate meaningfully in the March they *had* to march in a bisexual

Are You Ready for a National Bisexual Network?

In October, bisexual men and women from all over the country travelled to D.C. to march with the National Bisexual Contingent for the March on Washington for Gay & Lesbian Rights. The Fourth Annual Conference on Bisexuality, produced by the East Coast Bisexual Network in May, was attended by some 250 bi's from 16 states. For some of us, these two recent events clearly demonstrate the need for a National Bisexual Network, a political body that would facilitate communication and political action among the 20+ bi networks that already exist nationwide. The potential for such a network is enormous. The question is whether the bisexual movement in America has gained enough momentum to drive a national network.

The increased visibility of bisexuals both within the straight world and the gay and lesbian community is inevitable. More and more bisexuals are coming to realize that unless we promote and protect our rights to live and love the way we want to, nobody else will. Gays and lesbians are years ahead of us in their organized struggle for liberation, and our liberation has been enhanced through their efforts. However, gay issues and bi issues are not identical. We need our own movement to serve our own emotional and political needs.

Now is the time to assess those needs. Would you like to see the founding of a National Bisexual Network? What should a national network do to foster bi awareness and activism? What actions or events should it undertake? Should it perform an educational function? Do we need to educate ...lves, heterosexuals, gays & lesbians, politicians, the media, the Pope, all of the above? How could a national network best serve the bi community?

Those of us who organize regionally know what it's like to work for networks with large mailing lists and tiny member participation. A national network would fail in its mission to represent bi's without active participation from different regions and different kinds of bi's. A handful of people cannot mobilize a whole country. What role would YOU be willing to play in a National Bisexual Network? Would you be willing to serve as a regional representative on a National Steering Committee? Would you contribute to or edit a newsletter? Would you travel, perhaps a long distance, to attend a bi conference? Would you give money? a lot? The Big Question: would your involvement in a National Bi Network be limited to being on the mailing list? Besides assessing our needs, we must also assess our collective energy and the strength of our commitment.

Perhaps the idea of a National Bi Network is premature. Perhaps we should take stock again two years from now, or five years from now. On the other hand, perhaps the time is NOW!

ARE YOU READY FOR A NATIONAL BISEXUAL NETWORK? WHAT ARE YOU WILLING TO DO??

Start by filling out this handy coupon. Mail it to: National Bisexual Network, c/o Bi-Pol, 584 Castro Street, Box #422, San Francisco, CA 94114. Feel free to check off more than one of the boxes below.

Fig. 4.2. "Are You Ready for a National Bisexual Network?" BBWN flyer distributed at the 1987 March on Washington for Gay and Lesbian Rights.

contingent . . . In the continuing 'march' toward gay liberation, bis cannot be left behind. We cannot leave bi liberation in the hands of gay liberationists."[80] The 1987 National Bisexual Contingent is consistently marked as a turning point in bisexual history. This key bisexual space is formed within lesbian and gay territory, but also functions as a sign of a future, separate bisexual space, linked both to a national movement and local communities nationally. The National Bisexual Contingent at the 1987 March on Washington was also personally significant for individual bisexuals. Matthew le Grant writes of "march[ing] proudly with the NATIONAL BISEXUAL NETWORK contingent," and relates this to what he sees as "the last major step in my own personal coming out process."[81] The event thus emerges as a pivotal moment in the early formation of a contemporary U.S. bisexual imaginary, cementing the relationship between individual identity, local community, and national movement as reciprocal and mutually productive, and marking the coming of age of bisexual identity.

Indeed, within four months of the October 1987 March on Washington, BiPOL had received over 150 responses to the "Are You Ready for a National Bisexual Network?" flyer, and more than $500 in donations.[82] The feedback from the flyer was overwhelmingly in favor of establishing a national bisexual network, and by February 18, 1988, Lani Ka'ahumanu and Autumn Courtney were able to distribute a national mailing:[83]

Dear Nascent National Bisexual Networkers:

Yes we are ready! Yes we will go for it. Yes, from one low key flyer you responded from all over the USA. Yes, we're making history . . . It's time to COME OUT as a movement![84]

Again we see the transformation of local and individual experiences into a national narrative: here, it is not individual bisexuals but the national movement itself that must "come out," must cease to hide itself within lesbian and gay community and narrative, as if it had existed all along. Through this rhetoric, despite its inception almost a decade after the first regional or local groups were established, the national bisexual movement is positioned as waiting for participation rather than waiting to be formed. Before it has met in any form, before it has any formal members, the national bisexual network is retrospectively positioned as preceding, and hence allowing for and giving rise to, individual and local bisexual identity. The mailing asked networkers to prioritize the aims of the network, and included the first written mention of the 1990 NBC: "Would it be possible to attend a conference in June, 1990, during Lesbian/Gay Pride Week and march as a contingent in the Parade? Who would seriously think about attending?"[85]

The most sustained responses to Ka'ahumanu and Courtney's

questionnaire came from groups in Boston, Seattle, Washington, D.C., and Charlotte, North Carolina. Individual enthusiasm proved difficult to maintain, however, and decisions about the structure of the network were repeatedly postponed. Eventually, "nascent-network" members were advised that the "North American Bisexual Network In-Formation will (hopefully) hammer out the final statement of purpose and by-laws at the [1990 International Bisexual Conference] to form a fully fledged organization."[86] There were two subsequent national mailings to network members prior to the conference. The first, sent in April 1989, functioned primarily as a vehicle to distribute the call for workshops and performers for the conference, and to reinforce the decision that "[t]his is where the NABN [North American Bisexual Network] will give birth to itself."[87] The second, sent in October 1989, was a proposal for the structure of NABN from the "North American Bisexual Network working group of the 1990 San Francisco conference on Bisexuality Committee."[88] In a variety of rhetorical and organizational ways, then, the 1990 NBC was explicitly conceived of as a space to mark the inception of the national bisexual movement.

Bisexual Landmarks

The 1990 NBC itself was simply titled "Celebrate!"[89] It began on Wednesday, June 20, with an opening reception at the Mission High School, and ended on Saturday, June 23, with a closing ritual, following the report on the "Official Formation of the National Bisexual Network" that afternoon. There was a social event each evening of the conference: Thursday, An Evening Celebrating Bisexuality: The Third Path; Friday, Clean and Sober Get Acquainted Social, in honor of the Bisexual People of Color Caucus; and Saturday, to end the conference, the Free Clean and Sober Dance. Every lunchtime participants could join in on the NBN committee meetings, the "open mike" performances, or a bisexual twelve-step meeting. The three-day program included six general assemblies and six workshop spaces. Workshops were grouped into eleven tracks—People of Color, Feminism, Androgyny and Gender, Writing/ Publishing, Sexuality, Relationships, Therapy, AIDS, Spirituality, Politics, and Coming Out—with the number of workshops varying from two in the Spirituality track to thirteen in the AIDS track. The emphasis on bisexuality and AIDS at the conference highlighted the influence of its San Francisco location. Ka'ahumanu remarks that when she went to a bisexual conference in Boston in 1989 and spoke about AIDS "nobody in the Boston area had had anyone they knew die of AIDS. By that time in '89, I had stopped counting ... In San Francisco ... some of our leadership had died of AIDS already."[90] The 1990 National Bisexual conference coincided with the 1990 International AIDS conference, also being held in San Francisco. The centrality of AIDS was also marked by the presence on the main stage of the auditorium of three panels from the AIDS Memorial Quilt commemorating members of the bisexual community who had died of AIDS.[91] In total, 449 delegates attended the conference over the three days, compared to the preconference estimate of 125.[92] Of these, approximately two-thirds were from California, 71.5 percent of whom were from the San Francisco Bay Area (which includes San Francisco, Berkeley, Oakland, and San Jose); almost ten percent were from Massachusetts (mostly Boston); and the rest of the nationally based contingent from New York and Seattle of the overseas participants, over half were from England and Scotland.[93]

In keeping with the positioning of the 1990 conference as the pivotal event in the creation and consolidation of bisexual community and identity, the San Francisco Board of Supervisors officially proclaimed June 23, 1990 as Bisexual Pride Day in San Francisco.[94] The bisexual contingent for the 1990 Lesbian and Gay Freedom Day Parade was marked in advance as historic in its advertisement in the National Bisexual conference brochure (fig. 4.3). It read "The largest gay pride parade featuring the largest Bi marching contingent in the world begins at 11:00am at Spear & Market Streets and ends at the Civic Center.... This will be a Bistoric event! Let's all march together and proclaim our diversity, our strength, our numbers, our PRIDE!"[95]

Before the occurrence of either the conference or the parade, the former was already being written about as precipitating the "largest Bi marching contingent in the world." The bisexual contingent at the parade was, indeed, the largest ever, with one estimate that there were 250 participants,[96] and another that there were over 300.[97] The significance of the 1990 conference for a linear narrative of bisexual history culminating in the inevitable emergence of bisexual pride is also emphasized throughout the conference, whose opening "welcome" paragraph reads, "Just as Stonewall marked the crystalization of the gay and lesbian liberation movement, so does this conference mark the beginning of the coalescing of our bisexual community. This is an historic occasion which will shape the growth of bisexuals across the nation. We are here to celebrate our strength as a community and as a people. Through discovering the diversity and the talents of each other, we can realize our true power. It is through the National Bisexual Network that we can be connected to our history and our community."[98]

The local press response to the conference endorsed this parallel. Sarah Murray wrote in the *San Francisco Sentinel* that "more than 400 bisexuals from as far away as Boston and Great Britain converged on Mission High School to see what a bisexual movement might look like."[99] In an article aptly titled "Conference Marks Bisexuals' Stonewall," Carol

"7-8-9-10, We Love Women, We Love Men!"

1990(BI)/LESBIAN/GAY FREEDOM DAY PARADE & CELEBRATION
"The Future Is Ours"

The largest gay pride parade featuring the largest Bi marching contingent in the world begins at 11:00am at Spear & Market Streets and ends at the Civic Center.
Check the Conference Information Board for
Bi Marching Contingent Information.

This will be a Bistoric event! Let's all march together and proclaim our diversity, our strength, our numbers, our PRIDE!
A Motorized Cable Car will be available.

"Come On Now, Let's Hear You Shout Bisexuals Come On Out!"

Fig. 4.3. Advertisement for the 1990 Lesbian and Gay Freedom Day Parade in San Francisco from the 1990 National Bisexual Conference brochure.

Queen is cited as saying, "We're thinking of this as our Stonewall 20 years later."[100] And Greta Christina confirmed in an article for the *San Francisco Bay Times* that "References to Stonewall were commonplace" throughout the conference.[101] Here once again, bisexual history is placed in relation to a lesbian and gay context—the 1969 Stonewall Riots in New York City—and simultaneously detached from that history. Bisexuals now had their own founding moment in the 1990 National Bisexual Conference.

One major difference between the two events paralleled here, of course, is that the Stonewall Riots were a local (and then national) reaction to homophobic violence, whereas the 1990 NBC was a preplanned event emphasizing unity and celebration with (as far as I know) no casualties. Unlike other identity movements of this century— the suffrage movement, the black civil rights movement, and the lesbian and gay movement, to name but three—this founding moment in bisexual history was not born from a mass public response to violence and oppression, but from a conscious desire for unity, for a community and movement to give the term *bisexual* contemporary political meaning. It is important to note here too that Stonewall's status as the founding moment of gay and lesbian politics and culture is highly contested. George Chauncey, for example, has painstakingly documented New York's vibrant and visible homosexual community in the early twentieth century, and Warren Blumenfeld and Diane Raymond write that "at least one hundred years prior to the Stonewall Riots there was a healthy, homosexual rights movement."[102]

This vision of bisexual unity could also be seen in terms of a later-twentieth-century understanding of bisexual marketability. As Donaldson notes, the solidification of bisexual identity could be seen as "an attempt to create an exploitable bisexual market along the lines of the rapidly growing gay and lesbian markets, and even to seduce consumers away from them."[103] In these terms, the 1990 NBC could be seen as the promotion of bisexual culture and products (from safer sex to T-shirts) as well as the creation of the contemporary bisexual consumer who might buy such products. The Bisexual Conference Committee certainly understood the power of self-publicity: the conference was professionally filmed for a two-hour video,[104] and many of the conference workshops were audiotaped; the conference was always bound to be a salable historical memory. Of course, the advertising strategies of the committee mean that the conference is effectively easier to research than any other. I am only too aware of my own gains as a researcher as a result of these strategies, and of the production of a different kind of saleable reality from an academic standpoint.

Part 2: Bisexual Home

As well as providing a historic bisexual landmark, the 1990 conference committee sought to create a sense of home for the more than four hundred people in attendance. This section examines the creation and use of the notion of "bisexual home" in the promotion and execution of the 1990 NBC. I am particularly interested in the discursive mechanisms whereby a sense of bisexual home is secured and regulated before and during the conference, as well as what is excluded in order for that home to feel safely and uniquely bisexual. Marking the conference experience as one of safe refuge from a biphobic outside world, Ka'ahumanu exclaimed at the final assembly, "Standing here today, I feel like I've clicked my heels three times and come home."[105] In this sense home is not simply geographical, but a site of meaning within which one both recognizes oneself and is recognized in turn. The conference was the first time some participants had met another bisexual person, let alone several hundred.[106] The emotional connections among participants were heartfelt, and the "hidden stories, the secret stories, the untold stories of our community" formed the "constant backdrop" to the conference.[107] Throughout the three days, regular emphasis was placed on the relationships among the larger bisexual community (both present and in process), regional groups, and individual bisexuals. Thus, the general assembly meetings that took place twice a day alternated between providing a space for individual testimony, local group histories, and discussions of a larger bisexual movement.

The opening plenary session of the conference was planned as a way of dramatizing this individual and community relationship. People on stage and previously designated members of the audience who stood up and said their name and two things about themselves—for example, "I'm Lani Ka'ahumanu; I'm a lesbian-identified bisexual; and I'm a parent."[108] The process was then opened up to the general audience. As Ka'ahumanu recalls, "[t]here was all of a sudden people standing up on stage, all different kinds of bisexuals, it was mind-boggling. . . . So people started coming forward and saying, 'I'm blah-blah, and I'm from a small town in Ireland, I'm a school teacher and I'm a bisexual too.' It was . . . so moving, because people were from all over, people couldn't stop cheering and screaming."[109] The desired generation of bisexual home is achieved by an appeal to and emphasis upon diversity within bisexual community. The conference space was planned as one in which all participants could see themselves represented and catered to. A draft of the Conference Statement of Purpose began, "This conference will bring together bisexuals of all colors, classes, ages, abilities, . . . etc. who are community organizers, scholars, artists, regular folks to share our experience, theories, strategies, skills, artistic expression and our history."[110]

The conference committee demonstrated its commitment to this ideal of an inclusive bisexual home through a number of important practical measures. Committee members attended disability/access awareness training before the conference,[111] and presenters were "strongly encouraged" to make their workshops as inclusionary as possible.[112] The People of Color Caucus was planned in November 1989,[113] and met several times before the actual conference.[114] American Sign Language interpreters were booked for hearing-impaired individuals and for the plenary assemblies, and conference signs were printed large and bold for partially sighted participants. Advertising and signage was in English and Spanish. Child care arrangements were prepared well in advance, with a budget of $1000 set aside for this purpose. Registration fees were on a sliding scale and were waived for those attending from other countries.[115]

At the conference itself organizers attempted to make the spaces as open as possible. Participants were asked not to use scented products to protect those with allergies, and most of the social spaces were alcohol and smoke-free zones.[116] Wheelchair access to the conference site itself was limited, however, with only one elevator; and most of the sessions took place on the second floor.[117] As well as the People of Color Caucus, a Special Needs Caucus met during the conference and a special needs page was included in the conference brochure, drawing participants' attention to each other's needs and to the overall shape of the conference space. Ka'ahumanu makes the salient point that whatever the designs of the conference organizers, many participants with special needs discovered that their requirements were not being respected,[118] a distinction that I return to in discussing the negotiation of race and racism during the conference. The conference committee's extended efforts to make the 1990 conference space accessible in a variety of ways were usually attentive and most participants acknowledged this in the conference evaluation sheets.

This practical attention to differences at the 1990 conference is secured by a rhetorical invocation of unity running through the plenary speeches, published materials, and conference vision. The discursive use of "unity" allows all participants to gain a sense of what they share as more significant than the way in which they differ from one another. Ka'ahumanu argues that an overarching notion of "bisexual home" needs to be created at the conference, so that delegates can return to their various geographical homes with a strong sense of their own position within a larger bisexual movement.[119] The sense of unity was envisioned as a mechanism to generate sufficient energy within individuals and regional groups for the conception of other regional bisexual spaces. She notes that "we wanted to get across to people, and talked about this from the stage quite a bit . . . that we recognize that . . . you're going to have to go home, and you're going to crash. We're going to crash. . . . We talked a lot about the early days when it was only . . . six of us or seven of us [in San Francisco] doing these wild things . . . making the community look very big, even though it wasn't. And we talked a lot about that . . . emphasizing the organizing."[120]

The tone in the conference workshops was, similarly, of a bisexual group unity formed through its internal diversity. Naomi Tucker opens the conference with her jubilant declaration, "This is the bisexual harmonic convergence!"[121] At his session, "Bisexuals as an Ethnic Minority," Fernando Gutierrez makes a case for viewing bisexuals as having a distinct history, and stresses that we need to "create [our] own sense of sameness and continuity as bisexuals," to "create culture for ourselves in the here and now."[122] Gutierrez also confirms the status of the conference as a historical landmark, suggesting that bisexuals "are making history . . . by participating in this Conference."[123] At his workshop, "Labels: Can't Live with Them, Can't Live without Them," Michael Beer proposed, "Either we can take the established route of creating just another ghetto. . . . Or we can take a leap and cast a very wide net. We can try to be as diverse as possible and almost try to come up with a synonym for the word 'sexual.' We can make this really be a movement not only about sexual liberation, but about ending lookism, racism, sexism, ageism, That's my dream. That's my utopia."[124] This rhetoric works by making difference the core of bisexual identity rather than that which will pull it apart. A bisexual movement can be figured as a force for unity across differences between bisexuals and other groups, as well as within bisexual community. Throughout the conference, bisexuality is everywhere presented as having the potential to heal the splits caused by sexual, gender, racial, age, and class differences, both within the world and within the bisexual self. The bisexual movement is presented as a panacea not only for sexual oppression, but also for any number of other social and political ills: it both represents and is a move toward an ideal future. The comment from workshop participant that "I will be who I will be" is typical.[125] That participant uses what I call the "future utopic grammar" of the bisexual self and community produced at the 1990 NBC. This grammar constructs a bisexual home of possibility that can only be sketched, never built, an architect's fantastic blueprints that defy the laws of structure and gravity. In this way the specificities of what might constitute a bisexual home are endlessly deferred by reference to an imagined future of bisexual possibility.

Not everyone is convinced by this call for a unified celebration of differences in the name of bisexual diversity, however. Greta Christina, in her *San Francisco Bay Times* article, comments that by the end of the conference she was frustrated with "the lack of clarity over long-term goals [and the] vagueness of vision," and criticizes the "tendency for a number of workshops to be somewhat simplistic and imprecise, as well as . . . the speeches, several of which were cliched [*sic*], long-winded, and self-indulgent. The judgment may seem harsh, but the power and excitement of a newly conscious sexual minority in its embryonic stage is much too valuable to be diluted by the atmosphere of an awards ceremony."[126] While I agree with Christina's assertion that such an atmosphere is frustrating. I would argue that this "awards ceremony" atmosphere is not what holds the "newly conscious" bisexual movement back, but what effectively creates it. The rhetorical invocation of differences is not located within a demarcated bisexual space or set of boundaries other than those the conference provides. The "awards ceremony" atmosphere, then, is precisely what locates this bisexual space. The enthusiastic assertion of unity is the thread connecting the conference space of bisexual difference, without which there would be no "newly conscious sexual minority" at all.

Bisexual Difference

The lack of specificity in delineating bisexual home at the conference proves particularly problematic when organizers and delegates are forced to consider the ways in which bisexuality may be different from other identities. Despite Beer's call for lack of labels as the basis for bisexual identification, the desire for a uniquely bisexual space insistently raises the question of who is or who is not the subject of that space. Although the conference committee is adept at identifying and emphasizing differences among bisexuals (and within the term *bisexual*), differentiating bisexual identity, community, and space from "others" proves far more problematic. This is particularly true in relation to lesbian and gay communities, since bisexuals have devoted considerable time and attention to highlighting the commonalties between bisexuals and lesbians and gay men in order to lay claim to acknowledgment within queer spaces, and have had to counter accusations of "really" being heterosexual, lesbian, or gay themselves. In other words, any articulation of difference from lesbians and gay men must not have the effect of positioning bisexuals as part of heterosexual space, whether or not some bisexuals feel themselves to be located more comfortably there. Along these lines, any articulation of similarity must be figured plainly within a bisexual context to avoid being understood as effectively lesbian, or gay.

As a result of these histories and tensions, the discourse of bisexual difference from lesbian and gay subjects and communities is ambivalent. For some conference participants, bisexuals are an inseparable part of lesbian, gay, or queer communities: Carol Queen, for example, remarks that bisexuals' "same sex connections are very powerful and precious . . . That's what makes us bisexual instead of heterosexual. We're not heterosexual people,"[127] and Autumn Courtney emphasizes that: "Whether or not they are a part of our community, we are a part of theirs. We have always been a part of the lesbian gay community and we will always be there."[128] David Lourea also argues in favor of viewing bisexuals as both "apart and separate" from the lesbian and gay community.[129] Other commentators, such as Ellyn, see bisexual space as equally separate from lesbian, gay, and heterosexual spaces—"straight society sees us as perverted, and gays see us as selling out."[130] And still others suggest that we need to work toward establishing a space of inclusion, one that can incorporate bisexual, lesbian, gay, and straight difference: "I don't want a bi community; I want there to be a unified sexual minority community."[131] The conference organizers are clear from the outset that the bisexual conference space should be consolidated adjacent to or within lesbian and gay space, which is partly a reflection of the conference's location in San Francisco, but not all the participants endorse that emphasis. Several use the feedback sheets to complain of the lack of focus on heterosexual issues: for example, "Please address heterophobia in your next convention," and "not everyone comes to bisexuality through lesbigay groups."[132]

Rather than attempt to differentiate bisexual space from "other" space, then, the question of concrete bisexual space is deflected, and posed instead as enigmatic and joyfully inclusive, as a space with no actual place. The "Bi Artist's Manifesto" (fig. 4.4) written by Rachel Kaplan and Keith Hennessy, the coordinators of "The Third Path: An Evening of Performances by Members of the Bisexual Diaspora," is a case in point. The authors stress the importance of acknowledging bisexuals, as they declare, "WE WANT YOU TO KNOW THAT WE EXIST.... We want the bisexual story to be added to the truth as it is known.... WE DECLARE THE 90s [sic] AS THE FIRST *official* DECADE OF OUR EMERGENCE. WE WILL COME OUT AND BE WITNESSED."[133] The specific nature of bisexuals' visibility and where it might be witnessed remains opaque. In the "Bi Artists' Manifesto" bisexuals are "post-Stonewall" and "post-feminist" but we are also "not 100 percent pure grade anything. We want to be acknowledged as ALLIES to the GAY and LESBIAN communities and as MEMBERS of a larger community of SEX RADICALS in pursuit of PLEASURE. Rather than identifying as homo or hetero, bisexuals find themselves in an essential state of FLUIDITY and NON-IDENTITY, a third path.... OUR INNER CHILDREN WANT TO COME OUT.... We acknowledge the possibility of free-falling towards ALL of our DESIRES."[134] Bisexuals are thus represented as in a state of perpetual motion, allies to one community, members of another, never reducible to a single category: "We build bridges from ourselves to art/sex/activists everywhere [sic],"[135] but where we start from or end up cannot be mapped. This is a similar problem to the one I identified at the close of chapter 2. In both contexts, claims are made for a separate bisexual identity and community, but what separate space bisexuals can claim as theirs alone seems impossible to articulate. It is small wonder that bisexuals are often avid science fiction or Internet enthusiasts, or that, as Kaloski notes, "bisexuals can be identified by their . . . addiction

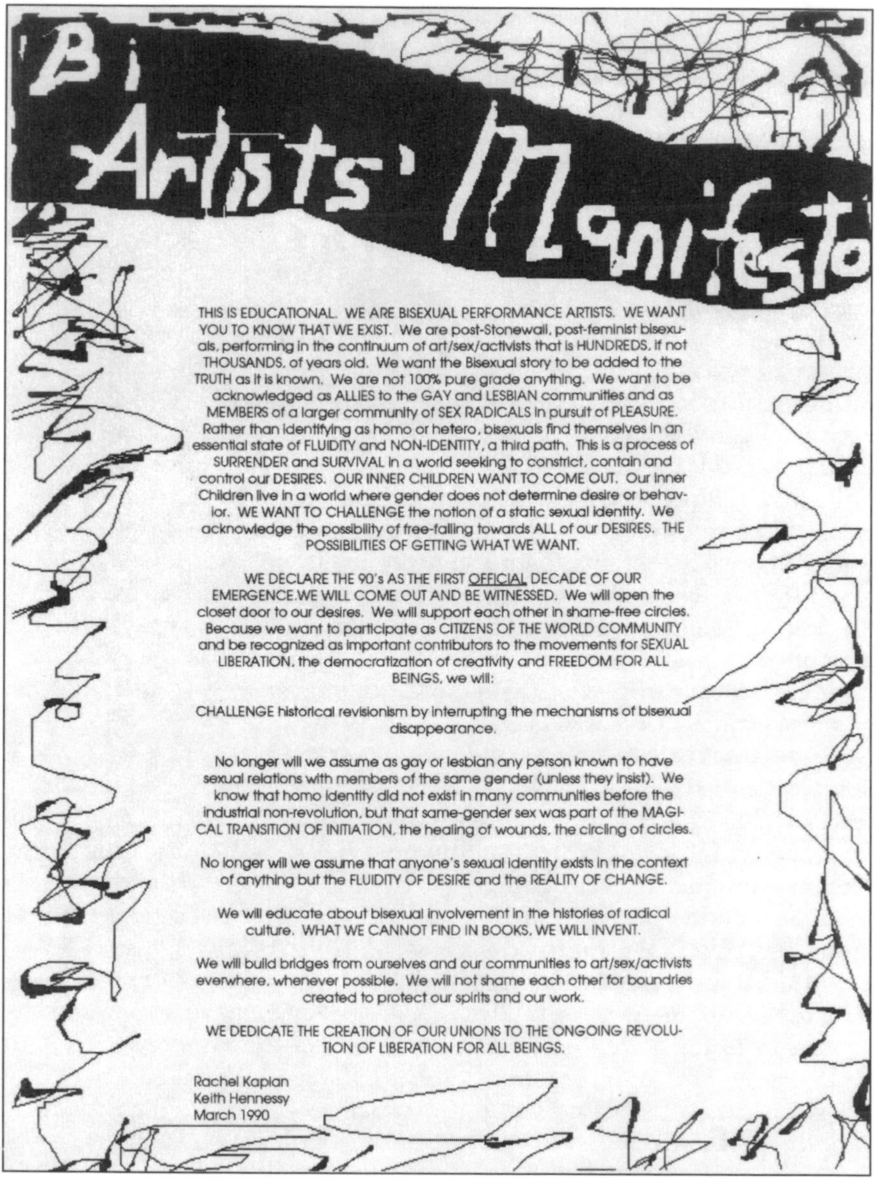

THIS IS EDUCATIONAL. WE ARE BISEXUAL PERFORMANCE ARTISTS. WE WANT YOU TO KNOW THAT WE EXIST. We are post-Stonewall, post-feminist bisexuals, performing in the continuum of art/sex/activists that is HUNDREDS, if not THOUSANDS, of years old. We want the Bisexual story to be added to the TRUTH as it is known. We are not 100% pure grade anything. We want to be acknowledged as ALLIES to the GAY and LESBIAN communities and as MEMBERS of a larger community of SEX RADICALS in pursuit of PLEASURE. Rather than identifying as homo or hetero, bisexuals find themselves in an essential state of FLUIDITY and NON-IDENTITY, a third path. This is a process of SURRENDER and SURVIVAL in a world seeking to constrict, contain and control our DESIRES. OUR INNER CHILDREN WANT TO COME OUT. Our inner Children live in a world where gender does not determine desire or behavior. WE WANT TO CHALLENGE the notion of a static sexual identity. We acknowledge the possibility of free-falling towards ALL of our DESIRES. THE POSSIBILITIES OF GETTING WHAT WE WANT.

WE DECLARE THE 90's AS THE FIRST <u>OFFICIAL</u> DECADE OF OUR EMERGENCE. WE WILL COME OUT AND BE WITNESSED. We will open the closet door to our desires. We will support each other in shame-free circles. Because we want to participate as CITIZENS OF THE WORLD COMMUNITY and be recognized as important contributors to the movements for SEXUAL LIBERATION, the democratization of creativity and FREEDOM FOR ALL BEINGS, we will:

CHALLENGE historical revisionism by interrupting the mechanisms of bisexual disappearance.

No longer will we assume as gay or lesbian any person known to have sexual relations with members of the same gender (unless they insist). We know that homo identity did not exist in many communities before the industrial non-revolution, but that same-gender sex was part of the MAGICAL TRANSITION OF INITIATION, the healing of wounds, the circling of circles.

No longer will we assume that anyone's sexual identity exists in the context of anything but the FLUIDITY OF DESIRE and the REALITY OF CHANGE.

We will educate about bisexual involvement in the histories of radical culture. WHAT WE CANNOT FIND IN BOOKS, WE WILL INVENT.

We will build bridges from ourselves and our communities to art/sex/activists everywhere, whenever possible. We will not shame each other for boundries created to protect our spirits and our work.

WE DEDICATE THE CREATION OF OUR UNIONS TO THE ONGOING REVOLUTION OF LIBERATION FOR ALL BEINGS.

Rachel Kaplan
Keith Hennessy
March 1990

Fig. 4.4. Rachel Kaplan and Keith Hennessy, "Bi Artists' Manifesto," from the 1990 National Bisexual Conference brochure.

to *Star Trek*."[136] Marge Piercy's *Woman on the Edge of Time* is possibly the most frequently cited "bisexual text"; it cannot be accidental that the narrative takes place for the most part in a "future utopic" world.[137] Similarly, the proliferation of bisexual Internet lists and interest makes perfect sense: the Internet functions here as a "world" without circumference, a potential space for a bisexual utopia and for home to be created without exclusion.

This lack of specific bisexual location is presented as positive, as part of the future utopic grammar of bisexuality that propels bisexual desire and identity toward somewhere it will never arrive. The free-falling bisexual is not expected to land. This future utopic bisexual grammar also refers "back" to a time before differentiation, of course, the "memory" of an uncircumscribed sexuality propelling the bisexual community to a like future. Kaplan and Hennessy's invocation to reclaim our inner children comes as no surprise in this context. Their representation of an imaginative bisexual space is reminiscent of a pre-oedipal polymorphous perversity: "We will open the closet door to our desires. We will support each other in shame-free circles."[138]

In the flyer design for "The Third Path: An Evening of Performances by Members of the Bisexual Diaspora" (fig. 4.5), this sense of bisexual placelessness is further confirmed. The flyer shows two hands and forearms clasped, meeting at the center point from which three arrows branch out. There is no information to indicate where the hands come from—they break the blackness only at the point where they meet. There is no indication of permanence to the hold (though it does seem firm), and no hint of where they might next surface. The image is an attempt to make bisexuality visible without specifying the different trajectories that might lead to this bisexual moment, this bisexual space. Bisexuality might spring forth at any moment, it seems, and at the meeting point of any three identities, desires, experiences, or histories. In a sense this is a reversal of the dynamic of bisexuality as middle ground enabling the homosexual or heterosexual direction of desire. Bisexuality still occupies the middle ground, but is refigured as the *result* of diverse desires and trajectories rather than their *origin*.

Kaplan and Hennessy's employment of the term *diaspora* is interesting and problematic here. Historically, of course, the term refers to the dispersion of Jews after the destruction of Israel, and to the sense of connection that links the Jewish people. The use of the term *bisexual diaspora* suggests that sense both of dispersion and connection, but as with the persistant invocation of the conference as the "bisexual Stonewall," there is no oppression or destruction that can be said to have caused the scattering of bisexual peoples in a comparable way. In contemporary postcolonial theory, *diaspora* is used more broadly to refer to the exile of and connection among peoples of color, indicating less an originary moment a dispersed imaginary, a sense of subjectivity formed from

Fig. 4.5. Rachel Kaplan and Keith Hennessy, "The Third Path," from the 1990 National Bisexual Conference brochure.

a number of different locations. Kaplan and Hennessy's invocation of the "bisexual diaspora" suggests that the bisexual occupies borderlands not unlike Gloria Anzaldúa's mestiza subject, in other words, whose identity is formed in the "borderlands" between and among dominant identities.[139] Michael du Plessis likewise advocates the bisexual use of the strategy of "para-naming," whereby "'bisexuality' can work in ways not unlike the 'oppositional consciousness' of which Chela Sandoval writes in relation to the contradictions of 'U.S. third world feminism.'"[140] Para-naming is the process of naming the self through negation: for example, the bisexual slogan "'Not half gay; not half straight, but totally bisexual,' in which 'bisexual' achieves its meaning through its refusal of both adjacent terms."[141] I have already mentioned my concerns about such a sexual/racial slippage that relies on bisexuality being located as the middle ground between (white) heterosexuality and homosexuality alone. In the context of the 1990 conference, the blithe reference to "bisexual diaspora" without accompanying specificity raises a question about the ethics of such bisexual appropriation of postcolonial geographic imagery. For third world feminists diaspora is located and locatable, the result of specific exile and relocation, hybridity, and fusion. Anzaldúa's mestiza subject is formed by and acts upon very particular influences: Mexico, Tex-Mex culture, and California. The bisexual utopia invoked by Beer, Tucker, Kaplan, and Hennessy at the 1990 conference, however, precludes the possibility of mapping "bisexual diaspora," relying as it does on an appeal to undifferentiated unity. The use of the term *diaspora* here, then, reads as a strategy for understanding bisexuality as inclusive of the ethnocultural differences suggested by that term, rather than as a way of mapping bisexuality's own difference. In this context, du Plessis's para-naming (we are not gay, not straight, etc.) also reads as strategy for creating an imaginative bisexual space free of exclusion thought the refusal to specify bisexual location.

The representation of bisexual spaces as no place and every place is not unique to the 1990 NBC in San Francisco. The logo for the U.K. Eighth National Bisexual Conference in Edinburgh (fig. 4.6), also held in 1990, is a kite, reflecting the same theme of bisexual desire as free-floating and blown by chance winds that Kaplan and Hennessy promoted here in the United States. Consider, too, the logo for the Second International Bisexual Conference, held in London in 1992, in which arrowless Cupids hover over either side of the world (fig. 4.7). The juxtaposition of the world (denoting inclusivity and difference) and the Cupids (denoting innocence and arbitrary desire) produces a similar effect to the "Third Path" text in its appeal to both a past and a future bisexual "innocence." The Fifth International Bisexual Conference, held at Harvard in April 1998, utilized a similar notion of pre- and postdiscursive unity. Through the conference title, "One World, Many Faces: Unity and Diversity in Bi Communities, Queer Communities, and the World" (see fig. 4.8),

Fig. 4.6. Flyer for the Eighth National Bisexual Conference, Edinburgh, September 7–10, 1990.

bisexual conference space is once again imagined as a unifying space. Once again a visual image of the world provides the backdrop to the conference information. In an unsettlingly similar genre to the "one world" Benetton advertisements, the Fifth International Bisexual Conference is presupposed as both containing and moving beyond difference, even though the conference itself was predominantly white and almost exclusively Northern European and North American. There is no shadow

Fig. 4.7. Flyer for the Second International Bisexual Conference, London, June 23–24, 1992.

of doubt here, no question mark—One World, Many Faces?—to suggest the possibility that this space might not in fact be inclusive.

What I have been describing in this section is the production of the 1990 National Bisexual Conference space through a future utopic bisexual grammar that presupposes bisexual inclusivity and anchors itself in relation to a future perfect lack of differentiation. Its presumed inclusivity is thus untraceable, reiterated as unquestioned unity of difference

FIFTH INTERNATIONAL BISEXUAL CONFERENCE

ONE WORLD, MANY FACES
Unity and Diversity in Bi Communities,
Queer Communities, and the World

Harvard Gay, Lesbian, Bisexual
and Gay Graduate Students
Harvard Bisexual, Gay, Lesbian,
Transgendered and Supporters
Alliance
Bisexual Resource Center
Multicultural AIDS Coalition
Biversity Boston
BiNet USA
Boston Bisexual Women's Network

Cambridge, Massachusetts, USA
April 3-5, 1998

Fig. 4.8. Cover for the Fifth International Bisexual Conference program, Cambridge, Massachusetts, April 3–5, 1998.

in general rather than through the delineation of specific bisexual inclusions and exclusions. The difficulties suggested by the question of who is "other" to bisexuals are discursively resolved by the relentless invocation of bisexuality *as difference*. The reality of the conference space and experience is unsurprisingly distinct from, though still articulated in relation to, this vision. The attention to access discussed above suggests that insistent issues of power and difference could not be solved by a "will to inclusion" alone. Ka'ahumanu spends considerable time describing her feelings of loss at her realization that the bisexual community could not "remain" an innocent community. Of a series of conflicts and betrayals over the role of feminism in the conference, Ka'ahumanu states, candidly, "It was so painful. . . . It was hard for a lot of [reasons]. Mostly it was the innocence, the level of trust that we had all been operating on. . . . It was like rape; it was violent. . . . There was this sense of loss."[142] As my discussion of the role of the Bisexual Center in the consolidation of bisexual community in San Francisco makes clear, bisexual community had not existed in a state of prepolitical innocence. However, the belief that it did, and the rhetorically expressed desire to "return" to an inclusive bisexual space, propelled the narrative of the 1990 Bisexual conference in significant ways. This desire for "innocence renewed" is one factor determining which identities, communities, and political perspectives are in fact embraced or rejected in the creation of the bisexual conference space.

Bisexual Identity

In this section I explore further the tensions, contradictions, and decisions influencing who is and who is not included in the term *bisexual* and in the 1990 NBC space. An extract from BiPOL's statement of purpose, revised for the 1990 conference Brochure reads, "BiPOL is an independent Bisexual/Lesbian/Gay political action group founded in 1983 which supports Bisexual identity and rights. While BiPOL works in tandem with the more personal, social and support Bisexual Groups, BiPOL supports more militant public methods to EDUCATE, ADVOCATE and AGITATE for Bisexual visibility and inclusion. BiPOL is a progressive, feminist, political organization. We believe in fighting to end the oppression of all people regardless of sexual or gender orientation, different abilities, race, age, culture, ethnicity, class or religion."[143] This politically focused statement stands in tension with Elizabeth Reba Weise's declaration on the first day of the conference that, as bisexuals, it is "humanity . . . that defines us. . . . We can be all things simultaneously and that scares people."[144] In BiPOL's statement of purpose, bisexual politics is unequivocally intertwined with lesbian and gay politics, and is firmly established as occupying feminist and antiracist position, among others. BiPOL was the organizing and sponsoring group for the conference, its politics setting the tone as a whole, as indicated by the printing of statement of purpose at the front of the conference brochure. These seemingly opposed views of bisexuality as either metonymic for "humanity" or as politically biased in order to achieve eventual inclusion are reflective of the historical strands of bisexuality that tend to prioritize either a sexual liberation or a feminist political model of the bisexual movement, run throughout the conference. The conference is a site where these different historical trajectories come together, where there are attempts to resolve the differences between the two perspectives. In fact, this desire to integrate humanist and feminist perspectives at the conference is one way in which a sense of national bisexual unity is imagined, and a further sign of the location of the conference as a landmark in the bisexual imaginary.

In this section I focus on the ways in which the politics of both gender and race are formative in the creation of the bisexual conference space. First, I discuss the extent to which feminism is viewed by turns as foundational to and disruptive of an individual and collective bisexual self. Second, I am concerned with the integration and displacement of race and ethnicity in the formation of a bisexual space and identity. As suggested at the beginning of this chapter, a bisexual self is partly formed through a cultural repudiation of gender and race that manifests through (attempted) rejection of feminism and (attempted) incorporation of multiculturalism.

Bisexual Feminism

The shift from bisexual movements of the 1970s to those of the 1990s is marked partly by the change in leadership from predominantly men to predominantly women. One reason for this change is the premature death in the 1980s and 1990s of many bisexual men from AIDS-related illnesses. Thus, Stephen Donaldson remarks that "the change [in bisexual leadership] may reflect how AIDS has decimated the male population and stigmatized bi men as AIDS infectors of the straight majority."[145] Another reason is that most of the women leaders of the bisexual movement came out as bisexual after identifying as lesbian (and often as lesbian separatist): these women have been concerned to safeguard radical feminist politics within the bisexual movement. Many of the articles in the anthology *Closer to Home: Bisexuality and Feminism* reflect this trajectory for individual authors, as do those in the more recent anthology *Bisexual Politics*.[146] The mutual implication of bisexuality and feminism occurs at a theoretical and political level too, as suggested by Amanda Udis-Kessler's fusion of bisexual and feminist movements in the 1980s. In her introduction to *Closer to Home: Bisexuality and Feminism*, Weise makes the case for bisexual and feminist identities being mutually implicated in one another because of the challenges she perceives they both make to hierarchical sex and gender difference. She writes, "Those of us who consider ourselves feminist are excited about the possibilities of a bisexuality informed by the understanding that sex and gender are classifications by which women are oppressed and restricted. We see bisexuality calling into question many of the fundamental assumptions of our culture: the duality of gender; the necessity of bipolar relationships [and] the demand for either/or sexualities."[147] For many of the women involved in bisexual organizing, bisexuality and feminism cannot be separated. Thus, Maggi Rubenstein states that, for her, feminism and bisexuality "co-incided. Getting into feminism and my power as a woman gave me the courage to come out as bisexual."[148] Weise suggests that the increased feminist focus within the bisexual movement can be attributed to the fact that the "two largest women-only groups, Boston's and Seattle's, are both staunchly feminist-identified. Other groups have grown more out of a sexual liberation model."[149] Joan Hill of the Seattle Bisexual Women's Network remarks that this group "was founded by women who think that feminism is relevant to their lives,"[150] and Robyn Ochs of BBWN also emphasizes her group's feminist, collective organization, as well as its distance from the Boston Bisexual Men's Network.[151] Both the Boston and Seattle women's groups were instrumental in the discussions about a national bisexual network prior to the NBC, and in the planning of the conference itself. The inception of BiPOL in 1983 marked the desire for an explicitly feminist political agenda within the bisexual movement in San Francisco, and this perspective was maintained throughout the organizing of the 1990 National Bisexual Conference. Thus, Ka'ahumanu notes that "Autumn [Courtney] and I were really clear that we always brought up feminism at every meeting."[152] In addition, Courtney and Ka'ahumanu drafted a policy document for committee members, "Bisexual Politics: What It Is?" that situated bisexual feminism as fundamental to the conference and to bisexual identity and community more generally.[153]

This feminist emphasis is not universally accepted within the bisexual movement, however. Donaldson remarks, for example, that the "imbalance of gender is a problem. Bisexual leadership at all levels must reach out to men, and men in the movement must take responsibility for developing remedies. The intellectual discourse of the bi movement, which often appears to be dominated by 'Women's issues,' must be broadened, or the movement may be perceived by men as a primary vehicle for arcane intrafeminist controversies."[154] Donaldson clearly deems feminism both a concern for women only and a source of tension between the interests of the (feminist) leadership of the movement and the grassroots membership. This tension took material form within the 1990 NBC committee. In the early meetings (late 1988–early 1989) one of the conference committee members frequently challenged the feminist emphasis of the planning. Ka'ahumanu outlines the story of this rift in my interview with her: "You know, 'Feminism, what does it mean, why do we have to deal with sexism? I'm oppressed too.' One of those kinds of men." Despite this man's being a "provocateur," Ka'ahumanu explains that "he would challenge pieces but he would listen . . . so it *felt* OK."[155] With Weise and Lisa Jean Moore, this committee member organized the first national mailing informing network members and regional bisexual groups about the 1990 Conference in San Francisco. At the last moment he removed his name from the letter and altered its contents, adding the word *feminist* at inappropriate points. His action was intended as "an alert," to make people aware that "it was . . . basically 'fascist feminist people' running this organization."[156] The letter went out before the sabotage was identified by the other members of the conference committee. The perpetrator did acknowledge his culpability in altering the letter and taking his name off, but despite the fact that the committee sent out another mailing immediately to "clean it [all] up as quickly as possible without targeting him or anything,"[157] the realization that bisexual identity—like all identity—is a messy business could no longer be ignored. In other words, the assertion of feminist unity that marked the early days of the conference organizing could not account for disagreement, human maliciousness, or error. The committee was required to reconsider its assumption that an inclusive bisexuality is always already both radical and ethical, or indeed, that there could be common agreement about the meaning of those terms in the first place. Clearly, "the saboteur" considered it his ethical duty to "warn" potential conference delegates of the feminist emphasis of the committee, while feminist committee members considered such an emphasis to be at the heart of an "ethical bisexuality." Effectively the antifeminist letter forced the Committee out of a state of presumed innocence, forcing its members to take a more explicitly political position in relationship to feminism. From this point onward, continued insistence on a feminist focus—"People across the country had to know that this was feminist"[158]—was combined with a knowledge that this would inevitably lead to the exclusion of those who disagreed. The committee recovered from this antifeminist "violation," but as Ka'ahumanu laments, "we'll never be that innocent again,"[159] and the meanings of feminism in the context of the conference were radically altered. Although this incident is understood as provoking the devastation of bisexual innocence, one might also see it as marking the inception of a bisexual community aware that however strong the desire for unity, each decision about bisexual meaning differentiates that community from what and whom it is not.

In July 1987 a bisexual woman who attended the ECBN conference wrote, "The men I met all indicated sympathy for feminism, but I also suspect some were motivated to come by sexual adventurism."[160] Sexual adventurism and feminism are clearly viewed as mutually exclusive terms and choices here, in a way that reminds me, somewhat ironically, of the association of bisexual women with "the sexual" and lesbians with "the political" during the Northampton debates. Here it is bisexual (feminist) women who are assumed to be "political," and bisexual men who are cast as "sexual" (and therefore apolitical). This personal response mirrors the accounts I have been describing that divide bisexual community history into pre- and postfeminist eras, with the distinction between the two being a move from the creation of bisexual social space (humanist) to the creation of bisexual political space (feminist). In the wake of the split within the committee around issues of feminism, however, the conference becomes imagined as a site for resolving this humanist/political tension without relinquishing a feminist premise. In this way, the conference is the site for an attempt to recuperate feminism for a humanist model of bisexuality as wholly inclusive of difference.

An exchange in the *Bay Area Bisexual Network Newsletter* just prior to the conference makes plain this desire to make humanism and feminism compatible. In their article "Feminism and the Conference" NBC organizers Naomi Tucker and Paul Smith explain "why feminism is part of the statement of purpose of this upcoming June conference."[161] They begin their article by stating that a feminist conference "means that we strive to be inclusionary in our visions of community,"[162] an assertion that frames the rest of the article. Tucker and Smith argue that without feminism women will continue to be oppressed, making equal relationships among individual men and women impossible and precluding the development of a bisexual community "that is truly for everyone."[163] For the authors a feminist politics is about creating equality among men and women of all races, classes, ages and cultures. They write, "The progressive, feminist politics of BiPOL necessitate actively struggling to end the oppression of all people regardless of sexual or gender orientation, different abilities, race, age, culture, ethnicity, class or religion. . . . We need more than a nondiscrimination statement of purpose. We need active outreach to diverse communities; we need an organizational structure that strives for . . . parity and reflects the diversity of our community."[164] In their article, Tucker and Smith attempt to refute any lingering notions of feminism as divisive and sectarian by claiming it as fundamental to a revolutionary vision of bisexual wholeness, as central to abolishing hierarchical "us/them" oppositions, and as allowing "the beauty of [bisexual] diversity" to emerge.[165]

W. L. Warner is not convinced by Tucker and Smith's arguments for a integrative feminist bisexuality, however. Responding directly to their article, Warner warns against "binding" links between the bisexual and feminist movements, arguing that "the bisexual movement is in danger of being hampered by the considerable baggage of the radical feminisms of the past."[166] In Warner's view, the feminist movement's insistence on "feminine superiority" is incompatible with "creating space 'in which we can all feel good about being bisexual.' "[167] Interestingly, Warner uses the past tense for describing both the feminist movement and "the cultural oppression of women,"[168] implying that feminism is a tool of yesteryear. His/her own suggestion for the present and future is "to establish our own gender-centrist movement, truly inclusive, and [discard] the exclusionary trappings of both male and female chauvinism."[169] Warner's narrative of the bisexual movement reverses the tendency to place sexual liberation models in the naïve past, writing feminism as the outdated politics of naïveté instead, and humanism as the politics of a mature bisexual movement. Tucker and Smith respond in the same letters page by reemphasizing the points they made in their original article. In addition they reject the "doctrine of female superiority espoused by a monolithic movement of guilt and shame,"[170] and underscore that in the context of the bisexual conference feminism means accessibility and equality for all. This feminism, unlike the "doctrine of female superiority," is "*NOT* the female parallel to chauvinism" but a way of "freeing women *AND* men from the traditional sex roles that bind and oppress us. Our goal is not, as you seem to fear, to have women dominate men. Rather we seek to affirmatively create a culture where women and men are equally valued."[171] The tone of Tucker and Smith's letter is conciliatory and defensive, where their initial article was vibrant. Tucker and Smith reinforce Warner's image of a feminist demon to be consigned to the paranoid past, in order to convince him/her that the feminist "organizing principle of the conference" is not *that kind* of feminism, and does not mean exclusion.[172] Their feminism, not unlike the "gender-centrist movement" Warner favors, is one where no one need feel bad about structural oppression as long as the mistakes of the past are not perpetuated in the present. In both letters, bisexual men's "fears" of dominant women are given the same symbolic and political weight as the "oppression of women in the past millenia."[173] The difference is that Warner invokes this fear (of "female chauvinism"), where Tucker and Smith dismiss it. Neither letter considers the possibility that these "fears" might themselves reproduce the structural oppression of women that has been so neatly consigned to an ignorant past. Neither letter names this outdated feminism as *lesbian* feminism either, although the repeated references to "feminine superiority," and isolation from men clearly mark it in this way. This failure to name lesbian feminism is particularly notable given the number of women involved in both the bisexual movement and the conference who previously identified as lesbian, as discussed earlier. In this context, Tucker and Smith's letter reads as less a justification of the conference committee's advocacy of feminism, and more as reassurance for bisexual men that the marker *lesbian*, which would signal their potential exclusion has been removed from the feminism of the past in order to create an inclusive bisexual feminism for the future.

This attempt to distance the bisexual feminism of the conference from lesbian feminism continues through the conference itself. The panel of speakers at the "Bisexuality and Feminism" session was, significantly, comprised of two women and two men,[174] all of whom saw feminism as a way of moving beyond the confines of the gender oppositions that oppress both men and women, enabling women and men to forge egalitarian relationships with one another. Thus, one panel member, Tom, states that feminism enables us to "overcome [the] false divisions in our society based on gender. . . . Part of our goal is to transcend them [and] build unity across divisions." Significantly, these divisions are "outside, not within" us;[175] in other words, they are wholly societally imposed rather than reproduced in gender relations to any extent. The other male speaker on the "Bisexuality and Feminism" panel, Bill Mack, similarly argues that men are "systematically hurt by the way society is organized."[176] For both speakers, bisexual feminism is a strategy for building the utopian future of gender, race, and class equality that lies beneath, or before and after, social stratification or exclusion. In this context, feminism becomes a way of activating the bisexual challenge to gendered dualism, a way of returning to a desired bisexual innocence. None of the speakers on this panel addresses the question of the ways in which gendered subjectivity may be formed in and through society, whether or not we "choose" such formations.

Joan Hill, one of the women speakers on the panel, provides a brief history of feminism, differentiating between radical feminism, which she defines as emphasizing the socially constructed nature of gender, and "cultural feminism," which she defines as a "reactionary movement" creating an opposition between men and women on the basis of a natural "feminine" superiority, and encouraging women to withdraw from men.[177] In a similar way to Tucker, Smith, and Warner, Hill consigns the usefulness of a "cultural feminist" movement to a less enlightened past.[178] Instead, she links bisexual feminism to radical feminism in its visionary accentuating of utopian possibility. The lesbian center of both radical and cultural feminism is, of course, not mentioned, as to do so would necessitate admitting that the term *feminist* (radical, cultural, or otherwise) does indeed place a question mark over the role of bisexual men. Instead, the panel isolates cultural/lesbian feminism as the reactionary force preventing male-female harmony, effectively positioning men as feminism's oppressed or excluded other, shifting the gaze away from male responsibility (as individuals or as a group) for the oppression of women. Clearly, women advocates of a humanist bisexual feminism at the conference use the term to mark out their position as "not lesbian" without having to state that as such. In the discussion after the panel presentations at the "Bisexuality and Feminism" workshop, one participant raises a series of questions about the relationship between bisexuality and feminism. She expresses doubts about bisexuality's ability to "fix men," and asks for more information and less rhetoric about the ways in which race, sex, and class may be aligned within a bisexual frame.[179] Her questions are greeted with a noticeable initial silence; when she is eventually answered it is with a further rhetorical invocation of an authentic bisexual self, whatever the context.

The "Bisexuality and Feminism" panel and the conference as a whole structure debates about feminism in such a way that even to suggest that sexism affects women and men differently, let alone that men might actually gain from current social power structures, is to invite a scorn generally reserved for the demon lesbian separatists of the bisexual imagination. The rest of the discussion after the panel reaffirms the separation of bisexual feminism from lesbian feminism, although the word *lesbian* is only mentioned once. In response to a question about the difference between sexuality and gender, Tom argues that we must remember that we are "dealing with messy, gray, human areas . . . more than [with] ideological dogmatic areas."[180] In the context of this panel Tom's statement may be read as referring to the complex area of bisexual men and women's (human) desire and the rigid oversimplifications of lesbian politics respectively. In the run up to the conference, bisexual space was located (as I illustrated) between and among lesbian, Hispanic, and gay male space in San Francisco. In the context of the conference itself, however, feminism is used as a mechanism for securing a bisexual space outside lesbianism rather than within it.

In the process of separating the terms *bisexual* and *lesbian*, the meaning of feminism in a bisexual context is altered, too. Tucker and Smith's original assertion was that without feminism women continue to be oppressed, which in turn has implications for relationships among men and women. In the course of the conference this has been transformed into the assumption that men and women are equally oppressed, such that bisexual feminism becomes a unifying and healing, rather than critical, practice. This deemphasizing of male responsibility for sexist oppression is endorsed by the conference committee in the later stages of organizing. In an article on oppression attached to the steering committee minutes of May 5, 1990, Charlie Kreiner argues, "As a white/male/ heterosexual and so forth, it is important to take complete pride in your humanity, not your roles. As a human, take pride in your inherent human qualities: that you are alive, have a right to exist, are completely good, innocent, blameless, whole, worthwhile, powerful."[181] This view, that subjects can detach themselves from the societal oppression that informs them (and thus be entirely blameless), sets the tone for the discourse of "equal harm" to be healed by bisexual feminism that circulates at the conference. Thus, although Christina writes positively about the role feminism played in the 1990 conference, concluding that "there was an overriding sentiment that one of the best things about the bisexual movement was that it inherently challenges traditional attitudes about sex roles and relations between men and women,"[182] the conference space depoliticizes feminism such that it becomes simply a question of individual soul-searching. In the clash between humanism and feminism, it is feminism that is forced to shift its boundaries. Christina's obvious pleasure at the fact that "almost everyone I spoke to . . . identified as feminist" highlights instead for me that in the conference context *feminist* has become little more than a label signifying bisexual agreement with a generalized desire for equality.[183] Thus, Christina writes that everyone she spoke to at the 1990 conference "felt strongly that feminism had an important and valuable place in their personal life," but that it should not become a "politically correct" agenda.[184] This desire for bisexuality to always already equal inclusion and equality rather ironically results in the denial of political, social, and individual differences.

Bisexual Multiculturalism

When viewed as the space in between lesbian and gay and straight communities, bisexual community is considered uniquely positioned to provide a home for, and a parallel to, other mélanges—of gender, as we have seen, and also of race. Thus, Margaret Mihee Choe suggests that "not being black or white in America may make bisexuality easier. One could even say that bisexuals are the Asians of sexual America: you're not one or the other, so you're overlooked."[185] Choe suggests that being neither "gay/straight" nor "black/white," bisexuality and Asian Americanness occupy parallel spaces of exclusion and facilitate one another. Alternatively, bisexuals are written contemporarily as the magpies of sexual culture, piecing together their identities from different locations: "Out of this comes a sense of a bisexual hybridity."[186] In these ways bisexuality is produced as either inherently or culturally situated in unique relation to communities and discourses of race. Brenda Marie Blasingame ties racial diversity and bisexuality together in a slightly different way, arguing that racism is one root of biphobia within lesbian and gay communities.[187] Blasingame explains that the model for a queer existence is a white model and that queers of color whose experiences do not "match up" to that model are often rejected on the grounds of being bisexual.[188] The presumed multiculturalism of the bisexual community serves the additional function of providing a platform of moral superiority for bisexuals to occupy in relation to a predominantly white U.S. lesbian and gay movement. I would argue, however, that merely because both bisexuals and other queers of color experience their relationship to lesbian and gay communities as compromised does not means that the two are fused in any more profound ways.

In reality, this discursive production of bisexuality and multicultural-ism as theoretical and cultural allies with singular insight into one another is set against the knowledge the organizers have that the confer-ence will undoubtedly reflect the wider U.S. bisexual community in being a predominantly white space. While white bisexuals may see bisexual identity as incorporating racial diversity, bisexuals of color apparently do not—and certainly not in significant enough numbers to transform the desire for inclusiveness into a visible reality through their presence at bisexual events. There is a marked gap between the conference committee's desire for bisexual space to be inherently racially diverse and their certain knowledge that it will not be. This provokes a similar politi-cization around issues of race and ethnicity as occurred around feminism. From the earliest stage of the conference planning, the organiz-ers employed a policy of affirmative action as an attempt to counteract the default whiteness of the bisexual community. Affirmative action on the grounds of race or ethnicity was not contested within the committee, or by conference participants, unlike the committee's politicization of bisexual space through feminism. This is partly because the 1990 NBC space is positioned within the predominant American fantasy of the United States as a multicultural "melting pot" and, more specifically, within San Francisco, where the activism of people of color has consid-erable influence and the racial and ethnic diversity of the population is highly visible. Within the terms of the National Bisexual Conference space itself, affirmative action for bisexuals of color is accepted because the belief that bisexuality is uniquely positioned in terms of multicultur-alism needs to be made visible if it is not to remain purely a metaphor. The conscious politicization around race, therefore, produces a paradox of sorts. On the one hand it undermines the assumption that bisexuality is always already racially diverse; while on the other it seeks to produce a nonwhite centrality to, and visibility within, the conference space such that the bisexual desire for inclusiveness, and the representation of that inclusiveness, are drawn closer together.

The need for political action to include people of color at the confer-ence was initially recognized by Loraine Hutchins. In October 1989 Hutchins wrote to the steering committee of ECBN requesting that "[a]ny 'surplus' funds in our ECBN account be allocated as scholarships for bisexual people of color and PWAs [people with AIDS] to enable both of these groups' attendance at the June 1990 conference in San Francisco, as well as to facilitate advertising efforts about the availability of this resource to these segments of our bi community."[189] Hutchins places this request in the context of "several incidents of racism [she] witnessed . . . at the May conference at [the ECBN conference at] Harvard."[190] She reasons that the bisexual community needs to stop viewing bisexuals as white—"People of color are not special exceptions or additions to 'us'"[191]—and that this will occur only when bisexuals of color are enabled to attend bisexual events. For Hutchins, this task involves an understanding of the structural and actual poverty of U.S. people of color and a fundamental shift of the bisexual community's existing (white) perspective. She concludes by insisting that real transformation requires a "thorough and on-going self-examination and reorientation of resources and consciousness toward addressing and changing this racism among us and beyond us."[192]

Hutchins's suggestions were adopted by the ECBN steering committee. The announcement, "ECBN Offers Scholarship Fund," issued in *Bi Women*, states, "First priority will be given to low income bisexual people of color."[193] The 1990 Bisexual Conference Steering Committee also made concerted efforts to guarantee that the conference would be as racially and ethnically diverse as possible. In an effort to reach a racially diverse population in San Francisco and coalition with other groups, the conference committee coorganized a benefit dance with members of the Asian Pacific Lesbian Retreat and the Men of Color conference in June 1989.[194] And as part of a larger education outreach strategy, the committee organized a plenary at the October 1989 National AIDS/ARC Update conference in San Francisco entitled "Finding Answers to the Problems of Reaching Bisexual Communities in Regards to AIDS Education, with Emphasis on People of Color."[195]

With respect to internal organizing, the Bisexual Conference Steering Committee agreed that each subcommittee should not begin conference planning until it had at least one person of color on it,[196] and it was impressed upon workshop presenters that their sessions should be relevant to people of color's experiences.[197] As a way of facilitating the racial diversity of workshops, the committee also offered resources for presenters who did not know where to find pertinent information. In November 1989 plans were laid for a People of Color Caucus to organize both before and during the conference.[198] The caucus was established to influence conference decisions, to provide a voice for bisexuals of color, and "to foster visible and diverse leadership in the bisexual movement."[199] Before the conference, the People of Color Caucus issued a statement about their aims and an invitation to participants, stating, "The 1990 conference is the place for us to put forth our issues. We are forming a caucus to build multi-cultural alliances that will help us organize out [*sic*] agenda for the 1990s. Our visibility will support bisexual people of color who are coming out of the lesbian/gay and heterosexual closets. The strength and challenge of our emerging bisexual community/movement is in our diversity. . . . Please contact us. Let us know what is going on with you and/or your local community/ movement. What do you want to see at the conference?"[200] The establishment of the People of Color Caucus suggested that the bisexual community had learned valuable lessons from the historical exclusions of "different liberation movements," and could avoid repeating those exclusions: "We don't have to begin at zero."[201]

During the conference itself, the committee continued to emphasize the centrality of racial diversity and bisexual inclusiveness in the formation of the national bisexual community. The People of Color workshop track had nine sessions (compared to six in the Feminism track), and the general assemblies usually included at least one speaker of color, and stressed the importance of racial diversity and political coalitions among different communities. For example, Susan Carlton of the UC-Berkeley Multicultural Bi/Gay/Lesbian Student Alliance relayed her experiences of coalition building between queers of color and bisexuals to force the campus gay and lesbian groups to become more inclusive of "both" groups.[202] Christina describes Carlton's story as one of the most inspiring of the conference.[203] Carlton's narrative is "inspiring" here because it demonstrates one of the prevailing assumptions of the conference— that bisexuals and people of color are natural allies—in a concrete political realm. In similar fashion, Ron Franklin, a conference organizer and member of the People of Color Caucus, underlined the conference committee's hope that the bisexual conference space (and bisexual community more generally) could be an environment where the desire for racial parity to be part of bisexual meaning is made visible. As Franklin noted at the time, "One thing we're trying to do in organizing this is to be very inclusive of men, women, people of color, differently-abled. The push is to see that followed through so that it's not just statements on paper, it's not just wording: that there are people of color, differently-abled people, people from different classes, so that it becomes a true, very involved, very inclusive organization that addresses the special needs of people across the board."[204]

Despite their best efforts at racial and ethnic inclusion, however, the conference committee discovered that they could not account for the attitudes or experiences of conference participants. Ka'ahumanu acknowledges that while "the representation of people of color from the stage was very well thought out," the majority of (white) workshop presenters still presumed a white bisexual audience.[205] According to Ka'ahumanu, members of the People of Color Caucus were amazed at the lack of "sophistication around challenging white supremacy" from white bisexual participants.[206] The caucus and the ECBN scholarships were originally intended as strategies for insuring that the conference/movement would not be predominantly or structurally white. In the course of the conference, however, the caucus's role shifted to become one of highlighting how the conference space consistently fell short of those intentions—how, in fact, racial diversity remained marginal rather than central to bisexual community. People of color expressed their concern and anger at their marginal position by walking out of conference workshops that did not address issues of racial diversity, or in their responses on the conference evaluation sheets. There are no statistics for the conference in terms of breakdown of participants along the lines of race or ethnicity. Of the thirty-seven conference evaluation sheets I have seen, 13.5 percent were completed by people of color. This should not be taken as a percentage of people of color at the conference, of course. It seems likely that a disproportionately high number of people of color filled out evaluation sheets in order to signal their disappointment at the lack of "racial inclusion" to the conference organizers and to suggest future improvements. Those filled out by people of color all attest to their disappointment at the whiteness of the conference, and their longing for a more genuine attention to ethnic and racial difference. Here are three examples:

> Diversity can't just be "declared." There has to be real listening to nonwhite, working class and differently-abled people.

> Despite the commendable efforts to do otherwise, I found the ambience of the conference definitely skewed toward a white countercultural sensibility that tended to exclude those of us from working class or people of color origins.

> The conference is too white. Why aren't there more People of Color here?[207]

Despite the evident dissatisfaction of people of color at the conference, Christina celebrates the conference's diversity in her postconference news article, writing, "Although the crowd was largely white, middle-class, educated, and able-bodied, it was not overwhelmingly so: there was a strong presence of disabled people and people of color, in significantly more than token numbers. An entire track of workshops focused specifically on bisexual people of color, and organizers and participants alike expressed a strong interest in creating a bisexual community that is multicultural and hospitable to any and all bisexuals and bi-friendlies."[208] Readers are clearly supposed to be impressed by the existence of an "*entire* track of workshops focused on bisexual people of color," but in light of the above conference evaluations one wonders for whom the conference was not "overwhelmingly" white, middle class, and so on, and who decides what constitutes "token numbers," "strong interest," or indeed "hospitality." Ka'ahumanu describes her shame at the realization that, because the conference felt safe to her as a light-skinned woman of color, she had assumed it was safe for everyone: "There [were] a lot of places around I-pass-for-white privilege that I didn't understand."[209] Clearly the conference was not experienced as multicultural by people of color whose inclusion many white delegates were celebrating as evidence of bisexual diversity.

The tensions generated over the question of the racial inclusiveness of bisexual space were particularly marked in the National Bisexual Network track discussions. The preliminary material on the "National Bisexual Network In-Formation" in the conference brochure makes it plain that the task of consolidating the network during the conference would not be an easy one: "We have a great deal of work ahead to reach our vision of a community-based national Network. Please join us and help realize the dream together."[210] From the beginning of the network organizing during the conference, "meetings were . . . frustrating because it took such a long time to make decisions and discuss ideas."[211] This process is exemplified in extended initial discussions about the name of the network. The name "North American Bisexual Network" was decided upon by participants at Friday's meetings, but the next day, the name was changed by consensus to "North American Multicultural Bisexual Network."[212] This consensus decision is described as a "painful process,"[213] and the source of "extreme tension,"[214] causing rifts among participants of the track. Gwen Riles, for example, was angered by what she perceived as the politically motivated "highjacking" of the strand, as opposed to genuine interest in building an inclusive national network, accusing "some of the people present" of "not [being] committed to looking for a solution that everyone could agree on and support."[215] The name was changed because of the predominant view that the omission of the term *multicultural* was racist and exclusionary. This perception was strengthened by the fact that there were no people of color at the Friday afternoon meeting, as the meeting time conflicted with the meeting of the People of Color Caucus. A further NBN meeting had been planned for Friday evening at the Women's Building, but was canceled when the organizers realized that the meeting would clash, once again, with the meeting of the People of Color Caucus, and was not wheelchair accessible.[216] As Michele Moore notes, "The lack of diversity in the first two days of planning the Network was obviously a major problem."[217] Other participants of the Network track argued that since the majority of people in the United States bisexual community are white, the inclusion of the term *multicultural* would be inaccurate and tokenistic.[218] After a consensus decision to include the term was reached, organizers emphasized the need to ensure that the term not be a substitute for real efforts at racial and ethnic inclusion, noting, "Much work has to go into the multicultural development of the Network. This should be emphasized in the next meeting . . . Meetings of the Network should not interfere with any of the Multicultural events. The Network should clearly state it's [sic] commitment to Multicultural issues."[219] The addition of the term *multicultural* serves, then, as an indicator of both the bisexual community's sense of its own diversity, and of its apparent lack of diversity. Conference participants continued to be confused over what to call the national network, despite the fact that at the following meeting, *multicultural* was dropped once again. The struggle over the naming of a national bisexual network reflects broader struggles within the conference over the relationship between bisexuality and racial and ethnic identities—struggles that remain unresolved.

Race and gender are, clearly, central to the conference space, but not in terms of an inherent bisexual inclusiveness of all genders, races, and ethnicities. The centrality of race and gender to bisexual identity and community resides in the extent to which their contested position within bisexuality structures the emergence and experiences of this bisexual space. Where the 1990 Bisexual conference space is inclusive, this is not because of an innate bisexual ability to transcend difference, but because it is a site where organizers and participants are forced to negotiate the mechanisms of power that produce bisexual difference.

The 1990 NBC space is interesting precisely because it crystalizes the oscillation between bisexual *innocence* and bisexual *identity*. The nostalgia for a "future perfect" bisexual innocence rubs shoulders with the knowledge that identity formation produces particular exclusions. In that respect, the 1990 National Bisexual Conference space is not a middle ground uniting heterosexual and homosexual, white and black, or male and female, as organizers and participants initially wished. It is, rather, a space where the assumptions constituting that desire for bisexuality to occupy the middle ground are made manifest. Jo Eadie remarks that the desire for bisexuality to be inclusive in and of itself can be a way of forgetting "the fact that we are always caught up in *conflicts* of class, gender and 'race.' "[220] In the context of the conference, that same desire means that the conflicts cannot be forgotten. From early on, the conference committee realized that bisexual space and identity needed to be identified with some identities and practices, and differentiated from others, if it was not to replicate dominant discourses of power. In that sense, the process of creating the conference space is also a process of becoming bisexual, of differentiating bisexuality from other forms of sexuality, and of trying to do so ethically. Earlier in the chapter I cited Ka'ahumanu's playful queer reference to Dorothy in *The Wizard of Oz* in the final plenary of the conference: "Standing here today, I feel like I've clicked my heels three times and come home."[221] Then it stood as evidence of the discourse of the conference as a safe bisexual home; now it can be reread as an expression of the knowledge that home is where you wake up when the dream evaporates.

Part 3: Conclusion

Throughout this book I have sought to challenge the notion of bisexual location as the unquestioned, abstracted middle ground uniting hetero-sexuality and homosexual opposition. In doing so, I have endeavored to highlight the complex ways in which bisexuality is culturally, politically, and discursively positioned. I want briefly here to reflect on some of the ways in which bisexuality takes up space, bringing together some of the threads that run through this genealogy of bisexual meaning as a whole.

First, I contend that if we consider bisexual meaning in spatial terms, it becomes clear that bisexuality is not only a location between hetero-sexuality and homosexuality, binary genders or sexes, but also resides at the heart of lesbian community, between lesbian and gay communities, and in parallel with transsexuality within queer feminist terrain. As a result, a bisexual subject is capable of producing knowledge that is at odds with dominant and community formations of sexuality and gender, and for that reason alone is worth attending to.

Second, I have sought to show that where bisexuality meaning *is* generated from its position positioned as normative or transgressive middle ground, this is commonly the result of an abstraction of bisexual experience rather than an engagement with its specificities. Both kinds of bisexual abstraction exist in necessary tension with the bisexual cartogra-phies above, and are frequently part of an attempt to reposition bisexuality in order to reproduce and secure dominant discourses of sexuality and gender more generally. In the lesbian community context of Northampton, Massachusetts for example, women's bisexuality is described as occupying the normative middle ground between lesbian and heterosexual male spaces in order that the subject of lesbian territory not come under scrutiny. In queer feminist terrain, bisexual and transsexual subjects carry the weight of lesbian and gay desires for the queer subject to remain homosexual. And in San Francisco, bisexuality as transcendent middle ground between sexed, gendered, and raced "opposites" enables the continuation of a bisexual fantasy of inclusiveness. In the first two contexts, bisexuality is relentlessly produced as normative and then blamed for its failure to be subversive. In the latter context, bisexuality is equally relentlessly produced as subversive, its production within dominant discourse conveniently overlooked.

Third, I hope I have gone some way in showing that where bisexual identity or community is the result of these struggles over bisexual meaning, it is frequently at the expense of the specific nature of bisexual political and cultural location. When community is invoked rather than traced, and particularly where this relies on the abstraction of bisexual-ity as transcendent middle ground, the effect is either a lack of sustainable community, as in the Northampton context, or the rhetorical reproduc-tion of bisexuality as more inclusive of polarized differences than other identities or communities. In the former case, this seems to confirm accusations of bisexual inauthenticity; in the latter, it begs the question of which exclusions are not being attended to and why. In fact, attention to the conflicts of bisexual meaning in all these contexts yields a more interesting, more accurate, picture of the terrain in question and, I hope, offers a range of ways in which theorists and activists might take bisexual inquiry foward. Throughout this book I have indicated the ways in which and the extent to which the various vested interests in bisexuality as the abstract middle ground of sexual and gendered terrain actively prevent the tracing of different bisexual meaning, seeking as they do to universalize rather than particularize bisexuality.

In genealogical terms I believe this research also shows not just the problems with the fusion of dominant bisexual meaning with bisexual subjects, but the theoretical and political potency of meaning just prior to discursive (re)consolidation of the bisexual middle ground. A focus on bisexual locations within lesbian community, or on dissonant, partial bisexual narratives and temporalization, allows us to glimpse alternative alignments of sexual and gendered meaning that are culturally answerable, rather than discursively overdetermined. I want to be clear that I do not conceive of these alignments as "new," in the sense of dispensing with dominant formations, but I do think that they can seem impossible to articulate. As an example, take May Wolf's mismatching sense of the relationships among her desire, identity, and community that I discussed in chapter 2, which could so easily be refigured as straightforward heterosexism. An approach to bisexual meaning that focuses on its location within and among different spaces allows us to imagine a lesbian history with May Wolf, as one subject among, without needing Wolf to claim a bisexual identity.

To take bisexual knowledges seriously, then, is important not just in order that we may tell a more complex story of bisexuality—though this is significant in its own right. A focus on local bisexual knowledges found elsewhere, those not fully circumscribed by dominant formations of heterosexuality and homosexuality, also provides a strategy for resisting the narrativization of heterosexual and homosexual histories that rely on a denial of bisexual specificity. Instead of celebrating dubious bisexual transgressions of sex, gender, and sexual oppositions, I advocate an approach that insists that bisexuality's capacity to generate radical reconfigurations of those oppositions resides not outside but within social and cultural meaning.

NOTES

Introduction

1. There are some exceptions. Particularly important for this book have been the following lesbian inquiries into bisexual meaning: Jan Clausen, "My Interesting Condition," *Journal of Sex Research* 27. 3 (1990): 445–59, which provoked extended discussion of opposite sex behavior and lesbian identity in the pages of *Out/Look*, where it was republished in the same year; Julia Creet, "Anxieties of Identity: Coming Out and Coming Undone," in *Negotiating Lesbian and Gay Subjects*, ed. M. Dorenkamp and R. Henke (New York: Routledge), 179–99, and Paula C. Rust, *Bisexuality and the Challenge to Lesbian Politics: Sex, Loyalty and Revolution* (New York: New York University Press, 1995).

2. Jo Eadie, "Activating Bisexuality: Towards a Bi/Sexual Politics," in *Activating Theory Lesbian, Gay, Bisexual Politics*, ed. Joseph Bristow and Angelia Wilson (London: Lawrence and Wishart, 1993), 139–70; Maria Pramaggiore, "BI-ntroduction I: Epistemologies of the Fence," in *RePresenting Bisexualities: Subjects and Cultures of Fluid Desire*, ed. Donald E. Hall and Maria Pramaggiore (New York: New York University Press, 1996), 1–7; Elizabeth D. Däumer, "Queer Ethics; or, the Challenge of Bisexuality to Lesbian Ethics," Special Issue: Lesbian Philosophy, *Hypatia: a Journal of Feminist Philosophy* 7. 4 (1992): 91–105; Amber Ault, "Ambiguous Identity in an Unambiguous Sex/Gender Structure: The Case of Bisexual Women," *Sociological Quarterley* 37. 3 (1996): 449–63; Amber Ault, "Hegemonic Discourse in an Oppositional Community: Lesbian Feminist Stigmatization of Bisexual Women," in *Queer Studies: A Lesbian, Gay, Bisexual, and Transgender Anthology*, ed. Brett Beemyn and Mickey Eliason (New York: New York University Press, 1996), 204–16; Ann Kaloski, "Bisexuals Making Out with Cyborgs: Politics, Pleasure, Con/fusion," *Journal of Gay, Lesbian, and Bisexual Identity* 2. 1 (1997): 47–64; Merl Storr, ed., Steven Angelides, *A History of Bisexuality* (Chicago: University of Chicago Press, 2001). *Bisexuality: A Critical Reader* (London: Routledge, 1999), 1–12; Mariam Fraser, *Identity without Selfhood: Simone de Beauvoir and Bisexuality* (Cambridge: Cambridge University Press, 1999).

3. *Monosexuality* is the term bisexual writers commonly use to indicate desire for only one sex. I discuss the strategic use of this term to produce a viable bisexual identity in chapter 1.

4. Hélène Cixous, "Sorties: Out and Out: Attacks/Ways/Forays," trans. Betsy Wing, in *The Newly Born Woman*, ed. Hélène Cixous and Catherine Clément (Manchester: Manchester University Press, 1986), 63–132.

5. See, for example, Kathleen Bennett, "Feminist Bisexuality: A Both/And Option for an Either/Or World," in *Closer to Home: Bisexuality and*

Feminism, ed. Elizabeth Reba Weise (Seattle: Seal Press, 1992), 205–32; and Yasmin Prabhudas, "Bisexuals and People of Mixed-Race: Arbiters of Change," in *Bisexual Horizons: Politics, Histories, Lives*, ed. Sharon Rose, Cris Stevens et al. / Off Pink Collective (London: Lawrence and Wishart, 1996), 30–31.

6. Hall and Pramaggiore, eds., *RePresenting Bisexualities*, is exemplary in this regard.

7. Michael du Plessis, "Blatantly Bisexual; or, Unthinking Queer Theory," in Hall and Pramaggiore, eds., *RePresenting Bisexualities* 22–23.

8. See, for example, Sandra Harding, *Whose Science? Whose Knowledge? Thinking from Women's Lives* (Milton Keynes: Open University Press, 1991).

9. I analyze these exclusions in the development of bisexual conference spaces in chapter 4.

10. An early forerunner to this widely held view of bisexual identity as an indicator of particular mental health among bisexual activists and writers is Fritz Klein, *The Bisexual Option: a Concept of One-Hundred Percent Intimacy* (New York: Arbor House, 1978).

11. Off Pink Publishing, *Bisexual Lives* (London: Off Pink Publishing, 1988); Sue George, *Women and Bisexuality* (London: Scarlet Press, 1993).

12. Loraine Hutchins and Lani Ka'ahumanu, eds., *Bi Any Other Name: Bisexual People Speak Out* (Boston: Alyson Publications, 1991); Elizabeth Reba Weiser, ed., *Closer to Home*.

13. Rose and Stevens, eds., *Bisexual Horizons*; Naomi Tucker, ed., *Bisexual Politics: Theories, Queeries, & Visions* (New York: Harrington Park Press, 1995).

14. Creet, 179. I raise this issue briefly in "Locating Bisexual Identities: Discourses of Bisexuality and Contemporary Feminist Theory," in *Mapping Desire: Geographies of Sexualities*, eds., David Bell and Gill Valentine (London: Routledge, 1995), 41–55.

15. Jonathan Dollimore, "Bisexuality, Heterosexuality and Wishful Theory," *Textual Practice* 10. 3 (1996): 523–39.

16. Dollimore singles out two articles—one mine, the other Jo Eadie's—for critique. See Clare Hemmings, "Resituating the Bisexual Body: From Identity to Difference," 118–38, and Eadie, "Activating Bisexuality," 139–70 both in Bristow Wilson, eds., *Activating Theory*.

17. Storr, ed., *Bisexuality: A Critical Reader* 1.

18. Eve Kosofsky Sedgwick, *The Epistemology of the Closet* (New York: Harvester Wheatsheaf, 1991).

19. Sedgwick, "Introduction: Axiomatic," in ibid., 16.

20. Sedgwick, "Bi," "Queer Studies List," qstudyl@ubvm.cc.buffalo.edu, as of August 17, 1994.

21. Merl Storr, "The Sexual Reproduction of 'Race': Bisexuality, History and Racialisation," in *The Bisexual Imaginary: Representation, Identity and Desire*, ed. Bi Academic Intervention (London: Cassell, 1997), 73–88.

22. Sedgwick, "Introduction: Axiomatic," 27; emphasis in the original.

23. Ibid., 44–48.

24. Judith Halberstam, *Female Masculinity* (Durham: Duke University Press, 1998), 53.

25. Sedgwick, "Introduction: Axiomatic," 48.
26. Ibid., 26.
27. Ibid.; emphasis in the original.
28. Ibid.
29. Judith Butler, *Bodies That Matter: On the Discursive Limits of "Sex"* (New York: Routledge, 1993), and *The Psychic Life of Power: Theories in Subjection* (Stanford, CA: Stanford University Press, 1997); and Halberstam, *Female Masculinity*. I understand Halberstam as concerned with both a Sedgwickian historiographic and Butlerian performative project.
30. Judith Butler, *Gender Trouble: Feminism and the Subversion of Identity* (New York: Routledge, 1990), 31.
31. The relationship between queer theorists and a potential bisexual performativity forms the basis of chapter 3, so I restrict my framing remarks to Butler's work here.
32. Butler, "Melancholy Gender/ Refused Identification," in *The Psychic Life of Power*, 132–50.
33. Butler, *Gender Trouble*, 54, 57–77.
34. Alisa Solomon, "Strike a Pose," *Village Voice*, November 1991: 13–19, cited in du Plessis, 34.
35. Ault, "Hegemonic Discourse in an Oppositional Community," 206.
36. I have discussed the overlap between queer narration of bisexual and femme narratives in two previous articles. See Clare Hemmings, "Waiting for No Man: Bisexual Femme Subjectivity and Cultural Repudiation," in *Butch/Femme: Inside Lesbian Gender*, ed. Sally Munt (London: Cassell, 1998), 90–100, 234–38, and "'All My Life I've Been Waiting for Something:' Theorising Femme Narrative in *The Well of Loneliness*," in *Palatable Poison: Critical Perspectives on The Well of Loneliness Past and Present*, ed. Laura Doan and Jay Prosser (New York: Columbia University Press, 2001).
37. Ault, "Hegemonic Discourse in an Oppositional Community," 214.
38. Sedgwick, "Introduction: Axiomatic," 23.
39. Mariam Fraser also discusses the role of confession in the fashioning of a bisexual self, although she focuses on the public confession that relieves guilt to produce a viable subjectivity, where I am more concerned with the *incitement to confess* as structuring bisexual experience of intimacy in politically specific ways. Fraser, *Identity Without Selfhood*, 14–18.
40. I provide an account of this increase in chapter 1.
41. Gordon Brent Ingram, Anne-Marie Boutillette, and Yolanda Retter, "Marginality and the Landscapes of Erotic Alien(n)ations," in *Queers In Space: Communities, Public Places, Sites of Resistance* (Seattle: Bay Press, 1997), 13.

Chapter 1: Bisexual Spaces

1. An earlier version of the first part of this chapter was published as "Bisexual Theoretical Perspectives: Emergent and Contingent Relationships," in Bi Academic Intervention, ed. *The Bisexual Imaginary: Representation, Identity and Desire* (London: Cassell, 1997), 14–37.
2. Margaret Mead, "Bisexuality: What's It All About?" *Redbook* (January 1975): 29, 31; Charlotte Wolff, *Bisexuality: A Study* (London: Quartet,

1977); Fritz Klein, *The Bisexual Option: a Concept of One-Hundred Percent Intimacy* (New York: Arbor House, 1978).

3. Other writings that formed part of this renewed interest in bisexuality qua bisexuality in the mid-1970s include Julius Fast and Hal Wells, *Bisexual Living* (New York: Pocket Books, 1975); Philip Blumstein and Pepper Schwartz, "Bisexuality in Women," *Archives of Sexual Behaviour* 5 (1976): 171–81; and Janet Bode, *A View from Another Closet: Exploring Bisexuality in Women* (New York: Hawthorn, 1976).

4. Alfred Kinsey, Wardell Pomeroy et al., *Sexual Behavior in the Human Male* (Philadelphia: W.B. Saunders, 1948), 656.

5. Ibid., 656–59.

6. Ibid., 656–57.

7. Mead, 29. It is not clear why there was a gap in work on bisexuality from 1953 until the mid 1970s: work on bisexuality in this period still needs to be done. Gayle Rubin has written on probable causes of silence and repression of deviant sexual behavior in the 1950s and 1960s, but does not include bisexuality as a deviant sexuality. Gayle Rubin, "Thinking Sex: Notes for a Radical Theory of the Politics of Sexuality," in *Pleasure and Danger: Exploring Female Sexuality*, ed. Carole Vance (New York: Routledge, 1984), 269–91.

8. Clearly, "same" and "opposite-sex" sex has occurred, and been represented, since before the twentieth century. I am interested in tracing the contemporary meanings of the term *bisexual* in this book, however, and not with the development of a transhistorical account of bisexual desire.

9. Sigmund Freud, "Three Essays on the Theory of Sexuality," in *On Sexuality: Three Essays on the Theory of Sexuality and Other Works*, ed. Angela Richards; ed. James Strachey (London: Penguin, 1905), The penguin Freud Library, 55. Freud's position on bisexuality was not consistent, however, in line with his changing understandings of femininity and masculinity. I discuss this issue in more depth in chapter 3.

10. Magnus Hirschfeld, *Die Homosexualitat des Mannes und des Weibes* (Berlin: Louis Marcus, 1914); Otto Weininger, *Sex and Character* (London: William Heinemann, 1903).

11. Wilhelm von Krafft-Ebing, *Psychopathia Sexualis* (1886; Philadelphia: F. A. Davis Company, 1903); Havelock Ellis, *Studies in the Psychology of Sex, Volume 2: Sexual Inversion* (1897; Philadelphia: F. A. Davis Company, 1915).

12. Wilhelm Stekel, *Bisexual Love* (New York: Phsyicians and Surgeons Books, 1934).

13. Virginia Woolf, *Orlando: a Biography* (London: Hogarth Press, 1928); Radclyffe Hall, *The Well of Loneliness* (London: Jonathan Cape, 1928). *The Well of Loneliness* makes this trajectory explicit both by sexological reference within the pages of the text, and through its commentary on the 1928 edition by Havelock Ellis.

14. Off Pink Publishing, *Bisexual Lives* (London: Off Pink Publishing, 1988); Thomas Geller, ed., *Bisexuality: a Reader and Sourcebook* (Ojai, California: Times Change Press, 1990).

15. See the following: Loraine Hutchins and Lani Ka'ahumanu, eds., *Bi Any Other Name: Bisexual People Speak Out* (Boston: Alyson Publications, 1991); Elizabeth Reba Weise, ed., *Closer to Home: Bisexuality and Fem-*

inism (Seattle: Seal Press, 1992); Naomi Tucker, ed., *Bisexual Politics: Theories, Queeries, & Visions* (New York and London: Harrington Park Press, 1995); Beth A. Firestein, ed., *Bisexuality: the Psychology and Politics of an Invisible Minority* (London: Sage, 1996). See also the Bisexual Anthology Collective, *Plural Desires: Writing Bisexual Women's Realities* (Toronto: Sister Vision Press 1995), which is Canadian, but follows a similar format, although with a more sustained focus on bisexual women of color.

16. Sue George, *Women and Bisexuality* (London: Scarlet Press, 1993); Sharon Rose, Cris Stevens, et al./Off Pink Collective, eds., *Bisexual Horizons* (London: Lawrence and Wishart, 1996).

17. See, for example, Sharon Gonsalves, "On Bisexuals in the Lesbian Community," viewpoint, *Sojourner* (May 1989): 7–8, and Amanda Udis-Kessler, "Identity/Politics: A History of the Bisexual Movement," in Tucker, ed., *Bisexual Politics*: 17–30.

18. Weise, introduction to *Closer to Home*, ix.

19. The close relationship of bisexuality and feminism is by no means uncontested, however. I discuss the debates around the role of feminism within the U.S. bisexual community in chapter 4.

20. Fritz Klein, Barry Sepekoff, and Timothy Wolf, "Sexual Orienation: a Multi-variable Dynamic Process," Special edition on bisexuality, ed. Fritz Klein and Timothy Wolf, *The Journal of Homosexuality* 11. 1–2 (1985); Ron Fox, "Bisexuality in Perspective: a Review of Theory and Research," in Firestein, ed., *Bisexuality: The Psychology and Politics of an Invisible Minority*, 3–50.

21. For example: R. A. P. Tielman, M. Carballo and A. C. Hendrks, eds. *Bisexuality and HIV/AIDS: a Global Perspective* (Amherst, NY: Prometheus Books, 1991). Mark David, Gary Dowsett, and Ullo Klemmer, "On the Beat: A Report on the Bisexually Active Men's Outreach Project," in Rose and Stevens, eds., *Bisexual Horizons* 188–99; P. Aggleton, ed., *Bisexualities and AIDS: International Perspectives* (London: Taylor and Francis, 1996).

22. Naomi Tucker, "Bay Area Bisexual History: An Interview with David Lourea," in Tucker, ed., *Bisexual Politics*, 47–61. While researching this book I made use of the David Lourea Archives housed at the San Francisco Public Library.

23. Erich Steinman and Brett Beemyn, eds., "Bisexuality in the Lives of Men," special issue of *Journal of Bisexuality* 1. 2/3 (2001).

24. Jill Nagle, ed., *Whores and Other Feminists* (New York: Routledge, 1996); Annie Sprinkle, *Post-Porn Modernist* (San Francisco: Cleis Press, 1998); Carol Queen and Lawrence Schimel, eds., *Pomosexuals: Challenging Assumptions about Gender and Sexuality* (San Francisco: Cleis Press, 1997); Debra R. Kolodny, *Blessed Bi Spirit* (London: Continuum, 2000); there has also been a special issue of *Anything That Moves* on bi-trans coalitions; *Anything That Moves* 17 (1998).

25. *Bi Community News* 47 (2001).

26. *Bi Community News* 48 (2001).

27. BiCon 2001 was held in Coventry, England, August 25–27, 2001. See http://2001.bicon.org.uk/. BiCon's permanent website is http://bi.org/~bicon.

28. *Anything That Moves* is a relatively glossy magazine with feature articles, national and local advertisers, and its own merchandise. *Bi Community News* looks more like a local newsletter. See also Robyn Ochs, ed., *The Bisexual Resource Guide* (Cambridge, MA: Bisexual Resource Center), which is updated and reprinted annually.

29. National bisexual conferences began much later in the United States and take place less regularly than in Britain. For reasons of distance, it is more difficult to organize a National Bisexual Conference in the United States and more difficult and more expensive for people to attend than in Britain.

30. "Unity in Diversity: the Many Faces of Bi and Queer in the Americas," The North American Conference on Bisexuality, Gender and Sexual Diversity, August 9–12, 2001, University of British Columbia, Vancouver. I critically discuss this invocation of "unity" and "diversity" employed in the formation of bisexual conference spaces in chapter 4.

31. For an examination of the implications for bisexual desire of sex and gender "passing" in chat rooms, see Ann Kaloski, "Bisexuals Making Out with Cyborgs: Politics, Pleasure, Con/fusion," bisexual special issue, ed. Sharon Morris and Merl Storr, *Journal of Gay, Lesbian, and Bisexual Identity* 2. 1 (1997) 47–64. The *Anything That Moves* web page has an extensive bisexual resources listing section, including information on Internet resources; see http://www.anythingthatmoves.com/resources.htm/.

32. Information on the GLBT Historical Society can be accessed through their web page at http://www.glhs.org/baseinfo/glhsmisn.htm.

33. Merl Storr, review of *Vice Versa: Bisexuality and the Eroticism of Everyday Life*, by Marjorie Garber, *Bisexual Horizons* by Rose and Stevens, eds., and *Bisexuality and the Challenge to Lesbian Politics: Sex, Loyalty and Revolution*, by Paula Rust, *Feminist Review* 58 (1998): 103.

34. Elizabeth D. Däumer, "Queer Ethics; or, the Challenge of Bisexuality to Lesbian Ethics," special issue: lesbian philosophy, *Hypatia: a Journal of Feminist Philosophy* 7. 4 (1992): 91–105

35. The last Bi-Academic Intervention day conference was "Performing Bisexualities" at the University of York, November 1995.

36. Bi Academic Intervention, ed., *The Bisexual Imaginary: Representation, Identity and Desire* (London: Cassell, 1997); bisexual special issue, ed. Sharon Morris and Merl Storr, *Journal of Gay, Lesbian, and Bisexual Identity* 2. 1 (1997).

37. See Merl Storr, ed., *Bisexuality: a Critical Reader* (London: Routledge, 1999); and Mariam Fraser, *Identity without Selfhood: Simone de Beauvoir and Bisexuality* (Cambridge: Cambridge University Press, 1999).

38. Donald E. Hall and Maria Pramaggiore, eds., *RePresenting Bisexualities: Subjects and Cultures of Fluid Desire* (New York: New York University Press, 1996); Paula C. Rodríguez Rust, ed., *Bisexuality in the United States: A Social Science Reader* (New York: Columbia University, 2000).

39. Paula Rust, *Bisexuality and the Challenge to Lesbian Politics: Sex, Loyalty and Revolution* (New York: New York University Press, 1995), and Martin S. Weinberg, Colin J. Williams, and Douglas W. Pryor, eds., *Dual Attraction: Understanding Bisexuality* (New York: Oxford University Press, 1994) exemplify an empirical sociological approach to bisexuality.

40. Amber Ault, "Ambiguous Identity in an Unambiguous Sex/Gender Structure," *Sociological Quarterly* 37. 3 (1996): 449–63; and "Hegemonic Discourse in an Oppositional Community: Lesbian Feminists and Bisexuality," *Critical Sociology* 20. 3 (1994): 107–22.
41. *Journal of Bisexuality* 1. 1 (2000).
42. Paula C. Rust, "Two Many and Not Enough: the Meanings of Bisexual Identities," *Journal of Bisexuality* 1. 1 (2000): 31–68. Karen Yescavage and Jonathan Alexander, "Visibility: a Call for a Critical Update," *Journal of Bisexuality* 1. 1 (2000).
43. Steven Angelides, *A History of Bisexuality* (Chicago: Chicago University Press, 2001).
44. David Bell and Gill Valentine, eds., *Mapping Desire: Geographies of Sexualities* (London: Routledge, 1995); Gordon Brent Ingram, Anne-Marie Bouthillette, and Yolanda Retter, eds., *Queers In Space: Communities, Public Places, Sites of Resistance* (Seattle: Bay Press, 1997).
45. Lucy Bland and Laura Doan, eds., *Sexology in Culture: Labelling Bodies and Desires* (Cambridge: Polity, 1998); Lucy Bland and Laura Doan, eds., *Sexology Uncensored: the Documents of Sexual Science* (Cambridge: Polity, 1998).
46. S. O. Weisser and J. Fleischner, eds., *Feminist Nightmares: Women at Odds* (New York: New York University Press, 1994).
47. See, for example, Sally Munt, ed., *Butch/Femme: Inside Lesbian Gender* (London: Cassell, 1998); Andrew Medhurst and Sally Munt, eds., *Lesbian and Gay Studies: A Critical Introduction* (London: Cassell, 1998); Shane Phelan, ed., *Playing with Fire: Queer Politics, Queer Theories* (New York: Routledge, 1997).
48. See, for example, Joseph Bristow and Angelia Wilson, eds., *Activating Theory: Lesbian, Gay, Bisexual Politics* (London: Lawrence and Wishart, 1993). The *International Journal of Sexuality and Gender Studies*, ed. Warren Blumenfeld (New York: Human Sciences Press) has a bisexual-inclusive editorial board and demonstrates consistent inclusion of bisexual work.
49. Brett Beemyn and Mickey Eliason, eds., *Queer Studies: A Lesbian, Gay, Bisexual and Transgender Anthology* (New York: New York University Press, 1996), contains four articles with bisexuality as their central theme, and two articles on transgender theory, whereas Phelan, ed., *Playing with Fire*, has a single article on bisexuality and none on transgendered theory or politics.
50. Diana Fuss, "Inside/Out," in *Inside/Out: Lesbian Theories, Gay Theories*, ed. Diana Fuss (New York: Routledge, 1991); Teresa de Lauretis, "Queer Theory: Lesbian and Gay Sexualities: An Introduction," *Differences: a Journal of Feminist Cultural Studies* 3. 2 (1991): iii–xvii.
51. Shane Phelan, *Getting Specific: Postmodern Lesbian Politics* (Minneapolis: University of Minnesota Press, 1994), 96; emphasis added.
52. Phelan, *Getting Specific*, 152.
53. Pat Califia, "Gay Men, Lesbians, and Sex: Doing It Together," *Public Sex: The Culture of Radical Sex* (San Francisco: Cleis Press, 1994), 183–89; Julia Creet, "Anxieties of Identity: Coming Out and Coming Undone," in *Negotiating Lesbian and Gay Subjects* ed. M. Durenkamp and R. Henke (New York: Routledge, 1995), 179–99.

54. Creet 186. Significantly for this discussion, although speaking from a lesbian subject position when *Public Sex* was published, Califia has subsequently come to occupy a bisexual and transgendered subject position.

55. Marjorie Garber, *Vice Versa: Bisexuality and the Eroticism of Everyday Life* (New York: Simon and Schuster, 1995); Jonathan Dollimore, "Bisexuality, Heterosexuality, and Wishful Theory," *Textual Practice* 10. 3 (1996) 523–39.

56. Storr, review (see note 33), 105–6.

57. Dollimore, 529.

58. Malcolm Bowie, "Bisexuality," in *Feminism and Psychoanalysis: A Critical Dictionary*, ed. Elisabeth Wright (Oxford: Basil Blackwell, 1992), 26.

59. Kinsey, Pomeroy et al., 657.

60. Eve Kosofsky Sedgwick, "Introduction: Axiomatic," in *The Epistemology of the Closet* (New York: Harvester Wheatsheaf, 1991), 1–63.

61. Kinsey, Pomeroy et al., 657.

62. Freud, 66–67.

63. David Bell, "Perverse Dynamics, Sexual Citizenship, and the Transformation of Intimacy," In Bell and Valentine, eds., *Mapping Desire*, 304–317.

64. Judith Butler, "Melancholy Gender/Refused Identification," in *The Psychic Life of Power: Theories in Subjection* (Stanford, CA: Stanford University Press, 1997), 132–50.

65. Ann Kaloski makes this tentative connection in "Following my Thumbs: Towards a Methodology for a Bisexual Reading," Ph.D. diss., University of York, 1997.

66. Fraser, 14–15.

67. For accounts of the relationship between gender, sexuality and narrative in the formation of the contemporary subject, see Teresa de Lauretis, "Desire in Narrative," in *Alice Doesn't: Feminism, Semiotics, Cinema* (Bloomington: Indiana University Press); Kenneth Plummer, *Telling Sexual Stories: Power, Change and Social Worlds* (London: Routledge, 1995); and Judith Roof, *Come As You Are: Sexuality and Narrative* (New York: Columbia University Press, 1996).

68. Ann Kaloski, "Returning to the Lesbian *Bildungsroman*: a Bisexual Reading of Nancy Toder's *Choices*," in Bi Academic Intervention, ed., *The Bisexual Imaginary*, 90. In this article, Kaloski beautifully complicates the dismissal of lesbian coming out narratives as dull and pejoratively repetitive, arguing that it is precisely in this repetition that "the potential, indeed probability, of 'mistake', and of change" resides. Ibid., 92.

69. Deborah Gregory, "From Where I Stand: A Case for Feminist Bisexuality" in Sue Cartledge and Joanna Ryan, ed., *Sex and Love* (London: The Women's Press, 1983), 150.

70. Clare, in Off Pink Publishing, *Bisexual Lives*, 27.

71. See note 66.

72. Momin Rahman, *Sexuality and Democracy: Identities and Strategies in Lesbian and Gay Politics* (Edinburgh: Edinburgh University Press, 2000).

73. David Bell and Jon Binnie discuss these problems in *The Sexual Citizen: Queer Politics and Beyond* (Cambridge: Polity Press, 2000).

74. Mead, 29.
75. Stekel, cited in Garber, 202; emphasis in the original.
76. Hutchins and Ka'ahumanu, 370.
77. Liz A. Highleyman, "Identity and Ideas: Strategies for Bisexuals," in Tucker, ed., *Bisexual Politics*, 86.
78. Ibid., 87.
79. Elias Farajajé-Jones, "Fluid Desire: Race, HIV/AIDS, and Bisexual Politics," in Tucker, ed., *Bisexual Politics* 119–21.
80. Warren Blumenfeld and Clare Hemmings, "Reading 'Monosexual,' " *Journal of Gay, Lesbian, and Bisexual Identity* 1. 4 (1996): 319.
81. Ault, cited in Storr, ed., *Bisexuality*, 169.
82. Mariana Valverde, cited in Storr, *Bisexuality*, 115.
83. George, 4–24; Amanda Udis-Kessler, "Challenging the Stereotypes," in Rose and Stevens, eds., *Bisexual Horizons*, 45–57.
84. Garber, 206.
85. Cited in Jean Ulrick Désert, "Queer Space," in Ingram, Bouthillette, and Retter, eds., *Queers In Space*, 20.
86. Klein, 147–48.
87. Garber, 354–55.
88. Bi Academic Intervention, introduction, 3–4.
89. Bi Academic Intervention, editors' roundtable discussion, 208; emphasis in the original.
90. See Stephen Whittle, "The Becoming Man: The Law's Ass Brays," *Reclaiming Genders: Transsexual Grammars at the Fin de Siècle*, eds. Kate More and Stephen Whittle (London: Cassell, 1999), 15–33.
91. Däumer, 98.
92. Clare Hemmings, "Resituating the Bisexual Body: From Identity to Difference," *Activating Theory: Lesbian, Gay, Bisexual Politics*, ed. Joseph Bristow and Angelia Wilson (London: Lawrence and Wishart, 1993), 136.
93. Maria Pramaggiore, "BI-ntroduction I: Epistemologies of the Fence," in Hall and Pramaggiore, eds., *RePresenting Bisexualities*, 3.
94. Pramaggiore, "BI-ntroduction I," 3. See also Christopher James, "Denying Complexity: the Dismissal and Appropriation of Bisexuality in Queer, Lesbian, and Gay Theory," in Beemyn and Eliason, eds., *Queer Studies*, 217–40.
95. Stacey Young, "Dichotomies and Displacement: Bisexuality in Queer Theory," in Phelan, ed., *Playing With Fire*, 69.
96. Merl Storr, "The Sexual Reproduction of 'Race': Bisexuality, History and Racialisation," in Bi Academic Intervention, *The Bisexual Imaginary*, 73–88.
97. Fraser, 14–15.
98. Dollimore, 529.
99. Ibid., 528.
100. Ibid., 529.
101. Ibid., 531.
102. Janice Williamson, "Strained Mixed Fruit (after Gerber™): an Autobifictograph," in the Bisexual Anthology Collective, *Plural Desires*, 44–73.
103. Ibid., 48.
104. Ibid., 49.

105. Ibid.
106. Ibid.
107. Ibid.
108. Ibid.
109. Ibid., 59.
110. Young, 71.
111. Jo Eadie, "'That's Why She Is Bisexual': Contexts for Bisexual Visibility," in Bi Academic Intervention, *The Bisexual Imaginary*, 143.
112. Phelan, 96; emphasis added.
113. Kaloski, "Returning to the Lesbian *Bildungsroman*," 90–105.
114. Stacey Young, "Bisexuality, Lesbian and Gay Communities, and the Limits of Identity Politics," in Tucker, ed., *Bisexual Politics*, 219–33; Rust, *Bisexuality and the Challenge to Lesbian Politics*; Ault, "Hegemonic Discourse in an Oppositional Community," 107–22.
115. Young, "Bisexuality, Lesbian and Gay Communities, and the Limits of Identity Politics," 222.
116. Rust, *Bisexuality and the Challenge to Lesbian Politics*, 2.
117. Ault, "Hegemonic Discourse in an Oppositional Community," 214.
118. Elspeth Probyn, *Sexing the Self: Gendered Positions in Cultural Studies* (New York: Routledge, 1993), 16–17.
119. Claudia Card, cited in Mariam Fraser, "Lose Your Face," in Bi Academic Intervention, *The Bisexual Imaginary*, 42; Fraser's emphasis.
120. Elizabeth Wilson, "Is Transgression Transgressive?" in Bristow and Wilson, *Activating Theory*, 112.
121. Particularly interesting on this issue are Sedgwick, 15–16; and Sharon Holland, "From This Moment Forth We Are Black Lesbians: Querying Feminism and Transgressing Whiteness in Consolidated's *The Business of Punishment*," in *Beyond the Binary: Reconstructing Cultural Identity in Multicultural Context*, ed. Timothy B. Powell (Piscataway, NJ: Rutgers University Press, 1999), 139–62.
122. Sedgwick, 15.
123. Henry Abelove, Michèle Aina Barale, and David Halperin, eds., introduction to *The Lesbian and Gay Studies Reader* (New York: Routledge, 1993), xv.
124. Judith Butler, "Against Proper Objects," in *Feminism Meets Queer Theory*, ed. Elizabeth Weed and Naomi Schor (Indianapolis: Indiana University Press, 1997), 1.
125. A pernicious side effect of Butler's resonance within the academy as queer over feminist is that she is more commonly taught as part of a exclusively poststructuralist (queer) trajectory linking Jacques Lacan, Michel Foucault and herself, evacuating her texts of their sustained feminist engagement as well as critique. Students are thus more likely to be encouraged to follow up on the male predecessors Butler cites in *Gender Trouble* than the feminist contemporaries (Luce Irigaray, Julia Kristeva, and Monique Wittig) she locates herself in relation to; Butler, *Gender Trouble: Feminism and the Subversion of Identity* (New York: Routledge, 1990).
126. Rosi Braidotti, *Nomadic Subjects: Embodiment and Sexual Difference in Contemporary Feminist Theory* (New York: Columbia University Press, 1994), 16, 35, 98.

127. Donna Haraway, "A Manifesto for Cyborgs: Science, Technology, and Socialist Feminism in the 1980s," in *Feminism/Postmodernism*, ed. Linda J. Nicholson (1985; New York: Routledge, 1991), 190–233; Braidotti, *Nomadic Subjects*.

128. Probyn, 3.

129. Despite my desire not to separate feminist and queer epistemologies here, I do also want to be faithful to their respective histories. Thus, I will use the terms *feminist* or *queer* to denote particular traditions of inquiry (e.g., standpoint and perverse presentism, respectively), even while I acknowledge this separation to be problematic. Where the traditions cannot be separated even temporarily I will use the rather cumbersome term *queer feminist epistemology/ies*.

130. I take Joan Scott's essay "Experience" as exemplary of this challenge; Scott, "Experience," in *Feminists Theorize the Political*, eds. Judith Butler and Joan Scott (New York: Routledge, 1992), 22–40.

131. Probyn, *Sexing the Self*.

132. Ibid., 16.

133. Ibid., 17.

134. Braidotti, *Nomadic Subjects*.

135. Ibid., 35.

136. Donna Haraway, "Situated Knowledges: The Science Question in Feminism and the Privilege of the Partial Perspective," in *Simians, Cyborgs and Women: The Reinvention of Nature* (New York: Routledge, 1991), 192.

137. Haraway, "Situated Knowledges," 195.

138. See, respectively, Haraway, "Situated Knowledges," Braidotti, *Nomadic Subjects*, and Probyn, *Sexing the Self*.

139. Doreen Massey, "A Place Called Home?" *New Formations* 17 (1991): 9.

140. Sedgwick, 27; emphasis in the original.

141. Ibid., 22–27.

142. Haraway, "A Manifesto for Cyborgs," 191.

143. Ibid., 196.

144. Michael Keith and Steve Pile, "Introduction: the Politics of Place," in *Place and the Politics of Identity*, eds., Michael Keith and Steve Pile (London: Routledge, 1993), 2.

145. Fredric Jameson, "Postmodernism, or the Cultural Logic of Late Capitalism," *New Left Review* 146 (1984): 64.

146. Dick Hebdige, "Subjects in Space," *New Formations* 11 (1990): vii.

147. Nancy Duncan, ed., *Body Space: Destabilising Geographies of Gender and Sexuality* (London: Routledge, 1996), 1.

148. See, for example, Linda McDowell, "Spatializing Feminism," in Duncan, ed., *BodySpace*, 30–31.

149. See, for example, Elspeth Probyn, "Lesbians in Space: Gender, Sex and the Structure of Missing," *Gender, Place and Culture* 2. 1 (1995): 77–84; and Karen Monin and Lawrence Berg, "Emplacing Current Trends in Feminist Historical Geography," *Gender, Place and Culture* 6. 4 (1999): 311–30.

150. See, for example, V. Lawson, "The Politics of Difference: Examining the Quantitative/Qualitative Dualism in Post-Structuralist Feminist Research," *Professional Geographer* 47. 4 (1995): 449–57; K. V. L. Eng-

land, "Getting Personal: Reflexivity, Positionality and Feminist Research," *Professional Geographer* 46. 1 (1994): 80–89.

151. See, for example, I. Maxey, "Beyond Boundaries? Activism, Academia, Reflexivity and Research," *Area* 31. 3 (1999): 199–208, and C. Twyman, J. Morrison, and D. Sporton, "The Final Fifth: Autobiography, Reflexivity and Interpretation in Cross-Cultural Research," *Area* 31. 4 (1999): 313–26.

152. Michel Foucault, "Of Other Spaces," *Diacritics*, Spring 1986: 22–27.

153. Edward W. Soja, "Heteropologies: A Remembrance of Other Spaces in the Citadel–L.A.," in *Postmodern Cities and Spaces*, eds. Sophie Watson and Catherine Gibson (Oxford: Blackwell, 1995), 14.

154. Foucault, "Of Other Spaces," 22.

155. Michel Foucault, "The Discourse on Language," in *The Archaeology of Knowledge* (New York: Harper and Row, 1971), 215–37; and Michel Foucault, "Lecture One: January 1976," in *Power/Knowledge: Selected Interviews and Other Writings 1972–1977*, ed. Colin Gordon (Brighton, U.K.: Harvester, 1980): 82, 85.

156. Beatriz Colomina, introduction to *Sexuality and Space*, ed. Beatriz Colomina (New York: Princeton Architectural Press, 1992), ii.

157. Foucault, "Of Other Spaces," 24.

158. Ibid., 24.

159. Gordon Brent Ingram, Anne-Marie Bouthillette and Yolanda Retter, "Lost In Space: Queer Theory and Community Activism at the *Fin-de-Millénaire*," in *Queers in Space*, 3. John Bentley Mays attributes the first use of the term "queer space" to Gordon Brent Ingram, an environmental planner from Vancouver. Mays suggests that queer space is a particularly appropriate term to describe public spaces, such as parks or toilets, that are queered by "nocturnal sexual trysts and romps that have historically defined and sustained urban gay communities"; Mays, "Redefining Urban Space: The Controversial Concept of 'Queer Space' Breathes New Life into the Arid Subject of City Planning," *Globe and Mail*, October 1, 1994: C7.

160. Doreen Massey, "A Global Sense of Place," *Marxism Today*, June 1991: 24–29; and Gloria Anzaldúa, *Borderlands/La Frontera: The New Mestiza* (San Francisco: Spinsters/Aunt Lute Press, 1989).

161. For examples of how this works in a variety of different urban and theoretical contexts, see the range of articles in Bell and Valentine, eds., *Mapping Desire*, and Ingram, Bouthillette, and Retter, eds., *Queers in Space*.

162. Joan Nestle, "Restriction and Reclamation: Lesbian Bars and Beaches of the 1950s," Ingram, Bouthillette, and Retter, eds., *Queers In Space*, 65–66.

163. Ibid., 65.

164. Ibid., 63.

165. Ibid., 66.

166. David Lourea was a prominent member of bisexual community in the Bay Area and nationally for many years, as well as a founding member of the Bisexual Center.

167. The name change occurred in January 1999. The mission statement for the society now reads, "The Gay, Lesbian, Bisexual, Transgender (GLBT) Historical Society is a non-profit organization whose mission is to col-

lect, preserve, and promote an active knowledge of the history, arts, and culture of sexually diverse communities in Northern California and beyond." See http://www.glhs.org/baseinfo/glhsmisn.htm.
168. Foucault, "Of Other Spaces," 22.
169. Colomina, i.
170. A recent, and compelling, exception to this rule is Philip Hubbard, "Desire/Disgust: Mapping the Moral Contours of Heterosexuality," *Progress in Human Geography* 24. 2 (2000): 191–217.
171. Dell Upton, "White and Black Landscapes in Eighteenth-Century Virginia," *Material Life In America, 1600–1860*, ed. R.B. St. George (Boston: Northeastern University Press, 1988), 357.
172. Probyn, "Lesbians in Space," 79.
173. Adrienne Rich, "Notes Toward a Politics of Location," *Blood, Bread, and Poetry: Selected Prose 1979–1985* (London: Virago Press, 1986), 210–31.
174. Rich, 212. The influence on feminist and queer theory of Rich's text has been immense. Donna Haraway is clearly influenced by Rich when she emphasizes the importance of locating the Western "eye" not the "Other." In the 1990s, feminist researchers Elspeth Probyn and Chandra Tolpade Mohanty also explicitly reference "Notes Toward a Politics of Location." Haraway, "Situated Knowledges," Chandra Tolpade Mohanty "Feminist Encounters: Locating the Politics of Experience," in *Space, Gender, Knowledge: Feminist Readings*, ed. L. McDowell and J. P. Sharp (London: Arnold, 1997), 82; Elspeth Probyn, "Travels in the Postmodern: Making Sense of the Local," in *Feminism/Postmodernism*, ed. Linda J. Nicholson (New York: Routledge, 1990), 177.
175. Rich, 231; emphasis in the original.
176. Probyn, "Travels in the Postmodern," 184.

Chapter 2: Desire by any Other Name

1. "Strange Town Where Men Aren't Wanted," *National Enquirer*, April 21, 1992: 8.
2. Liz Galst, "What Price: Life in Northampton after *20/20*," Supplement to the *Boston Phoenix*, March 1994: 12–13. The *National Enquirer* article gave rise to a number of other articles on the town's lesbian community and was covered on *CNN* and *20/20* in September 1992.
3. There has not been any sustained academic work on Northampton's lesbian community—it appears most consistently in newspapers or magazine articles. The following list is not exhaustive but gives an indication of its lesbian significance: Barbara Kantrowitz and Danzy Senna, "A Town Like No Other: 'The Power and The Pride,'" *Newsweek*, June 12, 1993: 56–57; Paula Neves, "Northampton: How to Make a Lesbian Mecca," *Network*, July 1994: 34–35, 38–39; , Brenda MacCoy, "États-Unis: La Cité des Femmes," *Femina*, 1993: 21, 23–24; "Northampton, Paradis des Lesbiennes," *Gazelle: Le Magazin Des Lesbiennes* 3. 11 (1996): 18–19; Janet Cowley, "You Don't Have to Be a Lesbian to Live Here, But It Doesn't Hurt," *Chicago Tribune*, December 5, 1993: 10–11.
4. Michael Lowenthal, "The House O' Happy Queers at 281 State," *Sister and Brother: Lesbians and Gay Men Write About Their Lives Together*, ed. Joan Nestle and John Preston (London: Cassell, 1995), 75.

5. Elizabeth Mehren, "A Place to Call Home," *Los Angeles Times*, December 19, 1991: E1.
6. Stacey Young, "Bisexuality, Lesbian and Gay Communities, and the Limits of Identity Politics," in *Bisexual Politics: Theories, Queeries, and Visions*, ed. Naomi Tucker (New York: Harrington Park Press, 1995), 225.
7. Ibid., 219.
8. Although gay and bisexual men do make up a strong presence in Northampton, there is little organized community as such. In 1994 there was an attempt to forge community by setting up the *Valley Gay Men's Calendar*, with the support of the *Calendar*, Northampton's listings magazine for lesbian events in the area. It did not last more than a year, however. Carey Lambert, "Men In Northampton," the *Valley Advocate*, August 6, 1992: 3, 6.
9. In November 1994 I interviewed Bet Power about the relationship between the archives' transition and his own. The interview forms the basis of my article "From Lesbian Nation to Transgender Liberation," which gives more detailed information on the archives. I refer to Power as "she" throughout this chapter, since at the time of the Northampton controversy, Power identified as a lesbian. Clare Hemmings, "From Lesbian Nation to Transgender Liberation: A Bisexual Feminist Perspective," *Journal of Gay, Lesbian, and Bisexual Identity* 1. 1 (1996): 37–60.
10. The Stonewall Center is the lesbian, bisexual, gay, and transgender center at the University of Massachusetts at Amherst.
11. Jonathan Freedland, "This Town is Big Enough for the Both of Us," *The Guardian*, November 6, 1995: 7. How one might certify one's dykedom remains unclear. I do like the idea, though, of all women needing to insist that they are dykes in order to gain from a rare lesbian economic advantage.
12. This walk reflects Northampton's geography in 1995, at the close of the Northampton controversy, unless otherwise indicated.
13. This graffiti was reproduced in the *National Enquirer* article on Northampton. By 1997 this lesbian graffiti had been "cleaned up," and carried instead a pastel rendition of a hand wielding a large paintbrush. The sensationalism of Northampton's status as "Lesbianville" can cause problems. One woman talked openly of her experience at the hands of the *National Enquirer* journalists. She was photographed under false pretenses and had no idea that the picture of her with her lover was going to be nationally reproduced in the tabloid. Karen Bradway, "The Price of Visibility: Northampton's Uneasy Outing in the Media," *The Valley Optimist*, September 14, 1992: 6.
14. Press release, June 1989, Northampton Collection, NSMA.
15. Curtis and Swartz closed in June 1997.
16. To give some idea of the lesbian community's diversity in Northampton, in May 1997 both Ferron (an internationally-adored lesbian folk singer) and Sleater-Kinney (a riot grrl punk band with a generally younger following) played to packed audiences.
17. Pride and Joy had T-shirts printed with the slogan "Lesbianville, USA" after the media attention, as both a tourist souvenir and ironic momento for locals.
18. In May 1997, the Academy of Music showed both *Chasing Amy* and *Female Perversions*, two films that have central queer (and arguably bisexual) female protagonists.

19. The North Star bar was sold in November 1995 and ceased to be a specifically lesbian bar, after attempts to save a failing business in the winter by closing the restaurant. The North Star changed hands again in May 1996, becoming The Grotto, and returned to being a queer bar.
20. Katja Sarkowsky highlights this shift in lesbian and gay community from the anticapitalist 1970s to the consumer-oriented 1980s; Sarkowsky, "Race, Power, and Privilege: The Lesbian Community in Northampton, Massachusetts," term paper, Trenton State College, spring 1996.
21. Karen Bradway, "The Price of Visibility: Northampton's Uneasy Outting in the Media," *The Valley Optimist*, September 14, 1992: 6.
22. See http://www.amazonian.net.
23. Galst, 13.
24. Valle Dwight, "Valley Luring More Tourists," "Pioneer Business ''94," *Daily Hampshire Gazette*, February 28, 1994: 8
25. "Analysis of a Lesbian Community—Part One," *Lesbian Connection*, July 1977: 7–8.
26. Ibid., 7.
27. The Northampton Collection, NSMA.
28. This definition of *lesbian* is challenged in a very different way during the Pride March controversy, as I argue later in this chapter. *Just Because of Who We Are: Violence against Lesbians*, Heramedia Productions, 1976.
29. The Northampton Collection, NMSA; *Just Because of Who We Are*.
30. Stanley Moulton, "A Woman Violated," *Daily Hampshire Gazette*, March 11, 1993: n.p.
31. Laurie Loisel, "Vigil Held to Protest Pearl Street Incident," *Daily Hampshire Gazette* March 11, 1993: n.p.
32. Pat Califia, "San Francisco: Revisiting 'The City of Desire,'" in *Queers in Space: Communities, Public Places, Sites of Resistance*, ed., Gordon Brent Ingram, Anne-Marie Bouthillette, and Yolanda Retter (Seattle: Bay Press, 1997), 193.
33. Freedland, 7.
34. "Domestic Partner Law Defeated: Hamp Says No by 87 Votes," *Union New*,s November 8, 1995: n.p.
35. "Analysis of a Lesbian Community—Part Two," *Lesbian Connection*, September 1977: 9–10.
36. Lesléa Newman notes that the Northampton area has "more Jewish lesbians per capita than any other area (with the possible exception of the Park Slope section of Brooklyn"; Newman, "A Happy Coincidence: Lesléa Newman Rediscovers Her Heritage among the Jewish Lesbian Community of Northampton," *Metroline*, November 11, 1993: 32–33.
37. Sarkowsky, 7.
38. *Just Because of Who We Are*, video transcript, 3.
39. Ibid.
40. Ibid., 4–5.
41. Conversation with Zizi Ansell, WOW Productions, Northampton, March 1995.
42. The Outreach Committee of the GLB Community Center Project, Upcoming Meeting Times, Request For Funds, Community Input, Office Space, and Supplies, November 9, 1991, Northampton Collection, NSMA.
43. Bet Power, Trixy Halloween, Terri Dixon and Lesbians and Gays against Censorship and Self-Destruction, Western Massachusetts, "Why Wom-

onfyre Books Closed: How Lesbians Hurt Lesbians and Others in the Name of Feminism," *Valley Women's Voice*, May 5, 1989: 5.

44. Ibid.

45. Susie Bright, "Lesbian Censors Close Women's Bookstore," *On Our Backs*, March–April 1989: 9.

46. Rose Maloof and Madelaine Zadik, "Dear Feminist Friends . . . ," *Valley Women's Voice*, June 1989: 4–5; Frances Ryan, "To the Editor . . . ," *Valley Women's Voice*, June 1989: 5. The editors apologized to Lunaria. After the owner of Gazebo (the lesbian lingerie store) responded to rumors that the antipornography lesbians were about to fire-bomb her business, the women at Lunaria speculated that police infiltration into the lesbian community might have been responsible for these and other such rumors. "Attention Women," leaflet, April 1989, Northampton Collection, NSMA.

47. "Andrea Dworkin Speaks: Pornography and Civil Rights," Flyer, April 1989, Northampton Collection, NSMA.

48. One of the group's cofacilitators felt that her needs as the only woman of color in the group were not being met. Conversely, some members of the group felt that this woman took up too much space, and was not fulfilling her role as facilitator. None of this was dealt with directly, but discussed among cliques outside the group. The bad feeling escalated until the group fell apart, not through direct confrontation, but because members of the group (unsurprisingly) simply stopped going. Interview with former members of the Valley Bisexual Network, May 1995.

49. I was a member of the Bisexual Women's Support Group for several months in 1995. The information recorded here is gathered from my impressions while attending the group, and from follow-up interviews.

50. "What's the Background to All This? A Chronology of the Northampton Pride March," *Queer Nation Speaks*, 1991: 4.

51. Ibid.

52. Becky Logan, "It's That Time Again," Pride March Committee press release, 1989, Northampton Collection, NMSA.

53. Jodi Lew, "Pain and Politics: the Next Pride March," *Valley Women's Voice*, March 1990: n.p.

54. "What's the Background to All This?" 5.

55. "COMMUNITY ALERT," editorial, the *Calendar*, January 1990: 1, emphasis in the original. The editor of the *Calendar*, Pamela Kimmell, supported the original name of "Lesbian and Gay" throughout the controversy.

56. Ibid.

57. "What's the Background to All This?" 5.

58. Smith spoke of the importance of coalition building among diverse minorities, not just sexual minorities—"I have to believe in coalitions because those are the only kinds of politics that can save my life." Barbara Smith, cited in Paul Oh, "Gays, Lesbians Celebrate with March and Rally," *Daily Hampshire Gazette*, May 16, 1988: 19.

59. Oh, 19.

60. Lew, n.p.; Lis Brook and Sarah Dreher, "Letter to the Editor," *Gay Community News*, March 11–17, 1990: 3–4.

61. "Bisexuals and Other Politically Sympathetic Groups to March As Allies," *Calendar*, February 1990: 1.

62. Editoral, *Calendar*, March 1990: 1.

63. The Program for Gay, Lesbian and Bisexual Concerns was renamed the Stonewall Center in 1995.
64. Editoral, *Calendar*, March 1990: 1. Two of the other organizers of the meeting were former members of the PMC who had resigned after the January 10 vote to restore the original title of the march.
65. Bet Power, "Who Gets to 'Belong' in the Lesbian Community Anyway?" *Gay Community News* April 8–14, 1990: 5.
66. Micki Seigel, letters, *Valley Women's Voice*, March 1990: 2.
67. Seigel, 2.
68. Brook and Dreher, 3–4.
69. "What's the Background to All This?" 5.
70. Brook, cited in Meg Kroeplin, "10th Annual Pride March Marred by Controversy," *Daily Collegian*, May 3, 1991: 1.
71. The Committee for an All-Inclusive Pride March, announcement, *Queer Nation Speaks*, 1991: 6.
72. Dreher, cited in Kroeplin, 1.
73. Sarah Dreher, "Pride March Speech," *Calendar*, June 1991: 2.
74. http://www.northamptonpride.org. Note the continued association of lesbian and gay, and bisexual and transgender, through the placement of slashes. I discuss the linking of bisexual and transgender subjects within queer politics and theory in chapter 3.
75. "7th Annual Lesbian and Gay March," *Daily Hampshire Gazette*, May 13, 1988: 18.
76. Fred Contrada, "'Bisexuals May Protest Exclusion from March," *Union News*, May 3, 1990: 16.
77. Ibid.
78. Elisabeth Brook, "Lesbians Don't Fuck Men: Letter to the Editor," *Sojourner* 14. 11 (1989): 6.
79. Brook and Dreher, 3.
80. Robyn Ochs, "Self-Identifying as Bisexual: A Political Statement," *Gay Community News*, April 8–14, 1990: 5.
81. Fred Contrada, "Gay Pride March Slated Saturday," *Union News*, May 2, 1990: 12.
82. Krause, cited in Fred Contrada, "Gay Community Rally in 'Hamp,'" *Sunday Republican*, May 6, 1990: A-2.
83. Brook, cited in Contrada, "Gay Pride March Slated Saturday," 12.
84. Power, "Who Gets to 'Belong' in the Lesbian Community Anyway?" 5.
85. Amber Ault, "Hegemonic Discourse in an Oppositional Community: Lesbian Feminist Stigmatization of Bisexual Women," in *Queer Studies: A Lesbian, Gay Bisexual, and Transgender Anthology*, eds. Brett Beemyn and Mickey Eliason (New York: New York University Press, 1996), 204–16; Paula Rust, *Bisexuality and the Challenge to Lesbian Politics: Sex, Loyalty and Revolution* (New York: New York University Press), 58.
86. Sheila Jeffreys, "Bisexual Politics: a Superior for of Feminism?" *Women's Studies International Forum* 22. 3 (1999): 273–85.
87. The recently closed Silver Moon bookstore in London was a case in point.
88. Collective Lesbian International Terrors Collective (C.L.I.T. Collective), "C.L.I.T. Statement No.3," "C.L.I.T. Collection No.2," *Dyke: A Quarterly* 1. 2 (1976): 47. Throughout her 1990 letter Power capitalizes *Bisexual* and *Sadomasochist* as well as *Lesbian*. It is significant that in her letter Power alternates between capitalizing and lowercasing *Trans-*

vestite and *Transsexual*. At this time Power cannot be unequivocal about their status, either within the lesbian community, or as separately validated identities. Power, "Who Gets to 'Belong' in the Lesbian Community Anyway?" 5.

89. Editoral, *Calendar*, January 1990: 1.
90. Editorial, *Calendar*, February 1990: 1.
91. Contrada, "Gay Pride March Slated Saturday," 12.
92. Ibid.
93. Ara Wilson, "Just Add Water: Searching for the Bisexual Politic," Bisexuality Debate, *OUT/LOOK* 16. 4. 4 (1992): 28.
94. Lesley Mountain, Letters, *Bifrost: A Monthly Moagazine for Bisexuals* 17 (1992): 7.
95. Michele Moore, "Holding Bisexuals to a Double Standard," *Gay Community News,* April 8–14, 1990: n.p.
96. Ochs, 5.
97. Ibid.
98. The Boston Bisexual Women's Network was formative in the development of a U.S. national bisexual network in the late 1980s. I discuss its role in the national context in chapter 4.
99. Karin Baker and Helen Harrison, "Viewpoint," *Valley Women's Voice,* April 1990: 3.
100. Power, "Who Gets to 'Belong' in the Lesbian Community Anyway?" 5.
101. Dreher, "Pride March Speech," 2.
102. Ibid.
103. Ibid.
104. Ibid.
105. Sarah Lucia Hoagland, *Lesbian Ethics: Towards New Value* (Palo Alto, CA: Institute of Lesbian Studies, 1988), 3.
106. Dreher, "Pride March Speech," 2.
107. Kimmell, cited in Kroeplin, 1.
108. Brook and Dreher, 2.
109. Ibid.
110. Ibid.
111. Editorial, *Calendar*, June 1990: 1.
112. Editorial, *Calendar*, January 1990: 1.
113. Kroeplin, 1.
114. Apuzzo, cited in Contrada, "Gay Community Rally in 'Hamp,'" A-2.
115. Editoral, *Calendar*, January 1990: 1.
116. Editorial, *Calendar*, February 1990: 1.
117. Northampton Lesbians Fighting Pornography, "Why We Need Lesbian Occupied Territory: A Statement from Northampton Lesbians Fighting Pornography," "Viewpoint," *Valley Women's Voice,* Summer 1990: 3.
118. Ibid.
119. Ibid.
120. Ibid.
121. The pages of *Sojourner* carry debates about inclusion of male children at lesbian festivals at the same time as the debates about bisexual women's place in the lesbian community are being thrashed out. The debate seemed to assume that women could divided into lesbian and straight even though the terms of the debate were similar to those structuring the bisexuality discussions. See Margaret Randall, "Differences Enrich Debate," *Sojourner* 15. 11 (1989): 3; Sheila Anne, "A Commitment to

Lesbian Space," *Sojourner* 15. 3 (1989): 7–8; Dotty Johnson, "Bitterness and Resentment Mark Lesbian Festival," *Sojourner* 15. 3 (1989): 7.

122. Ault, "Hegemonic Discourse," 210.
123. The term *heterosexual privilege* refers to the freedom and rights accorded to heterosexuals that are not accorded to lesbians, gay men, and in a range of instances, bisexuals. Loraine Hutchins and Lani Ka'ahumanu define heterosexual privilege as "the benefit of basic civil rights and familial recognition that heterosexuals accord themselves as the 'norm' "; Loraine Hutchins and Ka'ahumanu, eds., *Bi Any Other Name: Bisexual People Speak Out* (Boston: Alyson Publications, 1991), 369.
124. Brook and Dreher, 2.
125. Ibid.
126. Collective Lesbian International Terrors, 41.
127. Monique Wittig, "One is Not Born a Woman," in *The Straight Mind and Other Essays* (Hemel Hempstead: Harvester Wheatsheaf, 1992).
128. Brook, "Lesbians Don't Fuck Men," 6.
129. Ibid.
130. Jan Clausen, "My Interesting Condition," *Journal of Sex Research* 27. 3 (1990): 445–59.
131. Rust, 17.
132. Ibid., 16–17.
133. Greta Christina, "Drawing the Line: Bisexual Women in the Lesbian Community," *On Our Backs*, May–June 1990: 14.
134. Christina, 14–15. A T-shirt at Pride and Joy in Northampton suggests the same homogeneity that Christina is critiquing here. The T-shirt has "100% lesbian" written on the front and the words "NO COMPRO-MISE" emblazoned on the back.
135. Pat Califia, "Slipping," *Melting Point* (Boston: Alyson Publications, 1993), 210.
136. Power, "Who Gets to 'Belong' in the Lesbian Community Anyway?" 5.
137. Northampton Lesbians Fighting Pornography, 3.
138. Elizabeth Armstrong, "Traitors to the Cause? Understanding the Lesbian/Gay 'Bisexuality Debates,' " in Tucker, *Bisexual Politics*, ed. 199.
139. Susan Ardill and Sue O'Sullivan, "Upsetting an Applecart: Difference, Desire and Lesbian Sadomasochism," *Feminist Review* 23 (1986): 36.
140. Dreher, "Pride March Speech," 2.
141. Brook, "Lesbians Don't Fuck Men," 6.
142. This is a similar point to the one I made about the structure of lesbian and gay coming out narratives in chapter 1: mistakes or interruptions to the lesbian narrative are acceptable as long as they are seen as such.
143. Brook, "Lesbians Don't Fuck Men," 6.
144. Colleen Urban, "Lesbians are not Bisexuals," *Sojourner* 15. 3 (1989): 4.
145. Brook, "Lesbians Don't Fuck Men," 6.
146. Dreher, "Pride March Speech," 2.
147. Editorial, *Calendar*, January 1990: 1.
148. Ibid. Note the lowercase *bisexual* and uppercase *Lesbian* distinction made here, as discussed earlier.
149. Seigel, 2.
150. Ibid.
151. Brook in Kroeplin, 1.
152. Jo Eadie, "Indegestion: Diagnosing the Gay Malady," in *Anti-Gay*, ed., Mark Simpson (London: Cassell, 1996): 66–83.

153. Brook, cited in Judith Kelliher, "Gay Pride March Set for May 4: Event's Title Still Excludes 'Bisexual,'" *Daily Hampshire Gazette*, April 12, 1991: 3.
154. Power, "Who Gets to "Belong" in the Lesbian Community Anyway?' 5.
155. Steve Boal, letter to Bet Power, April 7, 1990; Northampton Collection, NMSA.
156. Boal, 1.
157. Bet Power, letter to Steve Boal, April 21, 1990, 1–2; Northampton Collection NMSA.
158. Power, "Letter to Steve Boal," 2.
159. Brook and Dreher, 3.
160. Ochs, 5.
161. Lew, n.p.
162. Baker and Harrison, 3.
163. Robinson, cited in Chris Muther, "Despite Bi Controversy, 2000 Celebrate Northampton Pride," *Gay Community News*, May 13–19, 1990: 3.
164. Cynthia Van Ness, "Too Queer for the Hets and Too Het for the Queers," *Gay Community News*, April 15–21, 1990: 4.
165. "What's the Background to All This?" 6.
166. Editorial, *Calendar*, April 1990: 1. Once again, the announcement underlines the association of bisexuality with "the sexual," as discussed above. In this context, the capitalization of each identity is highly satirical.
167. Seccs Uelle, "Dyke and Bi Women's Factions Sling it Out," *Gay Community Nudes*, April 1, 1990: 43.
168. Ibid.
169. Marcia Deihl, "Where Allegiances Count," *Gay Community News,* May 6–12, 1990: 5.
170. F. Hutchinson, "Working Together for Sexual Freedom," *Sojourner* 14. 12 (1989): 38.
171. Ginny Lermann, "Appreciating All Our Choices," *Sojourner* 14. 11 (1989): 5.
172. Ibid.
173. Moore, n.p.
174. Marjorie Garber, *Vice Versa: Bisexuality and the Eroticism of Everyday Life* (New York: Simon and Schuster, 1995), inside cover.
175. Sharon Gonsalves, "On Bisexuals in the Lesbian Community," "Viewpoint," *Sojourner* 14. 10 (1989): 7. I briefly discuss Gonsalves's sexual narrative in "Bisexual Theoretical Perspectives: Emergent and Contingent Relationships," in Bi Academic Intervention, *The Bisexual Imaginary: Representation, Identity and Desire* (London: Cassell, 1997): 27–29.
176. Gonsalves, 7.
177. Ibid.
178. Ibid., 8.
179. Ibid.
180. Ibid.
181. Brook's letter, "Lesbians Don't Fuck Men" discussed above, appears in the July edition of *Sojourner* in part as a response to Sharon Gonsalves's article. Not only do lesbians "fuck men," but, according to Gonsalves, lesbian desire itself can be directed to women and men.
182. Elizabeth Däumer argues even more controversially that there should be

no reason why "a man [could not] resist his designated gender . . . and assume a lesbian identity"; Däumer's words provoke an ardent response from Jacqueline Zita, for whom the idea of a "male lesbian" remains a profoundly immaterial (in all senses) concept; Jacqueline Zita, "Male Lesbians and the Postmodernist Body," *Hypatia* 7. 4 (1992): 106–127.

183. Gonsalves, 8.
184. Henry Rubin, "Transformations: Emergent Female-to-Male Transsexual Identities," Ph.D. diss., Brandeis University, 1997.
185. Gonsalves, 7.
186. May Wolf, "From Where I Sit," *Gay Community News*, June 24–30, 1990: 4.
187. Ibid.
188. Ibid.
189. Ibid.
190. Ibid.
191. Ibid.
192. Ibid.
193. Ibid.
194. Ibid.
195. Ibid.
196. Ibid.

Chapter 3: Representing the Middle Ground

1. Bernice Hausman, *Changing Sex: Transsexualism, Technology and the Idea of Gender* (Durham: Duke University Press, 1995), 110–40; Janice Raymond, *The Transsexual Empire: the Making of the She-Male* (London: The Women's Press, 1980), 99–119.
2. Elizabeth Wilson, "Is Transgression Transgressive?" in *Activating Theory: Lesbian, Gay, Bisexual Politics*, ed. Joseph Bristow and Angelia Wilson (London: Lawrence and Wishart, 1993) 107–17; Ara Wilson, "Just Add Water: Searching for the Bisexual Politic," "Bisexuality Debate," *OUT/LOOK* 16. 4. 4 (1992): 24.
3. Collective Lesbian International Terrors Collective (C.L.I.T. Collective), "Bi-Sexuality," "C.L.I.T. PAPERS," *Dyke: a Quarterly* 1. 1 (1975–76): 27.
4. Leslie Feinberg, *Transgender Warriors: Making History from Joan of Arc to Ru Paul* (Boston: Beacon Press, 1996), x. Feinberg notes that "the word 'trans' is being used increasingly by the gender community as a term uniting the entire coalition," xi. I will occasionally use this term in this chapter.
5. Richard Ekins and Dave King, eds., *Blending Genders: Social Aspects of Cross-Dressing and Sex-Changing* (London: Routledge, 1996), 3.
6. Marjorie Garber, *Vice Versa: Bisexuality and the Eroticism of Everyday Life* (New York: Simon and Schuster, 1995), 15.
7. I am influenced in this aim by Jay Prosser's important work on transsexual narrative. Later in this chapter I highlight the significance for my own project of his debate with Judith Halberstam over the place of transgender and transsexual subjects within queer studies; Jay Prosser, *Second Skins: The Body Narratives of Transsexuality* (New York: Columbia University Press, 1998); Judith Halberstam, "Transgender Butch: Butch/FTM Border Wars and the Masculine Continuum," in *Female Masculinity* (Durham: Duke University Press, 1998), 141–73.

8. I discuss this "feminophobia" as part of the heterosexism of sexual narrative in "'All My Life I've Been Waiting for Something': Theorising Femme Narrative in *The Well of Loneliness*," in *Palatable Poison: Critical Perspectives on The Well of Loneliness Past and Present*, eds., Laura Doan and Jay Prosser (New York: Columbia University Press, 2001).

9. Stephanie Device, "Sometimes It's Hard to be a Woman/Caught in the Act," in Bi Academic Intervention, *The Bisexual Imaginary: Representation, Identity and Desire* (London: Cassell, 1997), 181–96.

10. Loren Cameron, "Self-Portrait Nude #46A," *Photo Gallery* (2000); http:// www.lorencameron.org.

11. Jacob Hale's rules for nontranssexuals in this regard can be found at http:// www.actlab.utexas.edu/~sandy/hale.rules.html. Cited in Halberstam, "Transgender Butch," 145.

12. Dallas Denny, "You're Strange and We're Wonderful: the Relationship between the Gay, Lesbian and Transgender Communities," *TransSisters: The Journal of Transsexual Feminism* 6 (1994): 23.

13. Sigmund Freud, "Three Essays on the Theory of Sexuality," *On Sexuality: Three Essays on the Theory of Sexuality and Other Works*, ed. Angela Richards; *The Penguin Freud Library*, ed. James Strachey (London: Penguin, 1905), 55.

14. Magnus Hirschfeld, *Die Homosexualitat des Mannes und des Weibes* (Berlin: Louis Marcus, 1914); Otto Weininger, *Sex and Character* (London: William Heinemann, 1903).

15. Wilhelm von Krafft-Ebing, *Psychopathia Sexualis* (1886; Philadelphia: F. A. Davis Company, 1903); Havelock Ellis, *Studies in the Psychology of Sex, Volume 2: Sexual Inversion* (1897; Philadelphia: F. A. Davis Company, 1915).

16. Jay Prosser and Merl Storr, introduction, "Part III: Transsexuality and Bisexuality," in *Sexology Uncensored: The Documents of Sexual Science* (Cambridge: Polity, 1998), 76.

17. Ellis, cited in Merl Storr, "The Sexual Reproduction of 'Race': Bisexuality, History and Racialisation," *The Bisexual Imaginary*, 79.

18. Storr, "The Sexual Reproduction of 'Race,'" 80; brackets in the original.

19. C. Allen, letter, *British Medical Journal* 1040, May 1954.

20. Prosser and Storr, 77.

21. Ibid., 76.

22. Ibid., 77.

23. Denny, 23.

24. Prosser, *Second Skins*.

25. Issue 17 of *Anything That Moves*, the national U.S. magazine for bisexuals, was devoted to bi-trans theoretical, personal and political alliances. "Bi-trans Coalitions," *Anything That Moves* 17 (1998).

26. The terms *FTM* and *MTF* do more than simply shorten "female-to-male" and "male-to-female" respectively. They denote a shift in political emphasis and in transsexual narrative progression away from the idea of moving from female to male, or vice versa, toward claiming transsexuality as an identity in itself.

27. Raymond, *The Transsexual Empire*, 103–4, 112.

28. Ibid., xix.

29. Stone, 283.

30. Stephen Whittle, "Gender Fucking or Fucking Gender?" in Ekins and King, eds., *Blending Genders*, 207.

31. Raymond, *The Transsexual Empire*, 99.

32. Ibid.
33. Janice Raymond, "The Politics of Transgenderism," in Ekins and King, eds., *Blending Genders*, 217. This article first appeared as the "Introduction to the 1994 Edition" of *The Transsexual Empire*.
34. Simone de Beauvoir, *The Second Sex* (London: Penguin, 1953), 528–34.
35. Del Martin and Phyllis Lyon, *Lesbian/Woman* (New York: Bantam Books, 1972), 66.
36. Ibid., 68.
37. Raymond, "The Politics of Transgenderism," 218.
38. Ibid., 223.
39. Judith Butler, "Introduction: Against Proper Objects," "More Gender Trouble: Feminism Meets Queer Theory," *Differences: A Journal of Feminist Cultural Studies* 6 Summer/Fall (1994): 18.
40. Luce Irigaray imagines the possibilities of female labial signification operating independently of the phallus in *This Sex Which Is Not One*, two years before the publication of *The Transsexual Empire*. As Butler says of Irigaray's work, "the feminine could not be theorized in terms of a determinate *relation* between the masculine and the feminine." Judith Butler, *Gender Trouble: Feminism and the Subversion of Identity* (New York: Routledge, 1990), 10; emphasis in the original. See also Luce Irigaray, *This Sex Which Is Not One*, trans. Catherine Porter (Ithaca: Cornell University Press, 1985), 205–18.
41. Hausman, 175–94.
42. Hausman is mentioned unfavorably in Jacob Hale's rules for nontranssexuals writing about transsexuality. Halberstam, while acknowledging the importance of Hausman's theoretical framework, suggests persuasively that she "quite simply tends to attribute too much power to the medical configuration of transsexual definition." Jacob Hale, "Suggested Rules for Non-Transsexuals Writing about Transsexuals, Transsexuality, Transsexualism, or Trans," at http://www.actlab.utexas.edu/~sandy/hale.rules.html; Halberstam, "Transgender Butch," 160.
43. Jay Prosser, review of *Changing Sex: Transsexualism, Technology, and the Idea of Gender*, by Bernice Hausman, and *Blending Genders: Social Aspects of Cross-Dressing and Sex-Changing*, Richard Ekins and Dave King, *Journal of Gender Studies* 6. 1. (1997): 3.
44. Martin and Lyon, 67.
45. Pratt, 19.
46. Julia Penelope, "Passing Lesbians: The High Cost of Femininity," *An Intimacy of Equals: Lesbian Feminist Ethics*, ed. L. Mohin (London: Onlywomen Press, 1996), 126–27.
47. Ibid., 147.
48. Ibid., 120.
49. Ibid., 127.
50. Sheila Jeffreys, "Butch and Femme: Now and Then," *Not a Passing Phase: Reclaiming Lesbians in History 1840–1985*, Lesbian History Group (London: The Women's Press), 171–72.
51. Joan Nestle, *A Restricted Country* (Ithaca : Firebrand Books, 1987); Joan Nestle, ed., *The Persistent Desire: A Femme-Butch Reader* (Boston: Alyson Publications, 1992); Madeline D. Davis and Elizabeth Lapovsky Kennedy, *Boots of Leather, Slippers of Gold: The History of a Lesbian Community* (New York: Routledge, 1993); Dorothy Allison, *Bastard Out of Carolina* (New York: Plume, 1993); Amber Hollibaugh, *My*

Dangerous Desires: A Queer Girl Dreaming Her Way Home (Durham: Duke University Press, 2000).

52. Sheila Jeffreys, *Anticlimax: A Feminist Perspective on the Sexual Revolution* (London: The Women's Press, 1990), 111, 115.

53. Jeffreys, *Anti-Climax*, 182.

54. Foucault's work has been central to this framework, of course, as, more recently, has Sedgwick's. See in particular Michel Foucault, *History of Sexuality, Volume 1: An Introduction* (London: Penguin, 1978), and Eve Kosofsky Sedgwick, *Epistemology of the Closet* (New York: Harvester Wheatsheaf, 1991).

55. Jonathan Ned Katz, *The Invention of Heterosexuality* (New York: Dutton, 1995); George Chauncey, *Gay New York: The Making of the Gay Male World, 1890–1940* (London: Flamingo, 1995); Halberstam, *Female Masculinity*.

56. See Gloria Anzaldúa, *Borderlands/La Frontera: The New Mestiza* (San Francisco: Spinsters/Aunt Lute Press, 1989), and Sasho A. Lambevski, "Suck My Nation—Masculinity, Ethnicity and the Politics of (Homo)sex," *Sexualities* 2. 4 (1999): 397–419.

57. Jay Prosser, "No Place Like Home: The Transgendered Narrative of Leslie Feinberg's *Stone Butch Blues*," *Modern Fiction Studies* 41. 3 (1995): 484.

58. Diana Fuss, introduction, *Inside/Out: Lesbian Theories, Gay Theories* (New York: Routledge, 1991), 2.

59. Marjorie Garber, *Vested Interests: Cross-Dressing and Cultural Anxiety* (New York: Routledge, 1992), 17.

60. Garber, *Vice Versa*, 206.

61. To give just two examples: Joan Nestle and John Preston, ed. *Sister and Brother: Lesbians and Gay Men Write about Their Lives Together* (London: Cassell, 1995); and Marla di Carlo, "I am a Lesbian . . . and This Is My Boyfriend," *Amazonian* 6 (2001): 1.

62. Nic Williams, "The Boy at the bar," *The Common Denominator* 1 (1995): 14.

63. Ibid.

64. Pat Califia, "Gay Men, Lesbians, and Sex: Doing It Together," in *Public Sex: The Culture of Radical Sex* (San Francisco: Cleis Press 1994), 185.

65. Ibid., 186.

66. Ibid., 185–186.

67. Graham McKerrow, *Gay Times*, January 29, 1993, cited in Jo Eadie, "Activating Bisexuality: Towards a Bi/Sexual Politics," in Bristown and Wilson, eds., *Activating Theory*, 150.

68. Eadie, "Activating Bisexuality," 150.

69. Carol A. Queen, "Strangers at Home: Bisexuals in the Queer Movement," *OUT/LOOK* 16. 4. 4. (1992): 33.

70. Elizabeth Wilson cites this same passage in her article "Is Transgression Transgressive?" Despite Queen's desire to be read as queer, Wilson sees this extract as an attempt to make heterosexuality transgressive, and as an example of a desire to "move beyond" sexual binaries without interrogating their political import; Wilson, 113.

71. Eve Kosofsky Sedgwick, "Bi," "Queer Studies List," qstudyl@ubvm.cc. buffalo.edu, as of August 17, 1994.

72. Sedgwick, "Bi."

73. Butler, *Gender Trouble*, 31.

74. Judith Butler, "Melancholy Gender/Refused Identification," *The Psychic*

Life of Power: Theories in Subjection (Stanford, CA: Stanford University Press, 1997), 132–50.

75. Judith Butler, *Bodies That Matter: On the Discursive Limits of "Sex"* (New York: Routledge, 1993), 86–88, 234–42.
76. Carole-Anne Tyler, "Passing: Narcissism, Identity, and Difference," *Differences: A Journal of Feminist Cultural Studies* 6. 2–3 (1994): 235.
77. These readings of Califia's butch/femme poems first appeared in Hemmings "Waiting for No Man: Bisexual Femme Subjectivity and Cultural Repudiation," in *Butch/Femme: Inside Lesbian Gender* (London: Cassell, 1998), 90–100.
78. Pat Califia, "Diagnostic Tests," in Nestle, ed., *The Persistent Desire*, 484.
79. Pat Califia, "The Femme Poem," in Nestle, ed., *The Persistent Desire*, 417.
80. This is suggested by her formulation of the penis as "(k)not the phallus." Tyler, 241–43.
81. Califia, "The Femme Poem," 416, 417.
82. Califia, "Diagnostic Tests," 485.
83. Susan Stryker, "My Words to Victor Frankenstein above the Village of Chamounix: Performing Transgender Rage," *GLQ* 1 (1994): 237–54; Stone, 280–304; Judith Halberstam, "F2M: the Making of Female Masculinity," in *The Lesbian Postmodern*, ed. Laura Doan (New York: Columbia University Press, 1994), 210–28; Halberstam, "Transgender Butch"; Jay Prosser, "No Place Like Home: The Transgendered Narrative of Leslie Feinberg's *Stone Butch Blues*," *Modern Fiction Studies* 41. 3 (1995): 483–514; Prosser, *Second Skins*; C. Jacob Hale, "Consuming the Living: Dis(re)membering the Dead in the Butch/FTM Borderlands," *GLQ* 4. 2 (1998): 311–48.
84. Bornstein, cited in Whittle, 211.
85. Gilbert Herdt, ed. *Third Sex, Third Gender: Beyond Sexual Dimorphism in Culture and History* (New York: Zone Books, 1994); Feinberg, *Transgender Warriors*.
86. Garber, *Vested Interests*, 16.
87. Ibid., 293.
88. Jennie Livingston, dir., *Paris Is Burning*, 1991.
89. Halberstam, "F2M," 211.
90. Jacqueline Zita, "Venus: the Looks of Body Theory," *Body Talk: Philosophical Reflections on Sex and Gender* (New York: Columbia University Press, 1998), 184–201.
91. Jackie Goldsby, "Queens of Language: *Paris Is Burning*," *Queer Looks: Perspectives on Lesbian and Gay Film and Video*, eds. Martha Gever, John Greyson, and Pratibha Parmar (New York: Routledge, 1993), 115.
92. Halberstam, "F2M," 211.
93. bell hooks, "Is Paris Burning?" *Z*, June 1991: 61.
94. "Voguing" is a slang/familiar term for the staged performance of the participants in ball contests; it was later appropriated and made popular by Madonna. Goldsby, 113.
95. Judith Butler, "Gender is Burning: Questions of Appropriation and Subversion," in *Bodies That Matter*, 125.
96. Prosser, *Second Skins*, 46.
97. Donna Minkowitz, cited in Hale, 313.
98. hooks, 61.
99. Jackie Goldsby makes the similar point that Livingston "can tell this

story because her identity is not implicated in it," because her "cultural and social privilege . . . is inscribed into the film, however unobtrusive she strives to be"; Goldsby, 115.

100. Butler, "Gender Is Burning," 133.

101. Ibid., 135.

102. That the white lesbian gaze can be theorized in a more reflexive, nuanced fashion can be seen in Zita's consistently critical engagement with what her "white look" is doing when she's watching *Paris Is Burning* with her evident queer pleasure; Zita, 185, 196–201.

103. Coco Fusco, "Who's Doin' the Twist? Notes towards a Politics of Appropriation," in *English is Broken Here: Notes on Cultural Fusion in the Americas* (New York: The New Press, 1995), 73.

104. Fusco, 74.

105. Halberstam, "F2M," 212.

106. Ibid., 219.

107. Kate More, "Excitable Speech: Kate More Interviews Judith Butler, Author of *Gender Trouble* and *Bodies that Matter* on Transsexualism," *Radical Deviance: a Journal of Transgendered Politics* 2. 4. (1997): 138.

108. Prosser, "No Place Like Home," 488; emphasis in the original.

109. Halberstam, "Transgender Butch," 146.

110. Ibid.

111. Ibid., 149.

112. Ibid., 147.

113. Stone, 296.

114. Ibid., 299.

115. Hausman, 143–44.

116. Stone, 299.

117. Hausman, 144.

118. Heather Findlay, "Losing Sue," in Sally Munt, ed., *Butch/Femme: Inside Lesbian Gender*, 133–45.

119. Ibid., 135.

120. Minnie Bruce Pratt also writes of her changing relationship to both her sexuality and gender identity in her relationship with Leslie Feinberg, transgendered activist and writer; Pratt, in particular 19–21, 83–84, 114–115, 142, 184.

121. Debra Bercuvitz, "Stand By Your Man," in *The Femme Mystique*, ed. Lesléa Newman (Boston: Alyson Publications, 1995), 92; emphasis in the original.

122. Ibid., 93.

123. Ibid., 94.

124. FTM transitioning may result in a transsexual man who has been part of a lesbian community leaving this behind, but for many FTMs and femme partners this is either not what is desired, or, indeed, can instigate feelings of personal and cultural dislocation. Gayle Rubin advocates tolerance and acceptance toward transsexuals in transition from butch to FTM from within lesbian community; Rubin, "Of Catamites and Kings: Reflections on Butch, Gender, and Boundaries," in Nestle, ed., *The Persistent Desire*, 475–476.

125. Marcy Sheiner, "What?" *Anything That Moves: The Magazine for the Bisexual-at-Large* 10 (1996): 20.

126. Raymond, *The Transsexual Empire*, 112.

127. Sheiner, 20.

128. Sue O'Sullivan, "I Don't Want You Anymore: Butch/Femme Disappointments," *Sexualities* 2. 4 (1999): 465–73.
129. Annie Sprinkle, "Beyond Bisexual," in *Bi Any Other Name: Bisexual People Speak Out*, Loraine Hutchins and Lani Ka'ahumanu, eds. (Boston: Alyson Publications, 1991), 103.
130. Raymond, *The Transsexual Empire*, xiv.
131. Ibid.
132. Donna Haraway, "Situated Knowledges: The Science Question in Feminism and the Privilege of the Partial Perspective," in *Simians, Cyborgs and Women: The Reinvention of Nature* (New York: Routledge, 1991), 183–201.
133. Carol Riddell, "Divided Sisterhood: A Critical Review of Janice Raymond's *The Transsexual Empire*," in Elkins and King, eds., *Blending Genders*, 178.
134. Stryker, cited in Cherry Smyth, "How Shall I Address You? Pronouns, Pussies and Pricks: Talking to Female-to-Male Transsexuals," *On Our Backs*, January–February 1995: 21.
135. Stryker, in Smyth, 40.
136. Ibid.
137. Hale, "Suggested Rules for Non-Transsexuals," rule 11; emphasis in the original.
138. Ibid.
139. *The Collins Paperback English Dictionary* (Glasgow: William Collins Sons, 1990), 301.
140. Hausman, x.
141. Prosser, *Second Skins*, 133.
142. Rosi Braidotti, "Signs of Wonder and Traces of Doubt: On Teratology and Embodied Differences," in *Between Monsters, Goddesses and Cyborgs: Feminist Confrontations with Science, Medicine and Cyberspace*, eds. Nina Lykke and Rosi Braidotti (London: Zed Books, 1996), 139.
143. Hausman, 200.
144. Loren Cameron, "Self-Portrait Nude #46A.
145. Stryker, in Smyth, 40.
146. Loren Cameron, "Triptych," *Body Alchemy: Transsexual Portraits—Photographs by Loren Cameron* (San Francisco: Cleis Press, 1996), 29–31.
147. Cameron, *Body Alchemy*; Cameron, *Photo Gallery*; Feinberg, *Transgender Warriors*.
148. Stryker, in Smyth, 21.
149. Prosser, "No Place Like Home," 488; emphasis in the original.
150. Cameron, in Smyth, 19.
151. Whittle, 214.
152. Jay Prosser, "Transitional Matter: The Body Narratives of Transsexual Autobiography," Ph.D. diss., City University of New York, 1996, 64.
153. Donald Hall, "BI-ntroduction II: Epistemologies of the Fence," in *RePresenting Bisexualities: Subjects and Cultures of Fluid Desire*, ed. Donald E. Hall and Maria Pramaggiore (New York: New York University Press, 1996), 9. Emphasis in the original.
154. Garber, *Vice Versa*, 288–89.
155. Sharon Rose, Cris Stevens, et al. Off Pink Collective, eds., *Bisexual Horizons: Politics, Histories, Lives* (London: Lawrence and Wishart, 1996), front cover.

156. Rachel Lanzerotti, untitled photographs, *Anything That Moves: The Magazine for the Bisexual at Large* 10 (1996): front cover, 24, back cover, 22.
157. Garber, *Vice Versa*, front cover, and between 527 and 528.
158. David Bell and Gill Valentine, ed. *Mapping Desire: Geographies of Sexuality* (London: Routledge, 1995), front cover.
159. Device, *fingerprints*, 1997.
160. Device, *silenced 1: missing, silenced 2: jealousy*, in Bi Academic Intervention, *The Bisexual Imaginary*, 90–91.
161. Device, letter to the author, March 15, 1997.
162. Ibid.
163. Ibid.

Chapter 4: A Place to Call Home

1. I have found the following texts particularly useful in tracing San Francisco's position in the gay imaginary. Edmund White, "San Francisco: Our Town," *States of Desire: Travels in Gay America* (New York: E. P. Dutton, 1980), 30–33; John D'Emilio, *Making Trouble: Essays on Gay History, Politics, and the University* (New York: Routledge, 1992) 74–95; Gilbert Herdt, *Gay Culture in America: Essays from the Field* (Boston: Beacon Press, 1992); Susan Stryker and Jim Van Buskirk, *Gay By The Bay: A History of Queer Culture in the San Francisco Bay Area* (San Francisco: Chronicle Books, 1996); Gordon Brent Ingram, Anne-Marie Bouthillette and Yolanda Retter, eds., *Queers in Space: Communities, Public Places, Sites of Resistance* (Seattle: Bay Press, 1997); Nan Alamilla Boyd, " 'Homos Invade S.F.!' San Francisco's History as a Wide-Open Town," in *Creating a Place for Ourselves: Lesbian, Gay, and Bisexual Community Histories*, ed. Brett Beemyn (New York: Routledge, 1997), 73–95.
2. Elspeth Probyn, *Sexing the Self: Gendered Positions in Cultural Studies* (New York: Routledge, 1993), 16–17.
3. Ka'ahumanu also coedited the first U.S. bisexual anthology; Loraine Hutchins and Lani Ka'ahumanu, eds., *Bi Any Other Name: Bisexual People Speak Out* (Boston: Alyson Publications, 1991).
4. As discussed in chapter 1, the GLHSNC was changed to the Gay, Lesbian, Bisexual Transgender (GLBT) Historical Society in January 1999.
5. D'Emilio, 93.
6. Ron Williams, "Deadly Conflicts," *Bay Area Reporter*, November 8, 1990: n.p.
7. Williams n.p.; Lloyd V. Reihl, "Illuminating Diatribe," *Bay Area Reporter*, November 8, 1990: n.p.; Rachel Pepper, "Without the Women," letter, 1990, Additional L.A.B.I.A. Materials, Focus Group: L.A.B.I.A./Women's Issues, Queer Nation Records; Gay and Lesbian Historical Society, San Francisco; Charles Gray, "'Castro Trash'?" letter, from General Meetings, September 12–December 10, 1990, Chronological files box I of 1(93–2), Queer Nation Records.
8. Alan Berubé, cited in David Bell and Jon Binnie, *The Sexual Citizen: Queer Politics and Beyond* (Oxford: Polity Press, 2000), 85.
9. Of course the "dot-com" boom in San Francisco in the mid to late 1990s has meant that to speak of "poor" neighborhoods anywhere in San Francisco has become something of a moot point.

10. Pat Califia, "San Francisco: Revisiting 'The City of Desire,' " in Ingram, Bouthillette, and Retter, eds., *Queers in Space*, 182–88.
11. D'Emilio, 74.
12. Califia, 182.
13. Ibid., 189.
14. The difference between what is signified by these terms must be due in part to the historical roots of lesbian bar culture in the 1940s, '50s, and '60s, as opposed to the development of women's bookstores and "women's culture" as feminist spaces in the 1970s.
15. Henry Rubin, "Report on the First FTM Conference of the Americas: A Vision of Community," *Journal of Gay, Lesbian, and Bisexual Identity* 1. 2. (1996): 176.
16. Ibid.
17. Gordon Brent Ingram, "Interview with Pat Califia," in Ingram, Bouthillette, and Retter, eds., *Queers in Space*, 191.
18. Califia, in ibid., 191.
19. Clare Hemmings, transcript, interview with Lani Ka'ahumanu: First National Bisexual Conference," February 1, 1995: 5.
20. Hemmings, interview with Lani Ka'ahumanu, 1.
21. Ibid., 13.
22. 1990 NBC Steering Committee, *Steering Committee Minutes*, April 17, 1989, September 17, 1989, April 22, 1990.
23. This final site was not confirmed until the beginning of May 1990, which may indicate the difficulty of securing bisexual space; ibid., May 5, 1990, and Hemmings, interview with Lani Ka'ahumanu, 1.
24. BiPOL, Conference Brochure of the 1990 National Bisexual Conference, June 1990: n.p.
25. Amanda Udis-Kessler, "Identity/Politics: A History of the Bisexual Movement," *Bisexual Politics: Theories, Queeries, and Visions*, ed. Naomi Tucker (New York: Harrington Park Press, 1995), 22.
26. Ibid.
27. Elizabeth Reba Weise, introduction to *Closer To Home: Bisexuality and Feminism*, ed. Elizabeth Reba Weise (Seattle: Seal Press, 1992), xii.
28. Udis-Kessler, 24.
29. Ibid., 18.
30. Stephen Donaldson, "The Bisexual Movement's Beginnings in the 70s: A Personal Retrospective," in Tucker, ed., *Bisexual Politics*, 33.
31. Liz A. Highleyman, "A Brief History of the Bisexual Movement," pamphlet, Boston Bisexual Resource Center, March 1993: 1–4.
32. The National Bisexual Liberation Group published what is probably the earliest bisexual newsletter, *The Bisexual Expression*. Ibid., 1.
33. Udis-Kessler, 22.
34. Highleyman, "A Brief History."
35. Danielle Raymond and Liz A. Highleyman, "Brief Timeline of Bisexual Activism in the United States," in Tucker, ed., *Bisexual Politics*, 334.
36. David Lourea, "The Bisexual Center: More Than Just a Social Club," press release, David Lourea Archives, San Francisco Public Library, n.d.
37. "Androgyny vs Our Patriarchal Culture," *The Bi-Monthly: Newsletter of the Bisexual Center* 3. 1 (1978): 1.
38. Derek Fung, "Trailblazing in the Seventies: Maggi Rubenstein," interview, *Anything That Moves: The Magazine for the Bisexual-at-large* 10 (1996): 34; brackets in the original.

39. Naomi Tucker, "Bay Area Bisexual History: An Interview with David Lourea," in Tucker, ed., *Bisexual Politics*, 49.
40. Fung, 35. In fact, there is fairly extensive discussion of transgendered and transsexual inclusion in *The Bi-Monthly*.
41. Hutchins and Ka'ahumanu, "Political Activism: a Brief History," in *Bi Any Other Name*, 361.
42. Tucker, "Bay Area Bisexual History," 49.
43. Fung, 35.
44. Tucker, "Bay Area Bisexual History," 48.
45. "Editors' Roundtable Discussion," in *The Bisexual Imaginary: Representation, Identity and Desire*, ed. Bi Academic Intervention (London: Cassell, 1997), 202.
46. Tucker, 49.
47. Ibid, 51.
48. Ibid., 51; emphasis added.
49. Ibid., 50.
50. Ibid., 51; emphasis in the original.
51. The Bisexual Forum of New York, which had been running from 1975 as a social, educational, and support group, closed just prior to the opening of the Bisexual Center: "Because of general burnout, changes in life circumstances, and lack of new leadership, the last official meeting took place in 1983." As in San Francisco, the bisexual movement in New York gained new energy in the mid-1980s, with the New York Area Bisexual Network (NYABN) and the Bisexual Political Action Committee (BIPAC) of NYABN in the mid- to late-1980s; Hutchins and Ka'ahumanu, "Political Activism," 360.
52. Fung, 35.
53. BiPOL, "Statement of Purpose," San Francisco, 1983.
54. Tucker, "Bay Area Bisexual History" 54.
55. Ibid.
56. Hutchins and Ka'ahumanu, overview, "Politics: A Queer among Queers," in *Bi Any Other Name*, 222.
57. Donaldson, 41.
58. Fung, 35; Hutchins and Ka'ahumanu, "Political Activism," 363.
59. Hutchins and Ka'ahumanu, "Political Activism," 362.
60. Ibid.
61. Stryker and Van Buskirk, 112. Proposition 102 was sponsored by U.S. Representative William Dannemyer in 1988.
62. Hutchins and Ka'ahumanu, preface to *Bi Any Other Name*, xv.
63. Ibid.
64. Ibid.
65. Rubenstein, in Weise, 10.
66. Cited in Stryker and Van Buskirk, 114.
67. Stryker and Van Buskirk, 106–7.
68. Sheila Manalo, "Making a Case for Community History," *Our Stories: Newsletter of the Gay, Lesbian, Bisexual and Transgender Historical Society of Northern California* 15. 2 (2000): 8.
69. Weise, introduction to *Closer to Home*, xiii.
70. Weise, "Seattle Bi Women's Network," Feminist Workshop track, 1990 National Bisexual Conference, San Francisco, June 23, 1990, audiotape.
71. Weise, introduction, xiii.
72. The growth of the BBWN is documented by a number of writers. See Beth Reba Weise, Ann Schneider, Kim Christensen, Sue, Joyce Kravets

and Loraine Hutchins, "Bisexuality Conference," *Off Our Backs*, July 1987: 10; Hutchins and Ka'ahumanu, "Political Activism," 360; and Robyn Ochs, "From the Closet to the Stage," in Hutchins and Ka'ahumanu, eds., *Bi Any Other Name*, 210–3.

73. Weise et al., "Bisexuality Conference."
74. BBWN, "Call to Bisexuals," flyer distributed before the March 1987, on Washington for Gay and Lesbian Rights; Hutchins and Ka'ahumanu, "Political Activism," 365.
75. BBWN, "Call to Bisexuals."
76. BBWN, "Are You Ready for a National Bisexual Network?" flyer distributed at the National March on Washington for Gay and Lesbian Rights, Washington D.C., October 11, 1987.
77. Liz Nania, "Speaking Out," *Gay Community News* 15. 21 (1989): 5.
78. Ibid.
79. Ibid.
80. Lucy Friedland, "Bis Need Political Organization," *Sojourner* 13. 8 (1988): 3; emphasis in the original. Clyde Dillard of Bi-Ways, a Washington, D.C. bisexual group, sets the number at fewer than fifty; Dillard, letter from Bi-Ways, Washington, D.C., to BiPOL, December 12, 1987, 2.
81. Matthew le Grant, "The 'b' word," in Hutchins and Ka'ahumanu, eds., *Bi Any Other Name*, 208, 209.
82. Ka'ahumanu and Hutchins, "Political Activism," 366, Hemmings; "interview with Lani Ka'ahumanu, 8.
83. Autumn Courtney was one of the main organizers of both the NBN and the 1990 conference, and a member of BiPOL.
84. Lani Ka'ahumanu and Autumn Courtney, "Dear Nascent Bisexual Networkers," national mailing, February 17, 1988.
85. Ibid.
86. Ka'ahumanu, Courtney, and Weise, "Dear Nascent North American Bisexual Network-in-formation," national mailing, June 1988. Weise joined the group in June 1988. This title was later amended to the 1990 National Bisexual Conference, given that its organizing was entirely U.S.-based.
87. Ka'ahumanu and Courtney, "Dear North American Bisexual Network-in-Formation," national mailing, April 30, 1989.
88. North American Bisexual Network Working Group of the 1990 San Francisco Conference on Bisexuality Committee, national mailing, October 1989.
89. BiPOL, Conference brochure, n.p.
90. Hemmings, interview with Lani Ka'ahumanu, 10.
91. BiPOL, conference brochure, n.p.; 1990 NBC Steering Committee, Steering Committee Minutes, January 21, 1990.
92. Hemmings, interview with Lani Ka'ahumanu, 2.
93. 1990 NBC Finance and Logistics Committee, *1990 National Bisexual Conference Report* 1990.
94. Hutchins and Ka'ahumanu, "Political Activism," 366; Richard McPherson, "Conference Marks Bisexuals' Stonewall," *Bay Area Reporter*, July 5, 1990: 21–22.
95. BiPOL, conference brochure, n.p. This conjunction of "diversity" and "strength" preempts the alternative theme of the 1991 Pride March theme in Northampton: "Unity Is Our Power, Diversity Our Strength."
96. Greta Christina, "The First National Bisexual Conference: Hundreds

Celebrate an Emerging Community," *San Francisco Bay Times*, July 8, 1990: 8.

97. Liz Highleyman, "1990 National Bisexual Conference: A Report," *Bi Women* 8. 4 (1990): 4.

98. BiPOL, conference brochure, n.p.

99. Sarah Murray, "Bisexual Movement Comes Out Strong," *San Francisco Sentinel*, July 4, 1990: 13.

100. Carol Queen, cited in McPherson, 22.

101. Christina, 8.

102. George Chauncey, *Gay New York: The Making of the Gay Male World 1890–1940* (London: Flamingo, 1995); Warren Blumenfeld and Diane Raymond, *Looking at Gay and Lesbian Life*, updated and expanded ed. (Boston: Beacon Press, 1993), 276.

103. Donaldson, 42.

104. 1990 NBC Steering Committee, Steering Committee Minutes, June 3, 1990.

105. Ka'ahumanu, cited in Christina, 48.

106. Hemmings, interview with Ka'ahumanu, 11.

107. Hutchins, cited in Murray, 13.

108. Hemmings, Interview with Ka'ahumanu, 12.

109. Ibid.

110. 1990 NBC Committee, Conference Statement of Purpose, n.d.; text is per the original.

111. 1990 NBC Committee, Steering Committee Minutes, June 5, 1989.

112. 1990 NBC Committee, Steering Committee Minutes, January 21, 1990.

113. 1990 NBC Committee, Steering Committee Minutes, November 19, 1989.

114. 1990 NBC Committee, Steering Committee Minutes, March 3, 1990; March 18, 1990, April 22, 1990.

115. Hemmings, interview with Lani Ka'ahumanu, 6.

116. BiPOL, conference brochure, n.p.

117. Hemmings, interview with Lani Ka'ahumanu, 8.

118. Ibid., 9.

119. Hemmings, interview with Lani Ka'ahumanu, 11.

120. Ibid.

121. BiPOL, *First National Bisexual Conference, June 20–24, San Francisco*, unedited videotape of the conference, 1990: no. 1 of 4 tapes.

122. Fernando Gutierrez, "Bisexuals as an Ethnic Minority Group," People of Color Workshop track, audiotape, June 21, 1990, NBC, San Francisco: no. 1 of 2 tapes.

123. Gutierrez, tape no. 1.

124. Beer, cited in Murray, 13.

125. Anon, in Loraine Hutchins, "Interracial Bisexual Coupling," People of Color Workshop track, audiotape, June 22, 1990, NBC, San Francisco.

126. Christina, 48.

127. Queen, cited in McPherson, 21.

128. Courtney, cited in Christina, 8.

129. Lourea, cited in McPherson, 21.

130. Ellyn, cited in Christina, 8.

131. Anonymous, in Robyn Ochs, "Bisexual and Lesbian Women: a Dialogue," Feminist Workshop track, audiotape, June 23, 1990, NBC, San Francisco; no. 2 of 2 tapes.

132. 1990 NBC Conference Evaluation Sheets, 1990.

133. Rachel Kaplan and Keith Hennessy, "Bi Artists' Manifesto," conference brochure; emphasis in the original.
134. Ibid.
135. Ibid.
136. Ann Kaloski, "Bisexuals Making Out with Cyborgs: Politics, Pleasure, Con/fusion," *Journal of Gay, Lesbian, and Bisexual Identity* 2. 1 (1997): 47.
137. Marge Piercy, *Woman on the Edge of Time* (London: Women's Press, 1979).
138. Kaplan and Hennessy, "Bi Artists' Manifesto."
139. Gloria Anzaldúa, *Borderlands/La Frontera: The New Mestiza* (San Francisco: Spinsters/Aunt Lute Press, 1989). For an extended and subtle engagement with Anzaldúa's text from a bisexual perspective see Ann Kaloski, "Following My Thumbs: Towards a Methodology for a Bisexual Reading," Ph.D. diss., University of York, 1997.
140. Michael du Plessis, "Blatantly Bisexual; or, Unthinking Queer Theory," in *RePresenting Bisexualities: Subjects and Cultures of Fluid Desire* eds. Donald E. Hall and Maria Pramaggiore (New York: New York University Press, 1996), 22.
141. Du Plessis, 22.
142. Hemmings, interview with Lani Ka'ahumanu, 4–5.
143. BiPOL, conference brochure.
144. Weise, in BiPOL, *First National Bisexual Conference,* videotape of the conference: no. 1 of 4 tapes.
145. Donaldson, 37.
146. Sharon Gonsalves, "Where Healing Becomes Possible," 115–126; Nina Silver, "Coming Out as a Heterosexual," 35–46; Stacey Young, "Bisexuality, Lesbian and Gay Communities, and the Limits of Identity Politics," 219–28; and Vashti Zabatinsky, "Some Thoughts on Power, Gender, Body Image and Sex in the Life of One Bisexual Lesbian Feminist," 133–46, all in Tucker, ed., *Bisexual Politics.*
147. Weise, introduction to *Closer to Home,* ix.
148. Rubenstein, cited in Marcy Sheiner, "The Foundations of the Bisexual Community in San Francisco: An Interview with Dr. Maggi Rubenstein," in Hutchins and Ka'ahumanu, eds., *Bi Any Other Name,* 204.
149. Weise, introduction to *Closer to Home,* xiii.
150. Joan Hill, BiPOL, *First National Bisexual Conference,* videotape of the conference: no. 2 of 4 tapes.
151. Robyn Ochs, "Bisexual Groups around the U.S.: Local Flavors of Bisexual Groups," audiotape, June 21, 1990, NBC, San Francisco.
152. Hemmings, interview with Lani Ka'ahumanu, 2.
153. BiPOL, "Bisexual Politics: What It Is?" 1988/89.
154. Donaldson, 37.
155. Hemmings, interview with Lani Ka'ahumanu, 2.
156. Ibid.
157. Ibid., 3.
158. Ibid., 4.
159. Ibid.
160. Anonymous, in Weise et al., 11.
161. Naomi Tucker and Paul Smith, "Feminism and the Conference," *Bay Area Bisexual Network Newsletter* 2. 2 (1990): 1.
162. Ibid.
163. Ibid.

164. Ibid.
165. Ibid.
166. W. L, Warner, "Letter to the Editor," *Bay Area Bisexual Network Newsletter* 2. 3 (1990): 3.
167. Ibid.
168. Ibid.
169. Ibid.
170. Tucker and Smith, "Letter to the Editor," *Bay Area Bisexual Network Newsletter* 2. 3 (1990): 3.
171. Ibid., emphasis in original.
172. Ibid.
173. Ibid.
174. Vicki McGuire, "Bisexuality and Feminism," Feminist Workshop track, audiotape, June 22, 1990, NBC, San Francisco: tape no. 1 of 2.
175. Ibid.
176. Mack, in McGuire, tape no. 2 of 2.
177. Hill, in McGuire, tape no. 1 of 2.
178. The words of feminists such as Alice Echols and Hill have resulted in lesbian separatism being damned through its association with "cultural" rather than radical feminism, as being merely a reversal or retreat rather than a serious political position that is still part of a contemporary radical feminist movement. See Tania Lienert, "On Who is Calling Radical Feminists, Cultural Feminists (and Other Historical Sleights of Hand)," in *Radically Speaking: Feminism Reclaimed*, ed. Diane Bell and Renate Klein (Melbourne, Australia: Spinifex Press, 1996), 155–168.
179. Anonymous in McGuire, tape no. 2 of 2.
180. Tom, in McGuire, tape no. 2 of 2. .
181. 1990 NBC Steering Committee, Steering Committee Minutes, May 5, 1990.
182. Christina, 48.
183. Ibid.
184. Ibid.
185. Margaret Mihee Choe, "Our Selves, Growing Whole," in Weise, ed., *Closer to Home*, 22.
186. "Editors' Roundtable," 204.
187. Brenda Marie Blasingame, "The Roots of Biphobia: Racism and Internalized Heterosexism," in Weise, ed., *Closer to Home*, 50.
188. Blasingame, 51–52.
189. Loraine Hutchins, "'Dear ECBN . . . Letter from Loraine Hutchins," *Bi Women* 7. 6 (1989–1990): 5.
190. Ibid.
191. Ibid.
192. Ibid., 6.
193. "ECBN Offers Scholarship Fund," *Bi Women* 8. 2 (1990): 8.
194. The Dance, "Under One Flag," was held at the San Francisco Women's Building.
195. 1990 NBC Steering Committee, Steering Committee Minutes, September 17, 1989.
196. 1990 NBC Steering Committee, Steering Committee Minutes, January 9, 1989, September 17, 1989.
197. 1990 NBC Steering Committee, Steering Committee Minutes, January 21, 1990.

198. 1990 NBC Steering Committee, Steering Committee Minutes, November 19, 1989.
199. 1990 NBC Steering Committee, Steering Committee Minutes, March 18, 1990; Hutchins and Ka'ahumanu, "Political Activism," 366.
200. The Bisexual People of Color Caucus, "The Bisexual People of Color Caucus," *Bi Women* 8. 2 (1990): 8.
201. Ibid.
202. Carlton, in BiPOL, *First National Bisexual Conference,* videotape of the conference: no. 2 of 4 tapes.
203. Christina, 11.
204. Franklin, cited in Christina, 11.
205. Hemmings, interview with Lani Ka'ahumanu, 9.
206. Hemmings, "Interview with Lani Ka'ahumanu" 9.
207. *1990 NBC Evaluation Sheets,* 1990.
208. Christina, 11.
209. Hemmings, interview with Lani Ka'ahumanu, 9.
210. Lisa Jean Moore and Beth Reba Weise, "National Bisexual Network In Formation," conference brochure, n.p.
211. Lisa Jean Moore, "North American Multicultural Bisexual Network: Review of the Conference Organization," 1.
212. Gwen Riles, "North American Multicultural Bisexual Network Report," *Bi Women* 8. 5 (1990): 4.
213. Ibid.
214. Hemmings, transcript, interview with Robyn Ochs: Creating a National Bisexual Network," Boston, February 22, 1995.
215. Riles, 4.
216. Ibid.
217. Moore, 1.
218. Hemmings, interview with Robyn Ochs, 5.
219. Moore, 2.
220. "Editors' Roundtable," 204; emphasis in the original.
221. Ka'ahumanu, cited in Christina, 48.

PERMISSIONS

INDEX

Illustrations are denoted by page references in italics

Abelove, Henry, 38
AC/DC (bisexuals), 23–24
Activism, 3, 12, 18, 20, 65, 104,
    146–149, 155–156,
    159–162, 190
Activists, 5, 28, 63, 103, 134, 150,
    157–160, 173, 197
Affirmative action, 190
AIDS. *See* HIV/AIDS
Allison, Dorothy, 109
Amherst, 53
Androgyny, 16, 23, 102, 106, 146,
    156, 165
Angelides, Steven, 1, 20
Annie, Linda/Les *see* Halberstam,
    Judith
Anything That Moves, 18, 137–138,
    161
Anzaldúa, Gloria, 177
archives. *See* lourea; Northampton
Ardill, Susan, 81
Armstrong, Elizabeth, 81
Asian–americanness, 189
Ault, Amber, 1, 10, 19, 29, 36, 74,
    78

Baker, Karin, 75, 86
Bars
    Lexington women's, *151*
    North Star, *58–59*, 213n. 19
    Amelia's, *152*
Barthes, Roland, 107
Bay Area. *See* San Francisco
*Bay Area Bisexual Network News-
    letter* (BABNN). *See* newslet-
    ters
Bay Area Reporter, 157
Beer, Michael, 171

Bercuvitz, Debra, 125
Berkeley, 166. *See also* San Francisco
Berubé, Alan, 150
Bi Academic, 19, 35
Bi Artists Manifesto, 174
Bi Community News, 18
Bi-dykes, 81
Bi-Monthly, 161
BiCon, 18
BiFriendly, 159
Bifrost, 18
BiNet, 14, 18, 145
BiPOL, 158–162, 181–183, 185. *See
    also* San Francisco
Bisexual
    anthologies, 66
    cartographies, 44
    desire, 204n. 31
    epistemology, 33–37
    feminist epistemology, 39
    Femme/FTM Performativities, 124
    gay, 18, 55, 71, 102–103, 150
    imaginary, 4, 159, 164
    inclusion of the term, 63, 67, 71
    invisibility, 90, 160
    internet, 175
    landscapes (space), 12, 15, 17–25,
        27, 29, 31, 33–39, 41, 43,
        45, 47, 49, 51
    lesbian, 36
    pleasures, 112
    objects, 134–139
    sexual health action, 18
    subversions, 110
Bisexual Horizons, 4, 134, *135*, 137,
    139, 146

The Bisexual Imaginary (Stephanie Device), 30, 101, 139, 182
Bisexual Pride Day, 166
Bisexuals
as gendered subjects, 25
Bisexuality
challenge of, 19
celebration, 153, 165
definition, 22–24
and feminism, 185
in fiction, 16–17
male, 17–18
psychoanalytic theory, 16–17, n. 260
sex-work industry, 18
theoretical concepts, 16–36, 202n. 7
Udis-Kessler's fusion of, 155
US research, 19
Bisexuality in the United States (Paula C. Rodríguez Rust), 19-20
Blackness, 175
Blumenfeld, Warren, 168
Boal, Steve, 85
BOB. *See* butch
Body Alchemy, 129
Books *see* bookstore; press
Bookstore
San Francisco's Old Wives' Tales women's, 152
Lunaria, 63
Bornstein, Kate, 118
Boston, 5, 18, 49, 58, 66, 72, 75, 161, 165–166, 183
Boston's Bisexual Women's Network (BBWN) *see* Ochs, Robyn
Boundaries, 3, 30, 36, 43, 45, 48, 67, 80, 88, 100, 103, 111, 132, 172, 189
Bouthillette, Anne-Marie, 46
Bowie, Malcolm, 22–23
Braidotti, Rosi, 39, 40, 41, 44, 129
Brandon, Teena, 120
Bright, Susie, 63
Britain, 4, 6, 12, 15, 17–19, 24, 51, 61, 77, 113, 122, 166
British Bisexual Federation, 18
Brook Lis, 68
Brooklyn, 150

Bryant, Anita, 157
Buskirk, Van, 160
Butch
B.O.B (Butches Offended by Bis), 88
Califia, 117
Butler, Judith, 7, 9, 39, 107, 115, 117, 124, 146
critique, 121–124, 208n. 125

C.L.I.T., papers, 109
Califia, Pat, 61, 80, 112, 124, 150
California, 159, 166, 177
northern, 50
northern, lesbian historical society of, 18, 149
school system, 157
Cambridge, 180
Cameron, Loren, 129–134, 144
Self-portrait Nude, 130
Canada, 35, 161
Carlton, Susan, 192
Cartography, 44–46, 49, 53, 99, 101, 148–149, 154. *See also* Nestle
Castro (district). *See* San Francisco
Caucus
bisexual people of color, 165
color, 153, 170, 191–192, 194
special needs, 170
Censorship, 63, 80
Central americans, 150
Chauncey, George, 168
Chicago, 155, 161
University Press, 20
Choe, Margaret Mihee, 189
Christina, Greta, 80, 168, 171
Church, unitarian, 57
Class, 37, 61–62, 87, 96, 109–110, 119, 123, 150, 171, 181, 185, 187–188, 193, 195
Collectives
C.L.I.T., 74, 79, 100
coming out, 21, 26–27, 34, 58, 84–85, 90, 92, 94, 113–114, 156, 164–165, 191
Community
black & hispanic, 62
wider U.S. bisexual, 190–194

Conferences
  Bisexual Center's press, 157
  bisexuality, 171
  East Coast Bisexual, 86
  Fifth International Bisexual, 5,
    177–178, 180
  FTM, 152
  Men of Color, 191
  National Bisexual, 14, 18–19, 86,
    145, 148, 161, 165–168,
    174, *176–179*, 183, 190,
    195
  National Bisexual, brochure,
    166–*167*, *174*
  North American, 18
  Second International Bisexual, 177,
    179
  U.K. Eighth National Bisexual, 177
Connecticut River Valley, 53
Counters, Dreher, 81
Courtney, Autumn, 164, 172, 183
Cross-dressing, african male slaves,
  118
Cruz, Santa, 161
Cultural anxieties, 11, 35, 42, 101
Culture
  tex-mex, 177
  U.S., 22
  western, 44

D'Emilio, Washington, 161–162, 165
Daily Hampshire Gazette, 71
Darwin, 22
Däumer, Elizabeth D., 1
David Lourea Archives. *See* Lourea;
    Northampton
David, Mark, 17
De Beauvoir, Simone, 106
Deihl, Marcia, 88
Development. *See* sexual; Freud
Device, Stephanie, 101
  photographic work, discussion of
    139–144
  photos (fig. 3.4), *140–141*
  sexual location of, 142–143
Diaspora
  Hennessy's employment of the
    term, 175
  members of the bisexual, 173, 175
Displacement, 10–11, 24, 44, 182

Diversity
  racial, 189
  sexual, 18
Dollimore, Jonathan, 6, 21–22,
    33–35
Donaldson, Stephen, 155, 182
Drag balls, latino, 119
Drag queens, 69
Dreher, Sarah, 68–69, 76, 81
Duncan, Nancy, 44
Dwight, Valle, 60
Dworkin, Andrea, 63
Dyke, 56–58, 66, 77, 79, 88, 96,
    112, 114, 125

Eadie, Jo, 1, 35, 85, 113, 195
Edge of Time (Marge Piercy), 175
Edinburgh, 177–178
Ekins, Richard, 100
Ellis, Havelock, 81, 102
Empire Strikes Back, The (Sandy
    Stone), 102, 105, 123
England, 96, 166
Epistemology. *See* bisexual; queer
Ethnicity, 61–62, 121, 177, 181–182,
    185, 190, 193

Family, *70,* 86
  white American middle-class, 121
Feinberg, Leslie, 118, 130
Femininity, 106–109
Feminism, third world, 177
Feminist
  epistemology, 1, 15–22, 36–38, 44,
    207n. 29
  bisexuality, 185
  cartography, 44–45, 49, 53,
    148–149, 154
  genealogy, 8, 16, 41–42, 44–45,
    49–50, 52, 77, 90, 129,
    145–147, 196–197
  geographers, 44–45
  geography, 2, 5, 12, 16, 44–45, 48,
    52, 139, 209, 211–212
  politics, 185
  theory, 1, 15, 17–20, 37, 103, 127,
    145
  third world feminism, 177
  writers, 107

Feminophobia, 105
Femme, 8, 24, 60, 66, 88, 96, 104, 108–110, 115–117, 124–125, 133
Findlay, Heather, 124–126
Florence Heights, 62
Foucault, Michel, 45, 107
Franklin, Ron, 192
Fraser, Mariam, 1, 26, 33
Freud, Sigmund, 24, 102
  theory of sexual development, 107
Friedland, Lucy, 162
FTM (Female to Male), 104, 124–126, 220n. 26, 224n. 124
Fusco, Coco, 121
Fuss, Diana, 111

Galst, Liz, 60
Garber, Marjorie, 21–22, 30, 32, 36, 47, 100, 111, 118, 134, 139
Gay business guild, 60
Gay Community News, 54, 83, 93, 162
Gay ghetto, 149
Gay men, 21, 24, 29, 47, 53–54, 58, 61, 63, 68, 70, 72, 75–76, 80, 84–86, 89, 112–113, 119–120, 145, 149–150, 152, 160, 172
Gay Times, 113
Gays, 60, 75, 91, 150, 162, 173
Geller, Thomas, 17
Gender(s), 2, 32, 39, 93, 114, 157, 195–196
Genealogy, teratological, 129
Geographers, feminist, 45
Geography, cultural, 2, 44–45
GLBT (Gay, Lesbian, Bisexual, and Transgender historical society), 18, 49, 161
  Newsletter, 161
GLHSNC (Gay and Lesbian Historical Society of Northern California), 149, 160
Goldsby, Jackie, 119
Gonsalves, Sharon, 90, 95
Gordon, Stephen, 17
le Grant, Matthew, 164

Groups
  bisexual discussion, 65
  national bisexual liberation, 155
  Valley Bisexual Women's support, 65
  East Coast bisexual, various, 161
  Seattle women's, 183
Guardian, the (UK), 61
Gutierrez, Fernando, 171

Hadley, South, 53, 56
Halberstam, Judith, 8, 118–119, 123
Hale, C. Jacob, 118, 120, 128
Hall, Donald E. 134
Hall, Radclyffe, 103
Halperin, David, 38
Happy Valley. See Northampton
Haraway, Donna, 41–43
Harrison, Helen, 75, 86
Harvard University, 177, 190
Hasbian community, 92–93
Hausman, Bernice, 100, 107, 129
Hebdige, Dick, 44
Helms, Jesse, 114
Hemmings, Clare (previous articles), 201n. 36
Hennessy, Keith, 173–177
Heramedia, 60
Herdt, Gilbert, 118
Heteronormativity, 10, 110, 115, 120–121, 124–125
Heterosexual privilege, 8, 11, 29, 54, 74, 78–79, 87, 90, 95, 106, 109–110, 116, 193, 217n. 123
Heterotopias, 46
Highleyman, Liz A., 28, 155
Hill, Joan, 183, 187
Hirschfeld, Magnus, 102
Hispanic, 62, 138, 188
Historiographically, 10
HIV/AIDS, 5, 14, 17–18, 29, 35, 80, 134, 157–160, 165–166, 182, 190–191
Hollibaugh, Amber, 109
Hutchins, Loraine, 28, 190

Identification, 24–25, 33, 49, 79, 172

Identity, 69, 73–76, 85
  anxieties of, 20–22
  politics of, 88–90
imaginary. *See* bisexual
Ingram, Gordon Brent, 46, 153
intimacy, 142, 144
Ireland, 169
Israel, 175

Jameson, Fredric, 44
Joplin, Janis, quote, 159
Jeffreys, Sheila, 74, 109
Jews, 175. *See also* Northampton
Jones, Jordy, 123
Journal of Bisexuality, 18, 20

Ka'ahumanu, Lani, 28, 148, 153,
    159, 164–165, 169–170,
    181, 183–184, 192–193,
    195
Kaloski, Ann, 1, 26, 36, 157
Kaplan, Rachel, 173–*174*, *176*
Kennedy, Elizabeth Lapovsky, 109
Kimmel, Pamela, 74
King, Dave, 100
Kinsey Scale, 16
Klein, Fritz, 16, 20, 30
Knowledge, 1–2, 6–7, 9–10, 19, 32,
    40–43, 48, 55, 117,
    128–129, 132, 142, 148,
    152, 154, 184, 190,
    195–196
Krafft–Ebing, Wilhelm von, 102
Krause, Sue, 72
Kreiner, Charlie, 188
Kremensky, Robert, 61
Kristeva, Julia, 10

Labial signification, 107, 221n. 40
Lanzerotti, Rachel, 137
Latinos, 62
Lermann, Ginny, 88
Lesbian
  ethics, 19
  experiences, 90
  feminists, 32, 56
  festival, 56, 60
  politics, 75, 108, 168, 188
  Pride March. *See* Pride Marches
  rights, 161, *163*

sadomasochism, 81, 92
separatism, 232n. 178
space, 13, 54, 72, 78, 80, 82,
    88–89, 146, 152–153
  -straight debate, 216n. 121
  Student Alliance, 192
Lesbian Historical Society of
    Northern California, 18,
    149
Lesbian-feminist, 63, 105
Lesbianism, 10, 35–36, 53, 56, 73,
    75, 79–81, 93, 108, 110,
    125, 188
Lesbian-owned businesses, 56
Lesbian space. *See* Northampton
Lesbianville, U.S.A. (Northampton),
    53, 59–60
Lexington, 152
Liberation
  Bisexual, 27, 75
  Gay, 30, 75, 156, 164
Libraries *see* New Alexandrian;
    Neilson
Livingston, Jennie, 121
Llewellyn, Mary, 17
Location
  sexual, 142
  historical, 89
  politics of, 51–54
  San Francisco, 165
Los Angeles, 161
Los Angeles Times, 53
Lourea, David, archives, 50, 149,
    156–159, 172
Lowenthal, Michael, 53
Lunaria, 57, 63
LunaSea, *151*
Lyon, Phyllis, 106

Mack, Bill, 187
Manifesto, 102, 123, 173–174
Marginality, 4
Martin, Del, 106, 110
masculinity, female, 121–122
Massachusetts, 68, 95
Massey, Doreen, 41
McKerrow, Graham, 113
Mead, Margaret, 16, 27–28
Mestiza Anzaldúa's, 177

Methodology, 1–14, 2, 9, 12, 16, 19, 31, 36–37, 44, 50
Method, 6, 8, 36, 45, 181
Metonymic, 182
Mexico, 150, 177
Mission High School, 153, 165–166
Monosexism, 28–29, 75
Monosexuality, 3, 7, 5, 26, 28–29, 160
Moore, Lisa Jean, 184
Moore, Michele, 75, 89, 194
Mountain, Lesley, 75
Movements
   black civil rights, 89, 168
   gender minorities, 76
   history of the bisexual
   lesbian, 36, 76, 89
   power of the women's, 79
   US bisexual, 158
MTF (Male to Female), 104–105, 220n. 26
Multicultural issues, 194
Murray, Sarah, 166

Nania, Liz, 162
National Bisexual Conference (NBC), 145, 153–154, 159–161, 164–165, 168–169, 171, 177, 181, 183, 190, 195
National Bisexual Contingent, 161–162, 164
National Bisexual Network (NBN), 149, 161–162, 165, 194
National Enquirer, 53
Nebraska, 120
Neilson Library (Smith's), 58
Ness, Cynthia van, 86
Nestle, Joan, 47–48, 109
Networks
   Amherst–Based Valley Bisexual, 65, 67, 85–86, 214n. 48
   Bay Area Bisexual, 159–160
   Boston Bisexual Women's, 75, 161
   National Bisexual (USA), 14, 145, 154, 162, 165
   North American Bisexual, 165, 194
New Alexandria Lesbian Library, (NALL) 50, 55, 60, 61, 63

New York, 161–162, 168, 190, 228n. 51
New York Times, 56
Newsletters
   Bay Area Bisexual Network, 149, 185
   Bisexual Center's, 156
   Britain's National Bisexual, 18
Newsweek, 134, 137–138, 146
   front cover, *136*
Nicols, Les, 122
Noe Street, 149, 153. *See also* San Francisco
Non-transsexuals, 128
North American Bisexual Network (NABN), 165
North American Multicultural Bisexual Network Report, 194, 233n. 211-214
North Carolina, 165
Northampton (Massachusetts), 53–77
   antipornography lobby, 81
   gay community of, 67
   lesbian community, 80, 146, 153, 196
   prior analysis, 211n. 3
   as lesbianville, 212n. 9
   Pride March controversy, 90
   sexual minorities archive, 50, 55, 64, 69–71, 87
   woman-to-woman SM, 57
Nottingham, 19
NSMA (Northampton Sexual Minorities Archive), 55, 66

O'Sullivan, Sue, 81, 126
Ochs, Robyn, 72, 75, 86, 183
Ontology, 1, 6, 9, 12, 21, 23, 40, 76, 77, 101, 106, 117, 148
Orientation. *See* sexual
Orlando, (Woolf), 16
Out/look, 79
Outright Scotland, 18

Parades
   Freedom, 153–154
   Gay Freedom Day, 166–*167*
Paris Is Burning, 119, 120–121
Parody, 9, 104, 115–117, 120, 125, 138

Participation, 7, 49, 55, 75, 84, 133, 150, 159, 164
Passivity, 81, 106
Patriarchy, 28, 79, 92, 100, 105–106, 108, 110, 118, 127, 156
Pearl Street nightclub, 56, 61
Penelope, Julia, 108–109
Performativity, 6–10, 119, 121, 124
  as performance, 40, 57, 58, 100, 115, 117–124, *151–153*
  See also Butler, Judith
Phelan, Shane, 21, 36
Philadelphia, 161
Piercy, Marge, 175
Place
  placelessness, 175
  political places, 2, 36, 40, 52, 59, 89, 100, 190, 193
  sense of, 13–14, 122–133, 142–171
du Plessis, Michel, 3, 177
Pluralism, *87–88*
Policy, SM materials, 57
Politics
  bisexual, 4, 6, 162, 181–183
  lesbian, postmodern, 21
  politicization, 40–41, 94, 190
  San Francisco gay male, 150
Pomeroy, Wardell, 16
Pornography, 48, 57, 63–64, 78, 80–81. *See also* Northampton; lesbians
Post-feminist, 173, 185
Post-stonewall, 46, 156, 173
Post-structuralist, 7, 12, 16, 19, 37–41, 43–45, 51
Postcolonial, 175, 177
Postmodern, 21–22, 39–40, 43–44, 46
Posttranssexual, 102, 123
Power, Bet, 55, 61–63, 73, 76, 85, 212n. 9. *See also* Northampton; Sexual Minority Archives
Pramaggiore, Maria, 1, 32, 44
Pratt, Minnie Bruce, 99, 108
Pride marches, 13, 54, 57, 63, 65, 69–71, 73, 76–78, 80, 83–84, 86, 89, 97, 94, 104, 153, 166

night march, 77–78
SM (sado–masochist), 113
transgender, 71, 150
Probyn, Elspeth, 37, 39, 148
Prosser, Jay, 103, 118, 123
Pseudo-hermaphraditic, 8
Psychic, 11–12, 16, 23, 33–36, 44, 102, 133, 138, 156
Psychoanalysis, 1–10, 13, 16, 21, 24, 35, 45, 99, 101, 107, 115
  Freudian, 13, 107
Psychology, 16–17, 19–21
Puerto Rican communities, 62

Queen, Carol A., 69, 114, 168, 172
Queer
  epistemology, 20–21, 209n. 129
  space, definition of, 210n. 159
Queer Ethics (Elizabeth Däumer), 19
Queer theory, 2–3, 10–11, 15, 20–21, 27, 46, 50, 100, 104–105, 110, 112, 114–115, 117–118
Queers, 5, 46–47, 56, 189, 192

Race, 5, 14, 37, 61, 65, 110, 118–119, 137, 146, 148, 170, 181–182, 185, 187–190, 193, 195
Racialization, 102
Racism, 35, 170–171, 189–191
Radicals, 150, 173
Rahman, Momin, 27
Rally. *See* Pride Marches
Raymond, Diane, 168
Raymond, Janice, 100, 105, 107, 127, 128
Reflexivity, 4, 51, 128, 147–148
Relationships, 1, 15–17, 30, 32–33, 55, 66, 82, 90, 92, 94–97, 110, 126, 157, 165, 169, 183, 185, 187–188, 197
Religion, 62, 181, 185
Representation, 30, 101–102, 127, 129, 134, 136, 146–147
  Cameron's, 133
  Sheiner's, 126
RePresenting Bisexualities (Donald Hall), 134

Reproduction, 7–9, 49, 99, 102, 107, 196
Repudiation, cultural, 101, 182
Requeering, 121
Resistance, 9, 46, 123
Retter, Yolanda, 46
Rich, Adrienne, 51–52, 211n. *174*
Rickus, Janet, 139
Riddell, Carol, 128
Rights, 18, 27, 33, 61, 63, 68, 77, 84, 89, 156, 160–161, *163*, 168, 181
  civil, 61, 63, 68
  lesbian, 161, *163*
Riis Park, 47–48
Riles, Gwen, 194
Rogers, Gwen, 61
Rubenstein, Maggi, 156, 183
Rubin, Henry, 92, 152

Sadomasochism, lesbian, 81, 92
Same–sexuality, 113
San Francisco, 149, 152–153, 160
  Bay Area, bisexual community, 145, 149, 159, 166, 226n. 1
  Bisexual Network Newsletter *see* Newsletters
  Gay By The Bay, 160
  network. *See* Networks
  women's paper, 155
  bisexual community, 154–161
    political growth, 159–160
    SM, 157, 161
  Castro District, as a bisexual space, 149–154
    streetfairs, 150
  gay analysis, 226n. 1
  gay male politics of, 150
    Golden Gate Bridge road block, 160
  lesbian backbone of, 154
  post–Stonewall, 156
  Sex Information, 156
San Francisco Bay Times, 81, 168
San Francisco Sentinel, 166
Sandoval, Chela, 177
Sappho, 30, 103
Scotland, 18, 166

Sedgwick, Eve Kosofsky, 7–9, 11, 23, 32, 35–38, 41–43, 46, 49, 114
Seigel, Micki, 68, 83
Self
  sexual, 24–26, 33
  productive, 40–41, 43
  heteretopia as a mirror for the, 46
  author's sense of 51
  lesbian, 77, 82, 84–85, 90–91, 93–94, 107, 110, 115, 117, 123, 129, 147–148, 171, 177, 182, 188
Semiotics, 107
Separatists, 62, 88, 188
Sex-changing, 100
Sex-role, 105
Sex-work, 18
Sex-gendered, 24
Sexes, 2, 26–27, 32, 43, 81, 102, 114, 137, 196
Sexism, 32, 171, 184, 188
Sexological, 13, 16, 79, 99, 102, 137
Sexology, 7, 20–21, 33, 101, 103
Sexual
  behavior, 23–24, 28, 74–75, 79, 81, 84
  citizenship, 27
  diversity, 18
  freedom league, 155
  identity, choices, 25–26
  inversion, 102
  orientation, 16, 74, 102, 113, 137, 156–157, 181, 185
  politics, 67, 74, 106–107
Sexual minorities archive. *See* Northampton
Sexual-identity, 16
Sexualities, 2, 17, 24, 29, 31–35, 39, 44–45, 46, 104, 111, 157, 183
Sheiner, Marcy, 125
Shelix, 57, 63
Slater, Cynthia, 161
SM (sado-masochism) 34, 56, 96
Smith, Barbara, 68
Smith, Paul, 185
Society, 18, 21, 28, 30, 33, 49, 81, 105, 109, 111, 118, 127, 149, 161, 173, 187
Sociobiology, 13

Sociology, 16–19
Soja, Edward W.
Sojourner, 55
Space
  bisexual, 12–14, 18, 47–48, 54,
    78, 89, 145–149, 153–154,
    159, 164, 172–173, 175,
    177, 181–182, 188, 190,
    194–195, 226n. 1
  lesbian, 89
  lesbian–friendly, 150
  queer SM, 113
  queers in, 47
  terrain, 4, 12, 99–101, 142–143,
    148–149, 196–197
  territorial, 3, 48, 58, 77, 82, 85
Spanner trials, the (UK), 24
Spirituality, 18, 165
Spooner, Kiriyo, 62
Sprinkle, Annie, 122, 126
Star Trek, 175
Stein, Gertrude, 103
Stekel, Wilhelm, 16, 28
Stereotypes, 10, 27–30, 35, 93, 105,
    108–109, 137, 143,
    157–159
Stigmatization, 159
Stone, Sandy, 102, 105, 118, 123,
    124
Stonewall Conference, 166
Storr, Merl, 1, 5–7, 33, 102
Straight (straightness), 3, 5, 9, 14,
    29, 31, 38, 42–43, 47–49,
    57–58, 78, 80–81, 90–91,
    100, 109, 112, 115–117,
    119–120, 125–126,
    133–134, 157, 160, 173,
    177, 182, 189
Strained Mixed Fruit (Janice
    Williamson), 33
Stryker, Susan, 118, 128, 160
Subcultures, 46, 54, 58
Subversion, 75, 101, 114–121,
    123–124, 126–127, 196

Taxonomies, bisexual nonce, 11
Technology, 105, 107
Teratology, 129
Territory. *See* space, San Francisco,
    Northampton

Textualities, 101–102, 117
Theorists
  bisexual, 3–9, 19–22, 27–28, 42,
    44, 101, 115, 118, 134, 197
  femme, 109–110
  lesbian, 21
  poststructural, 40–42
  queer and feminist, 32–38
  transsexual 105–106
Theory
  british bisexual, 19
  queer. *See* queer
  spatial, 44–45
  wishful, 22, 33
Therapy, 20, 58, 165
The Third Path (Rachel Kaplan and
    Keith Hennessy) *176*
Tipton, Billy, 103
Transexual, *87*
  femininities, 126
  gazing, 129
  meaning (Hausman's), 128
  narrative, 219n. 7
  portraits, 129, 131
  representations of bisexuality, 127
  subversions, 110
  textualities, 101–102, 117
Transsexualism, 105, 111, 122,
    127–128
Transsexuality, 13, 47, 81, 99–105,
    109–111, 117–118,
    120–124, 126–128, 132,
    196
Transsexuals, 5, 13–14, 31, 76, 80,
    82, 92, 96, 99–107,
    109–111, 117, 119–129,
    131–133, 144, 152–154,
    196
The Transexual Empire (Janice
    Raymond), 105
Transgender
  activism, 103
  behaviour, 111–115
  bisexual, 18, 49, 71, 161
  definitions, 100–101
  performance, 117–124
  pride march, 71
  queer as transgendered, 20
  transgendered communities, 51,
    102–107, 150, 156, 161

transgender (*continued*)
  transition, 55
Transition. *See* Nicols, Les
Transvestite, 80, 87
Trisexual, 87
Truque, Mac, 88
Tucker, Naomi, 157, 171, 185
Tyler, Carole–Anne, 115

Udis-Kessler, Amanda, 29, 154–156, 182
Ultrasexual, 87
United Kingdom (UK)
  bisexual communities, 147
  Contemporary, 13, 54, 79, 164
  Twentieth–century, 22
United States (US), 4, 6, 12, 15, 17–19, 51, 53–54, 60, 74, 77, 92, 104, 145–147, 155, 161, 164, 177, 190
Upton, Dell, 51
Urban, Colleen, 81
Utopia, 154, 156, 171, 175, 177, 187

Valencia Street (bisexual space), 150–154
The Valley Advocate, 66
Valley Bisexual Network, 67
Valley Women's Voice, 63, 68, 77
Vice Versa (Marjorie Garber), 21–22, 30, 39, 111, 143
  film stills, 134
  front cover, 139
Violence, 8, 24, 29, 35, 48, 60–62, 74, 77–78, 94, 106, 120, 122, 160, 168
Visibility, lesbian and bisexual, 82–90
Voguing, 119, 121

Voyeurism, 33, 47, 128, 142

Warner, W.L., 185–187
Washington, D.C., 161–164
Weininger, Otto, 102
Weise, Elizabeth Reba, 17, 154
The Well of Loneliness (Radclyffe Hall), 17, 22
White, Edmund, 145
Whittle, Stephen, 105, 132
Wilde, Oscar, 30, 32, 103
Williamson, Janice, 33
Wilson, Ara, 74, 100
Wilson, Elizabeth, 100
Wittig, Monique, 79
The Wizard of Oz, 195
Wolf, May, 93, 95, 197
Women
  bi, 80, 191
  woman-hating-, 74
  woman-loving-, 93
  woman-to-, 57
  women-only, 17, 62, 89, 183
Women's bathhouse, *151*
Womonfyre Books, 60, 63
Woolf, Virginia, 16, 30
Working–class, 109
Workshops, 50, 66, 149, 165, 168, 170–171, 191, 193

Xtravaganza, Venus, 119–120

Yeskel, Felice, 68
Young, Stacey, 35–36, 54

Zita, Jacqueline, 119